Information Literacy and Workplace Performance

Information Literacy and Workplace Performance

Tom W. Goad

Q

QUORUM BOOKS
Westport, Connecticut • London

Library of Congress Cataloging-in-Publication Data

Goad, Tom W.
　　Information literacy and workplace performance / Tom W. Goad.
　　　p.　cm.
　　Includes bibliographical references and index.
　　ISBN 1–56720–454–6 (alk. paper)
　　1. Workplace literacy.　2. Information literacy.　3. Labor productivity.　I. Title.
　　LC149.7.G63　2002
　　302.2—dc21　　　2001031890

British Library Cataloguing in Publication Data is available.

Library of Congress Catalog Card Number: 2001031890
ISBN: 1–56720–454–6

First published in 2002

Quorum Books, 88 Post Road West, Westport, CT 06881
An imprint of Greenwood Publishing Group, Inc.
www.quorumbooks.com

Printed in the United States of America

The paper used in this book complies with the
Permanent Paper Standard issued by the National
Information Standards Organization (Z39.48–1984).

10　9　8　7　6　5　4　3　2　1

Librarians are dedicated to the cause of information literacy, ever ready to help us seek information and knowledge. It is only fitting that this book is dedicated to librarians everywhere. Your professionalism and service is truly appreciated.

Contents

Preface

Remember when all you needed was one skill and you could earn a living? When people were proud to type, operate a lathe, till the soil, teach the three Rs, sell things, work with numbers, and assemble parts to get on with their daily work life? There are still people who do these things, but for a greater number of us, technology leads us a merry chase through the workplace, making life and work more complicated, demanding ever-broadening information age skills—where with the blink of an eye, what you did yesterday isn't valid today. Is there still one skill we can count on, one skill we can master to fulfill our workplace dreams, regardless of what we do? The answer is yes, and that skill is information literacy, which is being able to locate, access, select, and apply information. Being information literate yields information power. Sounds simple enough, yet for so many jobs it can become a daily challenge. It's something we do every day, but we know it isn't always easy. And how important is it? "Having accurate, up-to-date information," we've been informed, "determines the difference between the rich and poor in the Information Age."[1] Some cases in point: when was the last time you used a typewriter? Have you toured a factory floor lately and counted the computers and robots? Do farmers pick up the *Farmer's Almanac,* or do they go to the Weather Channel Web site to check on the weather? How do you think Wal-Mart became the country's largest retailer?

Having information power—being information literate—is the tip of an iceberg. But it's a skill—actually, a system of interdependent and often overlapping skills—that can and must be mastered for success in the future workplace.

And the future is now. If Thomas Stewart's statement that "Information and knowledge are the thermonuclear competitive weapons of our time"[2] carries any measure of truth, then having information power is the only way such weapons can be delivered. It makes the difference between success and failure in the knowledge-intensive environment where global organizations conduct their business. The skills associated with the concept and levels of competence vary widely between practitioners.

This isn't a new buzzword nor is it a passing fad. Peter Drucker, a decade ago, brought it to our attention. "In this society," he stated, "knowledge is *the* primary resource for individuals and for the economy overall."[3] At first glance, it seems as though we're talking about how astute we are at using a library, or perhaps the Internet and its myriad of offerings. But there's more to it than being adept in the library—and on the information superhighway.

Libraries and dedicated librarians have taken the lead in helping our population become information literate. They go to great lengths to help students master the art and technology of obtaining information from the library. This ability is helpful in school, and to a great extent in the workplace, but it's not enough. Information comes from many sources and can be obtained in many ways. People at work must know all the ways and be adept at not only using them, but quickly choosing the most proficient one to use at any given time—in a time-compressed environment.

Fine resources exist about individual pieces of the information literacy puzzle—computer literacy, communications skills, how to be creative, and so on—but they haven't been brought together under the umbrella of workplace information literacy. Most of the material for information literacy deals with it at the level of profit and loss, such as how to account for intellectual capital as previously noted. This works well for the chief executive officer (CEO), but how about the people who must find and compute those accounting numbers, or conduct the work leading to the numbers in the first place?

ABOUT THE BOOK

Information literacy is a straightforward concept, one that has been practiced by people at work for some time. However, when expanded to include all the skills needed to make it happen most effectively, the process becomes monumental. The remainder of this book will define and describe information literacy, then lay out skills and considerations necessary for a person to be information literate. Each chapter is not intended to exhaust the particular topic, but rather to provide a detailed enough background for understanding and to provide a starting point from which to further expand the skills.

Chapter 1, "Information and Knowledge," provides the foundation upon which information literacy and all its ramifications are practiced.

Chapter 2, "Information Literacy," defines the process and provides an expanded description of it. A sixteen-step model provides a template applicable to most information-related job challenges. This is the framework within which all knowledge workers function.

Chapter 3, "Communicating in the Digital Age," lays out the communication skills needed to be information literate, including the traditional ones alongside digital skills. Communicating is something we do from the start to the finish of any information literacy activity.

Chapter 4, "Thinking and Decision Making Skills," describes the first of the sets of critical thinking and problem solving skills closely related to information literacy. This is how we apply the results of being information literate.

Chapter 5, "Creativity, Innovation, and Risk Taking," identifies the remaining thinking skills needed to be fully information literate. These skills further enhance and compliment the skill set above.

Chapter 6, "Computer Literacy," describes the skill that has almost taken over information literacy and is essential for so much of it. Being computer literate to some degree is mandatory for entry-level workers and executives alike.

Chapter 7, "Subject Matter Literacy," means just what it says, that you must know your job and know it thoroughly. The chapter delves into the various forms this takes, including business literacy and professional literacy, as well as emotional intelligence.

Chapter 8, "Learning How to Learn," describes the process of lifelong learning, which is necessary to continue being information literate. Technology begets change, and we must keep up with it. It's a process that keeps life interesting and challenging.

Chapter 9, "On-the-Job Help," addresses the availability of online and other help that can facilitate information gathering and usage. Electronic performance support systems (EPSS) are at the forefront of this type of assistance.

Chapter 10, "Humans Don't Live by Digits Alone," explores the concept that our work lives have become intertwined with our private lives and describes ways to cope successfully with this. Being able to do so contributes to success in information challenges as well as helps us make the most of everyday life.

Chapter 11, "The Future," provides food for thought regarding information literacy as we move into the new age. It also reviews the skill set required to be fully information literate.

In the next chapter you'll read about the foundations of work and organizational success today: information and knowledge. The skill set for information literacy, the one that will give you information power, is identified.

A NOTE TO THE READER

Throughout the book you'll find references to Web sites, which is to be expected in a book about being information literate. More and more of the information we need must be accessed electronically (although you'll be reminded that there's a lot to be found "nonelectronically"). As you're no doubt aware, sites continually change—they're here today and gone tomorrow in some cases, and even the tried and true ones change, sometimes for the better, and sometimes not. Please bear this in mind. If a site is no longer available, most likely others can be found that are comparable. Web sites are included to help you better understand the various topics covered in the book.

CHAPTER 1

Information and Knowledge: Foundations for Twenty-First Century Work

INTRODUCTION

Armed with buzzwords and high hopes, we enter the new age in full force, ready to tackle the jobs, competition, and challenges ahead of us. All the while, paradoxes abound: continuing layoffs and growing shortages of skilled workers; booming economies in one corner of the globe, and busts next door; technology reinventing itself overnight, and predictions of it replacing books, humans, and work that fail to materialize; diversity expanding and proving itself to be productive, along with continued, ofttimes increasing discrimination; more tools to obtain information, and more information than we can possibly use. Optimists would call it opportunity; skeptics, a vicious circle. Associated buzzwords include intellectual capital, knowledge management, and learning organizations. There are plenty more, but these are particularly important to review because of their close association with information power. Being able to effectively deal with information and knowledge is required in today's workplace. Information power, acquired by being information literate, is crucial for accomplishing work in the twenty-first century.

Knowledge work is an inherent element of the information age. As the subtitle to an article in *Fortune* noted, "Nations' real wealth doesn't reside in forests of rubber trees or acres of diamond mines, but in the techniques and technologies for exploiting them."[1] As we well know, people within those industries and organizations are the ones who decide which knowledge is needed. Michael Moynihan seconded this when he said that "Work in the United States will become less labor- and more knowledge-intensive as the labor market tightens now."[2] As noted above, the market for highly skilled labor continues to tighten.

This chapter reviews intellectual capital, knowledge management, and learning organizations, along with other current elements that impact how work is accomplished within organizations. The resulting knowledge worker who has mastered information literacy is introduced, for it is this person who will be progress in the workplace. The chapter concludes by identifying the skill set comprising information literacy, setting the stage for the remainder of the book.

BACKGROUND

Foundations for getting work done most effectively can be laid by reviewing the three concepts of intellectual capital, knowledge work, and learning organizations. Together, they have formed the essence of today's organization. Mary Park has identified several emerging information issues that affect managers, workers, and consumers of information alike, and they illuminate the importance of these three concepts when not treated appropriately. They include:

- Concepts people have in their heads about using information are either outmoded or devalued;

- Creative ideas of individuals and the collective knowledge of an organization are not recognized or organized so that they can be retrieved or used;

- There are, more often than not, no information policies, strategies, or standards that make high-quality internal or external information readily available or people accountable or willing to budget for it;

- If information is available, it is likely that there is no one within the organization who has the authority to ask the right questions;

- If one has the authority, many times one does not know how to ask the right questions to retrieve the information;

- In many cases, someone else in the company or organization already has the information, but is not motivated to share it;

- If information is retrieved, there is rarely someone who knows how to analyze it—or wants to;

- If the information is somehow retrieved and analyzed, it may never be acted upon;

- If acted upon, it may already be outdated, incomplete, or inaccurate;

- If outdated, incomplete, or inaccurate, it can cause a company, organization, or individual to fail in any given situation.[3]

Keep this startling list in mind as you progress through the steps in the information literacy process and the skills associated with it. It will help keep you on the information power track.

Intellectual Capital

How much value would you put on Jack Welch's head? Would it be more or less than the figures appearing on General Electric's annual statement for the value of the company's manufacturing facilities or office accouterments? Do the values change as he leaves and someone else takes over? Could you use this value system to help determine intellectual value to select his, or anyone else's, replacement? These aren't rhetorical questions. Given the amount of attention paid to intellectual capital, it's an idea whose time has come. To bring the thought closer to home, have you or the contents of your little gray cells appeared on a profit and loss statement lately? How much value would you place on your own information power?

Thomas Stewart, who has written extensively about intellectual capital for *Fortune*, defines it as "intellectual material—knowledge, information, intellectual property, experience—that can be put to use to create wealth."[4] Leif Edvinsson defines intellectual capital quite simply as human capital plus structural capital. Structural capital consists of those things we usually think of that can be measured in a reasonably accurate way, such as buildings, equipment, property, raw materials, and work in progress. Human capital, on the other hand, consists of knowledge, skills, creativity, company culture, and similar such things, all difficult to measure. Edvinsson's company not only espouses the concept, it includes it on financial statements, literally practicing what they preach.[5]

Intellectual capital takes the concept of the knowledge-driven workplace to a more detailed level. It means accounting for such things as how much training a person has had, how much experience and how many patents or awards for creativity. For an idea of just how detailed the accounting might be, and how difficult to measure, here's a list of potential items that might appear on an intellectual capital profit and loss statement:

- Training received by employees
- Number of patents obtained
- Types of skills for which workers are qualified
- Amount of investment in training and development
- Extent of use of technology (e.g., number of PCs, use of Internet, networks)
- Specific levels of technology expertise (e.g., software packages, systems)
- Indexes and surveys of employees, customers, and others

- Education levels of employees
- Research and development
- Turnover of employees
- Income per employee
- Market value per employee
- Experience level of employees
- Customer satisfaction indexes
- Customer loyalty
- Administrative rates of error

Placing value on the intellect within an organizational setting has brought about a variety of ways to do it. The Roundtable Group identified on its Web site three methods of accounting for intellectual capital. The return on assets method uses financial statement information to compute the return on assets for comparison against industry averages. The Market Capitalization Method reports a company's excess market capitalization over stockholder equity. The Direct Intellectual Capital method identifies the components (such as the ones listed above) and aggregates them. Numerous other methods have been developed. Two success stories of focusing on intellectual capital measurement are Dow Chemical and Glaxco Wellcome, companies who are knowledge driven entities. Dow shows that it generated over $125 million of new revenue from its patents, and Glaxco Wellcome has significantly increased its share value the past few years.[6]

No doubt that the corporate knowledge and skills resident in peoples' minds is what makes or breaks organizations. Flexibility to promote and use it is reality for organizations destined for dominance in their spheres of operation. Putting accurate dollar values on intellectual capital is difficult at best, but nonetheless, the demand to do so grows.

Knowledge Management

Explaining the term *knowledge management* is simple: it's the process of applying the accumulated knowledge of organizations. But, like intellectual capital, that knowledge isn't easy to measure. A manager can count the number of computer consoles in an office complex. But how do you measure the accumulated information and knowledge within the data stored in those computers, and moreover, to be able to precisely identify the level of expertise of the people who daily use those computers and the information they hold. More importantly, which items of knowledge are the ones to apply at a particular time? One evolution that has occurred is that the "management of knowledge ... is a skill, like financial acumen."[7] Intellectual capital provides the means to acquire knowledge; managing it to achieve organizational goals is the literal bottom line of organizations.

It's interesting to note that librarians are finding their niche in the corporate world. "In many large organizations, and some small ones, a new corporate executive is emerging—the chief knowledge officer. Companies are creating the position to initiate, drive, and coordinate knowledge management programs."[8] The CKO is as logical as any new development in organizations. Thus occurs a natural role for librarians.[9] Or almost natural. Of course, not all CKOs are librarians by training, but whoever holds the job must have the skills that resemble a combination of a master's of library sciences and master's of business. As a spokesperson for the library profession has noted, "Knowledge management, in some iteration, is entrenched in corporate America."[10]

Librarians tell us that the basic elements of knowledge management include being able to "recognize when information is needed and have the ability to locate, evaluate, and use effectively" in a way that benefits end users.[11] More simply stated, it is the facilitation of the process of turning information into knowledge that can be applied toward achieving the organization's mission, goals, and objectives. Today's workplace, in a nutshell, might be described as one

- that is knowledge driven and
- technology impacted; and where
- learning is lifelong, and
- change is the only constant.

CKO isn't the only term used. Chief information officer (CIO) and chief learning officer (CLO), among others, can also be found as the title given the person designated as the person in charge of knowledge in organizations. Whatever the title, the person wearing it must be knowledgeable about knowledge—how to find and acquire it, and how to use it to further the cause of the organization. *Training* magazine has called the position "Chief of Corporate Smarts," who they recognize as potentially a "trendy cipher or vital fixture."[12] The latter is the desired outcome. A market research effort conducted by the Special Libraries Association has identified the desired characteristics of the CKO, and they're formidable. In fact, they read like a combination of the skills discussed in this book that lead to being information literate and having information power—plus a dose of leadership skills thrown in for good measure.[13]

Key to believing in the concept of such a sharp focus on knowledge is to identify organizations that are doing it. A brief survey of the literature finds such organizations as the Central Intelligence Agency, Monsanto, Amoco, McKinsey & Co., Ernst & Young, Black and Veatch (whose CKO won an award of excellence), 3M, Booz, Allen, & Hamilton, IBM, Science Applications International Corp., Equiva (Shell and Texaco alliance), and many more organizations both large and small.

Learning Organizations

The learning organization has been defined as "an organization that facilitates the learning of all its members and continuously transforms itself."[14] Can organizations actually learn? Peter Senge thinks so. He named the concept, although profitable companies have been practicing it for years. A true learning organization contains most, if not all, of the following characteristics:

- Believes in and expects continuous learning and improvement
- Recognizes that there are many ways to learn and grow and provides the opportunity to do so
- Opens itself to new ideas and can easily adapt to them
- Promotes creativity and innovation as common events
- Allows people to fail—and learn therefrom
- Thinks in terms of the total system
- Practices collaboration on a large scale
- Believes in and promotes the concepts of competency and mastery of core competencies of both the organization and the employees—i.e., performance on the highest level
- Bases rewards on performance—and is often generous with them
- Orients itself toward teamwork, with teams the norm and people functioning as team players
- Facilitates acquisition of new skills before they're needed
- Spells out organizational mission and goals clearly and ensures that they are shared by all who work in the organization—and all actions are based on them

Senge notes that the learning organization continually expands its capacity to create its future. He identifies the disciplines of the learning organization as: systems thinking, personal mastery, mental models (assumptions, generalizations, images that influence how we see the world), building shared vision, and team learning.[15]

One of the most interesting things about learning organizations is that they were around long before the term itself became an everyday part of the pop management vocabulary. Take the eighteen companies studied by Porras and Collins in *Built to Last*, for instance.[16] The average age of the companies approaches one hundred years, yet they virtually started out applying the principles of learning organizations as the concept has become formally defined in recent years. In fact, most of them have thrived on taking risks, learning from their mistakes, all the while cashing in on their ability to continuously learn as organizations, and following the adage that success breeds success. They do what they have to do, and do it consistently, while continuing to profit and grow. By learning from all experiences, good and bad, the ability to excel seems to follow. The gist of this discussion is that people constantly learn, whether they're conscious of it or not. Organizations are people, so they, too, constantly learn. When effort is made to keep individuals and their organizations updated by being conscious of learning that leads to better performance, then everyone gains.

There are other buzzwords, new ideas, and highly touted panaceas, but these are enough to help paint the picture of what the new workplace is undergoing, and what it will likely continue to be in the future. By briefly reviewing a few key ongoing events, we'll have an even better assessment of the workplace, setting the stage to make the most of it.

Information as Power

Information has taken on a formidable new meaning, one with far wider impact than ever before. "There is less and less return on the traditional resources. . . . The major producers of wealth have become information and knowledge." Peter Drucker is telling us that information *is* power. Those people and organizations who have information and use it properly have the power to succeed. Drucker also noted that "information can empower and enable us" and pointed out that we 're challenged daily to use "basic information literacy skills . . . for survival in the Information Age."[17] As presented in the forthcoming chapters, we obtain information power by being information literate.

How serious can organizations be about becoming learning oriented? Marconi, PLC, a communications and information technology company operating in one hundred countries, has engaged The Forum Corp. to help them become a global learning organization. The intended result is an organization that will create a network of learning providers, divise a process for measuring learning return on investment, and provide advice for enhancing skills and knowledge learning policy.[18]

OTHER CURRENT EVENTS

One prediction is that the fastest growing job segment during the next five to ten years will be knowledge jobs—such as teachers, systems analysts, computer related, and Internet related jobs. By comparison, the current rate of people acquiring the skills needed to fill these knowledge jobs is falling short of the need by as much as 20 percent.[19] Finding ways to transform unemployed or underemployed people into those with the skills to fill this void will continue to be a priority. These factors, summarized in exhibit 1.1, are discussed in the following sections.

Exhibit 1.1
Other Factors Impacting Work

Many other factors impact work, including the following:

- Technology
    - Both improves and complicates work
    - Often drives the work
    - Involves more than computers
    - Can and often does create as many problems as it solves
- Global Competition
    - Knows no boundaries
    - Can occur quickly and without warning
    - Demands swift action to counter
- Lack of skilled workers
    - Paradox of excess workers and layoffs
    - Shortages of certain skills

Technology

Technology to many people is synonymous with personal computers (PCs) and silicon chips. Technology in action is multiplying gigabytes and megahertz, with new peripherals arriving daily. It's all this and more. Wired and wireless forms of telecommunications, medical machines and drugs that literally perform miracles, automation that simplifies life and makes it safer, and virtual reality and simulation that make anything seem possible, are also part of technology. Many fields, ranging from astrophysics to zoology, have both taken advantage of technology and invented their share of it in furthering their causes. Companies that embrace electronic technology have formed what has been called the electronic elite. One study of top companies in this group developed a corporate culture where the business is perceived as an ecosystem, the corporation a community, people within it as peers, management as facilitator, and change as a way to grow.[20]

But that's not all. We must also look at what technology does "to" us as well as for us. Not everything about technology is good. Even when it's good to some parties, it may be just the opposite to others impacted by it. Just what does this mean? How about a woman who is working to support two children who comes to work one day at the factory where she is an assembler, only to find out that she has been replaced by a robot? The robot adds to company profitability, but has a disastrous impact on the woman's economic well-being. The question arises about just how much making a continuous profit should take precedent over people. There are no easy answers.

Then there's the privacy issue. For people who work with computers, it's possible for the organization to literally know everything the person does, complete with a log of activities. Orwell's Big Brother is alive and well in the guise of technological improvements to the workplace. It's easy to scrutinize phone calls, e-mail messages, level of work activity, and more through the medium of digits, powerful software, mass storage devices, log-in and -off times, voice prints, and sometimes video records.

Other negative aspects of technology include its contribution to stress, fear of using computers and other devices, and the change it brings with it, which is already occurring too fast for many people. This will be discussed in greater detail in chapter 10.

Global Competition

One fallout of globalization is merger-mania. The coming together of companies, some already the largest at what they do, continues to maintain a high profile. Some of this is merely companies following the concept of if you can't fight them, join them. By banding together, progress can be achieved, or at least, attempted. In many cases, this is the process of two companies thousands of miles apart forming alliances. It's becoming more common to find archenemies of the marketplace teaming together for specific actions. Or perhaps two companies creating a new virtual corporation, where the new organization exists because of linked technology and databases, and may well be dissolved after a single mission is completed. Alliances on a global basis are facts of competitive life.

Lack of Skilled Workers

One of the most difficult facts to explain in the wake of massive layoffs and increasing numbers of people entering the workforce, both occurring on a global basis, is that a shortage of skilled workers remains. When we say *skilled*, the skills required are not ordinary. They have to do with specific industries and professions, and much to do with technology. Actually, it's how to use technology that contributes largely to this shortage. Electronics industry sources are clamoring for more skilled workers to the extent that they're asking for quotas to be lifted so these people can enter the United States to meet their pressing needs. The U.S. Congress has increased the quota for technology workers, satisfying the demands of high-tech industries (and creating controversy as well). Countries such as Costa Rica are recruiting high-tech workers from other Latin countries, so the beat goes on.[21]

Empowerment

Empowerment is one of those words people sometimes wish had never been invented. It's bandied about like it was holy water and the curse of the workplace—all in the same breath. Whatever your feeling, the term, and what it stands for when gone about properly, has done wonders to productivity. The reason is that when people are truly empowered to get work done, there's no longer the interference of heavy supervision and support from management—and the cost that goes with them. Empowerment frees teams to get large amounts of high quality work done. It includes the ability to acquire information and apply knowledge. It's no coincidence that this ability forms the basis of the definition of information literacy, which will be explored in more detail in the next chapter.

Stated in its simplest terms, empowerment means allowing employees to be self-managed and able to do their jobs the way they see fit, with no one looking over their shoulders—*after* they have been trained in how to be empowered, acquiring such skills as problem solving and decision making. This is a mandatory aspect of effective empowerment. It takes a conscientious effort on the part of management to implement a culture of empowerment. Often, however, empowerment occurs by default, resulting from a downsizing where the number of managers has been reduced. In this case, employees may be ill-prepared to act independently.

Whatever you choose to call it—empowerment, participatory management, reengineering, self-management—it's a process that pays off. When you consider that an organization may be virtual, with people participating via digital means only, from numerous spots around the world, it makes empowerment what it is—an absolute necessity. When you also consider all the telecommuters working from home and other remote sites, the need for empowerment becomes more apparent.

Information Overload

The greatest problem with information is that there is simply too much of it. "Society is being held hostage by a battery of information which threatens to exceed our ability to manage it" is the way one person sees the situation.[22] When there's too much, and it comes from so many directions, it causes such problems as accuracy, credibility, usability, and stress—collectively exacerbating an already massive problem. It's a situation that more than ever must be dealt with if we're to get at the information leading to the knowledge needed to make the best business decisions. Having the appropriate skills discussed in the following chapters appears to be the most plausible solution at this point.

Fortune calls it "infobog," a term that itself adds to the inundation of acronyms and buzzwords we're daily bombarded with. A few examples of what we mean by infobog: there were 11,900 million messages left in voice mailboxes in 1993; while an Internet information guide's hourly salary was $100, the number of secretaries was dwindling by over a half a million in number; all the while pain killer sales went up by a half-billion dollars.[23]

As often happens, the problem becomes part of the solution. A *Wall Street Journal* Technology report appropriately titled "Managing the Mountain," after describing some of the typical problems of information overload, stated that "In the past, society gradually adjusted to such developments as printing and telephones, and this time is no different. As people attempt to fit their life-styles to the information explosion, experts and entrepreneurs are on the hunt for technological solutions—applying the very tools that caused the data glut in a mission to help alleviate it."[24]

WHAT IT BOILS DOWN TO

The New Workplace

There are problems, as always, but this doesn't forebode doom and gloom. Quite the contrary. In the long run, improvements in how work gets done will benefit those who have a hand in doing the work and making the improvements. The more knowledge required, the more intellectually challenging the job. Of greater importance is to realize the new rules of the workplace. They're governed by information and knowledge, along with the tools used to acquire and use the information.

To help differentiate between information and knowledge, consider the statement "In the Information Age, what counts is not what information you have, but what you *know*."[25] Information must be turned into knowledge. Information must be turned into a benefit to the organization using it. For instance, a truckload of packing crates stuffed with sales receipts represents data, thousands of pieces of paper with numbers and names on them. After the crates have been shipped to Ireland for data entry, those numbers and names become lists of sales totals and identities of the people who made the purchases. This is information. In fact, quite useful information. If, for example, the analysis of the names and numbers shows that key customers are buying less, then the information becomes knowledge vital to the company's bottom line. Wisdom comes when the company takes positive steps to win back those customers. Another version of this concept might look like this:

Data—Personnel records showing skill levels of employees

Information—Identification of skills needed to maintain competitive marketplace position

Knowledge—Matching two items above and providing training needed by employees to close the skills gap

Wisdom—Looking ahead to determine what skills will be needed for long-term organizational viability

It's a process that builds, with the ability to glean and use information and turn it into knowledge as the central theme to organizational effectiveness. To doing well in life, for that matter.

What Others Are Saying about the Age of Information and Knowledge

Information and knowledge, and all that goes with them, have received plenty of press. Here are a few examples to illustrate their importance. These statements are made by people who are tuned in to the workplace and what goes on within it, and many are highly successful practitioners of creating organizational effectiveness.

- Handy, in *The Age of Unreason*, speaks of organizations "which receive their added value from the knowledge and creativity they put in rather than the muscle power."[26]

- Zuboff, *In the Age of the Smart Machine*, uses the term "informatting"—as opposed to automating, using smart machines in interactions with smart people.[27]

- Bellah and colleagues in *The Good Society* discusses the need to enlarge our paradigm of knowledge to include art, literature, ethics, philosophy, and so on.[28]

- Crawford, *In the Era of Human Capital* defines knowledge as the differentiation between knowledge and information: "Information is the raw material of knowledge just as wood is the raw material of a table." He goes on to say that "When you distinguish between information and knowledge, it is important to recognize that information can be found in a variety of inanimate objects from a book to a computer disk but that knowledge can be found only in human beings. Knowledge is understanding and expertise. Knowledge is the ability to apply information to specific work or performance. Information is useless without a knowledgeable human being to apply it to a productive purpose."[29]

- Davis and Davidson, in *2020 Vision* lay out an architecture of information, a matrix of data, text, sound, and image down the side (forms), and generation, processing, storage, and transmission (functions across the bottom). "The point is that the economic value from generating, using, and selling information is growing significantly faster than the value added by producing traditional goods and services."[30]

- Leonard-Barton in *Wellsprings of Knowledge* notes that organizations must have core capabilities, with knowledge-building capabilities—shared creative problem solving, new methodologies, experimentation, and learning from others—as ongoing activities.[31]

- A U.S. Department of Commerce report, *A Framework for Global Electronic Commerce*, notes that organizations are moving to a more flexible workplace, and "as more companies move to this method of work organization, the need to share information and knowledge across the enterprise will increase."[32]

Sources of Information

Information comes from sources as widely divergent as drum beats and orbiting satellites, shrugs of the shoulders during a business luncheon, and e-mail flowing around the earth. Some of the sources that come to mind, particularly regarding the workplace, are listed in exhibit 1.2. This list is incomplete. Such items as body language, sign language, billboards and neon lights, traffic signs and signals, pictures, and what is *not said*, along with numerous others, could easily be added. If this was a short list, say a half dozen or so familiar methods, work life would certainly be more simple. But it isn't, a fact we must not only contend with, but seize control of and turn to advantage.

THE RESULT: THE NEW KNOWLEDGE WORKER

What does the new knowledge worker look like? Is he under twenty-five, wears his ball cap backwards, and keeps his skateboard nearby? Does she go

Exhibit 1.2
Sources of Information—An Incomplete List

libraries	books	expert systems
computer outputs	periodicals	networks
scraps of paper	computer programs	info highways
co-workers	outside persons	facsimile
organizations	own memory	magnetic record
computer databases	films and video	market research
reports/studies	memoranda/notes	customers
manual files	microforms	old-timers
everyday life	audio recordings	competitors
art/graphics	archives	retirees
questionnaires	interviews	scrapbooks
signage	instruction manuals	trunks in attics
policy manuals	instruments	nosy neighbors
brainstorming	surveys	fortune tellers
grapevine	correspondence	billboards
conversations	telephone	sign language
television	journals/logs/diaries	body language
encyclopedias	experts in the field	graffiti

home from her job as a programmer and immediately fire up her mega-powered PC, then stay glued to its screen until three a.m.? Or is it the person who looks like any ordinary worker, just like most of us, including those of us who at one time dialed telephone numbers on a rotary device, and actually wrote memos on pieces of paper designed just for the purpose, complete with inserted carbons and a space for the reply? The answer is all the above. Even though not everyone could wear the badge of knowledge worker, most people have had their jobs impacted by the same things that drive technology and the workplace. For instance, mechanics must be, in addition to knowledgeable about cars, at home with computers because they play a big part in what mechanics do today. Even fast food workers have to push the correct buttons.

In discussing how to reeducate the corporation, Tobin notes that "not only do employees need higher levels of achievement in the three Rs, they're required to master a broad range of other skills. These 'thinking-literacy' skills include communication, mathematical, self-management, business, team, and specific functions."[33] The process individuals and organizations go through to acquire these skills closely parallels the information literacy process described in the next chapter. An aside here: the three Rs—reading, 'riting, and 'rithmetic—are as vital as ever in our workplace skills repertoire.

A U.S. Marine war fighter must be able to use sophisticated equipment, operate systems under computer control, and otherwise function just as much as a knowledge worker as the laid-back electronics industry guru who wears T-shirts and sneakers to work. The military must have personnel who are both highly motivated to serve, and experts in technology just the same as everyone else in the workplace. The army, too, has come to the same conclusion, that many of its troops are, indeed, knowledge workers. These are "people who produce not tangible results, but some form of processed or enhanced information."[34] A search through the Army's Research Area Web site turns up such terms and discussions as Knowledge Worker Information Management, model for Knowledge Worker Information Support, and the Knowledge Work Process. As you can see, there's no end to acronyms, buzzwords, and fancy new monikers within today's workplace.

However, information and knowledge are primary elements of knowledge jobs, and they demand skills that are different from those people who not so long ago had to have to survive and thrive at work. This is true even though there have always been knowledge jobs and knowledge-driven businesses. It's simply that the skills are critically different, and more of us need them.

The term is new; the person referred to by it is not. It's just that the concept is more concentrated and vital now that knowledge work and service-related organizations are prolific. Knowledge work ranges from preparing chicken sandwiches the way it was taught at Fast Food U., to sitting in front of a computer all day designing state-of-the-art engineering software packages and discussing the process with other engineers around the world. But make no mistake, the true, full-fledged knowledge worker earns his or her keep. A *Los Angeles Business Journal* report showed how the so-called knowledge worker made considerably more money that those on the lower end of the knowledge and skill scale.[35] Businesses and industries are joining the rush to embrace knowledge, which in turn requires that they prepare their employees to fulfill the role completely. It seems that Frederick Taylor and his work theories and stopwatches have given way to the likes of Peter Drucker, Rensis Likert, and Douglas McGregor. From automobile assemblers to those who manufacture chemicals and wood products, we have people rightfully acknowledged as knowledge workers. The organizations that will be succeed will be the ones that help their people excel at being information literate—and having information power.

Focus on Literacies

Literacy is one of the hottest topics these last few years and will continue to be so for some time to come. Among the "literacies" that have been identified are as follows:

- Functional, also called basic and simply literacy (see discussion below)
- Cultural, the arts, as well as cultural heritage
- Computer, the one that has run rampant (more on this in chapter 6)
- Scientific, part of the school systems' battle to raise test scores to match those of Japan and other countries that emphasize science and math study, sometimes at the expense of the three Rs
- Technical, which is taking on a broader meaning for all of us, but particularly in such professions as electronics, telecommunications, and the like
- Mathematical, similar to scientific literacy with the attendant concern
- Global, being a global thinker and accepting diversity; truly seeing the big picture
- Geographic, which includes knowing where all those new countries are located and what their names are
- Historical, which is becoming less distinct over time.
- Business, literally, understanding the nature of the organization for which you work, including its mission and goals and what contribution you can make to its bottom line, positive results (which applies to both the public and private sectors)

Note that each of these literacies assumes that a person is functionally literate, which means being able to read, write, speak, compute, make decisions, and otherwise operate within the realm of the specific literacy. Note also that same person must also be information literate to function in most jobs today. More on this in the following section. Also, many of these so-called "other" literacies are part of being literate in subject matter, something we all must do. This is the topic of chapter 7.

A critical literacy in the organizational world is that of business literacy. College graduates, for example, are being required to quickly learn, if they don't already know, what is the "bottom line" of the organization they join. This is particularly true for contingency workers who come and go frequently, yet must have virtually instant business knowledge. In the day of downsizing and empowerment, every member of the organization must make a positive contribution to that bottom line, whether it be profit, service, readiness, fund raising, or saving lives. This is a significant part of work and an integral part of information power and literacy. Consequently, it's addressed in more detail in chapter 7, along with the other literacies mentioned above.

The Special Problem of Functional Illiteracy

Functional illiteracy is "the inability of an individual to use reading, speaking, writing, and computational skills in everyday life situations."[36] This, in turn, impacts such a person's ability to get and keep a job in the first place. For instance, it most likely keeps the person from being able to fill out an application blank for a job or read the bus stop signs to find out which bus to catch to go to the initial job interview. The job here is entry level, requiring few skills other than one or two of those listed.

Difficult as it is to believe, over 20 percent of our population fits the category of functionally illiterate. Another 25 percent has been found to be just a cut above in basic skill level, with the shocking fact that the numbers are increasing. No wonder that over 40 percent of employers surveyed by *Training* magazine find themselves conducting basic literacy training for employees.[37] Teaching the three Rs is alive and well in corporate America. To further emphasize this distressing news, a recent American Management Association study showed that about one-third of job applicants tested lacked the literacy and/or math skills needed to perform the jobs for which they applied.[38] This situation is further impacted by the addition of persons with learning disabilities and those who speak English as a second language.

WHICH BRINGS US TO THE "BOTTOM LINE"

Information and Literacy

High hopes and being information literate—having information power—will help us as we enter the new age; buzzwords will not. In fact, buzzwords could well clutter up the path. What's needed is a set of tools—mastered skills—that will set individuals and the organizations they represent on the right path, the one towards organizational goal achievement. Knowledge by itself is meaningless. It must be integrated into a task—i.e., it must be used.

Within any organization, all knowledge must be integrated into a common task. Companies that recognize that people must be information literate, to be able to deal with information and knowledge in a profitable way, also recognize that those people must have the skills and tools to be so. In his book *Smart Training*, Carr notes that to the traditional process of "recognize, decide, and execute," we must add "assess and assimilate" and make it a closed loop model.[39]

Another way to look at it is to view how to train for a learning organization. Some of the abilities they need include these:

- Skills training (that get the job done)
- Learn how to learn skills
- Learning how to learn

The latter involves asking the right questions and knowing when to ask enough; identifying essential components within complex tasks and ideas; finding informal ways to measure understanding of pertinent material; and applying skills towards goals of specific training material and job tasks. It also requires that management create an environment where constant learning is the norm: proficient at all forms of training; everyone a trainer; continually reinforce the idea that learning is an essential part of every job.

This serves as a preview of the remaining chapters and the various skills that must be acquired. It is time now to delve into the overriding skill: information literacy. How the individual skills form the total, expanded set of skills required to be fully information literate is shown in exhibit 1.3.

The American Library Association a few years ago established nine standards for student learning, which they called "information power." Three of the standards relate to being information literate and deal with the process defined in the following chapter. The second three standards relate to independent learning, and the final three address social responsibility.[40] The specific standards are shown in exhibit 1.4. There's a close parallel between school learning and workplace skills. One provides a foundation for the other, and don't forget, learning is lifelong. In short, the process of information literacy, as discussed in the next chapter, has been well established. The challenge, as taken up by this book, is to bring it where it is sorely needed—in the workplace.

Exhibit 1.3
Information Literacy: The Expanded Skill Set

Chapter 2. A Person Who Is Information Literate
- recognizes that accurate and complete information is the basis for intelligent decision making,
- recognizes the need for information,
- formulates questions based on information needs,
- identifies potential search strategies,
- develops successful search strategies,
- accesses sources of information including computer-based and other technologies,
- evaluate information,
- organizes information for practical application,
- integrates new information into an existing body of knowledge,
- uses information in critical thinking and problem solving.[41]

Other skills:
Chapter 3. Communication—basic, electronic, diversity aspects
Chapter 4. Thinking skills—strategy, critical, problem solving, decision making
Chapter 5. Advanced thinking—creativity, innovation, risk taking
Chapter 6. Computer literacy—basic system, operating system software, applicatons software, Internet, communication, administrative
Chapter 7. Continuous learning.
Chapter 8. Whole person, whole life concept.
Chapter 9. Dealing with the future—business literacy, managing change

Exhibit 1.4
American Library Association's Nine Information Literacy Standards for Student Learning

---

The student who is information literate
1. accesses information efficiently and effectively,
2. evaluates information critically and competently,
3. uses information accurately and creatively.

The information literate student who is an independent learner
4. pursues information related to personal interests,
5. appreciates literature and other creative expression of information,
6. strives for excellence information seeking and knowledge generation.

The student who contributes positively to the learning community and to society
7. recognizes the importance of information to a democratic society,
8. practices ethical behavior in regard to information and information technology,
9. participates effectively in groups to pursue and generate information.[42]

CHAPTER 2

Information Literacy:
The One Skill

INTRODUCTION

Information literacy, the key to information power, can be briefly defined as the ability to search for, find, evaluate, and use information from a variety of sources. Looking back at the partial list of potential information sources (chapter 1, exhibit 1–2), things immediately get complicated. There are so many places to look. Then take the word *evaluate*, which is what we must do after we find information. It connotes something potentially more than making simple choices, though it can range anywhere from ordinary yes-no choices, to complex life and death matters. Using information is a key element of the equation. Information is obtained for a purpose, and in the business setting, it means making decisions based on that information. A simple definition isn't so simple after all for much of the information seeking and using we do.

Information literacy has also been called "a wholistic, interactive learning process encompassing the skills of defining, locating, selecting, organizing, presenting, and evaluating information."[1] Though stated in the context of education, the concept applies equally to workplace applications, perhaps more so. The same source noted that students who become information literate "develop confidence and control over their lives." A strong statement, this, and one that is most true. Lack of control over information does complicate life, and how about control over work, which is a fundamental component of life? More on this topic in chapter 10, when we discuss life beyond digits and electrons.

To fully comprehend information literacy, think of it as librarians would: "Information literacy is a process. Information literacy skills must be taught in the context of the overall process.[2] For the person who's left school and gone to work, it must be considered in context with the job at hand, from filling out a resume to developing a global marketing program.

A brief word about information technology (IT) is appropriate at this juncture. The term is found far more often than is *information literacy* in business literature. In its simplest form the term means anything we use to exchange information. Computers play a major role, but also included are transmission methods (wired and wireless, fiber optics and satellites), software packages, telephone systems, the Internet, the World Wide Web, storage media, and more. To put it into perspective with information literacy, a person must be capable of using information technology in order to be information literate. Business people will talk at length about IT, but those who work in successful organizations are the ones who know how to put IT to productive use. *Information technology* is not, then, a term that is interchangeable with *information literacy* or *information power*. It's simply a part of both. Chapter 3 on communications and chapter 6 on computer literacy will address information technology further.

The American Library Association defines information literacy as:

- knowing when information is needed,
- identifying the information needed to address a given problem or issue,
- finding the needed information,
- evaluating the needed information, and
- using the information effectively to address the problem or issue at hand.[3]

An expanded version of information literacy is identified next in this chapter, and then exploded into a sixteen-step process that covers most information gathering situations (which will form the framework for the remainder of the book). Following this, the chapter illustrates how the process works in varying levels of difficulty, identifies strategies for information searches, and provides examples of the process at work.

KEY STEPS IN THE PROCESS

Ten key steps, as identified by Christina Doyle in an extensive research process, are required to execute an information task. The 10 steps are:

1. Recognizes need for information
2. Recognizes need for accurate and complete information
3. Formulates questions based on needs

4. Identifies potential sources of information
5. Develops successful search strategies
6. Accesses sources including computer-based and other technology
7. Evaluates information
8. Organizes information for practical application
9. Integrates new information into existing body of knowledge
10. Uses information in critical thinking and problem solving[4]

Note how they subtly become more complex, each one requiring a bit more finesse and skill than the one before it—and how they build on each other, making it a total, systemic approach to being information literate. Let's now take a more detailed look at each of the steps.

1. Recognize the Need for Information

This would certainly seem logical, but may be more illusory than one might think. For instance, we're constantly surrounded and overwhelmed with information. Just when, exactly, might we need some of it, what information do we need, and how much of it might be used? Is it a real problem, or one that is only perceived and so no action is required? A final question is, do we already have it, or must we launch a search?

2. Recognize That Accurate and Complete Information Is Needed

This is where it becomes easy to slack off. For instance, how much of the information available on the millions of Web sites has been validated? Is there a more recent report than the one we found in the file drawer? How much time is there to ensure accuracy and completeness? Can we believe, and use, everything we see and hear from whatever source? Perhaps you've spent an evening in the library only to recognize that you've barely scratched the surface—and the position paper is due to your boss tomorrow morning. It's awfully easy to take the first data that shows up on the screen or that someone offers on the telephone, but its accuracy could easily be suspect, as well as its completeness. This involves determining how much is enough.

3. Formulate Questions Based on Information Needs

This involves getting into expanded skill sets, moving the exercise into a higher degree of processing, and applying requisite skills. This step goes back to the tried and true Socratic method of getting to the truth, by asking penetrating and provoking questions. This basic skill ages well and serves us most faithfully. As we'll see later, it's not the first time questions are asked in the process, nor the last.

4. Identify Potential Sources of Information

At this point, information overload takes on a more serious meaning along with the additional challenge of sometimes having to search for the proverbial needle in the haystack. The secret is to identify the best potential sources, which sets up the next step. The ideal situation is to identify just enough that includes the best sources and the ones that will get you what you need. The problem is, this is not always easy to do, nor can it happen often, given the sheer number of sources available. "Tried and true" are descriptors that come in handy here, but wariness must be exercised, particularly when the need is for a highly serious problem to be solved.

5. Develop Successful Search Strategies

This is exactly the point where the process takes a steep, upward skill turn. Strategy encompasses higher-level skills and experience and becomes especially demanding when time is of the essence, such as when competition is breathing down your neck. When strategy takes on a broader impact on the organization, information literacy strategy selection becomes central to long-term success. This step is further impacted when time is critical, which it usually is. The paradox is that time is money, yet it's information leading to knowledge that ultimately makes us money in one way or another.

6. Access Sources of Information Including Computer-Based and Other Technologies

But don't forget that not all information requires technology to access. This step also implies that knowing how to get your hands on the information, after having identified where to get it, requires greater effort and skill. This may range anywhere from remembering a password or telephone number, to gaining access to a well-guarded, exclusive database, possibly even reading a foreign language (which could also be the jargon of technology or a specialized discipline).

7. Evaluate Information

This is the second time information literacy skills take an upward turn. This steps implies a wide range of critical analysis considerations in light of the original objective to be accomplished with the information. Many of the skills expanding the concept of information literacy will come in handy here.

Evaluation occurs all up and down the line during the process, but this is the point when the decision must be made to act (or not act, if that is the case).

8. Organize Information for Practical Application

In other words, get it ready to use. For simple situations, this could be easy. But when the task is to obtain large amounts of critical information, it could take time to format into language and appearance others can understand and be easily distributed. If the information is used improperly, or not used at all, as often happens, then the effort has been a waste of time and money. In highly competitive business situations, this waste is intolerable, and when it occurs too frequently it can be fatal. This is a tempting step to skip, but, if done properly, can result in one with tremendous payoffs.

9. Integrate New Information into Existing Body of Knowledge

This is the penultimate step toward applying the newly gained knowledge. Information cannot be used out of context of what is already known without risking misuse. Fortunately, this is the way rational adults normally react, by putting things into a context they can understand and be comfortable with. Here's where good old fashioned common sense comes in handy. (See the section on emotional intelligence in chapter 7.) Another way to think of this step is that if the information doesn't fit easily into what is already known, there is a tremendous amount of risk involved, or else the wrong information was obtained.

10. Use Information in Critical Thinking and Problem Solving

This step is the only reason the effort was made in the first place. This results in a specific decision or action based on the information. If the results of the first nine steps are unusable, then you must reenter the process, perhaps at the top. This is also where the process starts over again as one piece of knowledge often leads to the need for more—and so on. It's possible you could skip some or all of the steps, such as for finding a piece of information that requires a simple e-mail to the resident expert, who e-mails you back the one piece of information you needed. But be careful not to skip any steps unless you have full confidence it's okay. Better to take an unnecessary step, except in the most dire of time-critical circumstances, than to skip a vital one. The overall process is impacted by the complexity of the situation; and in any given situation, any one or all of the steps could be made more complex.

AN INFORMATION LITERACY MODEL

Information flows through knowledge into action, as follows:

Situation	Your organization is fully aware that competition can make breakthroughs to catch up to you at any time, providing comparable products faster, cheaper, more customized, or more advanced.
Information needed	Competitive studies. What is the competition doing?
	Own status—when can you improve, update, reduce prices, open new markets, and so on.
	Marketplace—what do customers have to say, what are their needs, what are they buying?
Action	Apply information literacy model (expanded version shown below).
Results	Information becomes knowledge that can lead you to stave off the competition because your information search showed you had a competitive edge (i.e., beat them to the punch with improved, cheaper, or better products).

Another example could also have been a nonprofit agency being pressed to search for new funding sources; a church group trying to determine what kind of summer program to hold for kids; or a retiree wishing to build a Web page for a new business. In short, it applies to all information search situations.

The ability to execute this process is the essence of information literacy. Like the information literacy definition, its model is simple and practical. By using the model as the overall guide, and expanding the ten steps, we can develop a more detailed version of what information literacy is all about and apply it to business-related applications. Actually, using a living model is an excellent method of illustrating how a person properly executes the information literacy model. Acquiring information power is a major workplace challenge, but one worthy of vigorous pursuit.

Expanded Model

The result of this expansion are sixteen steps that apply when executing the information literacy process. The reason for adding steps is to make it easier to illustrate the potential complexity of information literacy and to present it in as much detail as possible. It's simply an expanded version of the widely accepted ten-step version:

1. Establish the need.
2. Break the subject down into its parts.
3. Identify the relationships and hierarchies.
4. Identify information sources.
5. Identify multiple sources.
6. Select a strategy.
7. Develop a question list.
8. Conduct the search.
9. Authenticate the information.
10. Filter the information while remaining focused.
11. Analyze the information.
12. Summarize the information once gathered.
13. Select the information that applies.
14. Put information into context.
15. Apply the information.
16. Evaluate the action taken and reenter as necessary.

The example we'll use to give meaning to the steps is a where a work process change is required in order to make a work team more effective and productive (bearing in mind that some information tasks may require but a few steps, others all of them).

1. *Establish the need*—e.g., a work team that processes work orders for a manufacturing operation is asked to investigate ways to make the processing more efficient in order to reduce throughput time (i.e., the competition is processing orders for anxious customers faster than you—or better yet, you simply want to improve on what already is the best).
2. *Break the subject down into its parts*—in this case, the parts might be the steps in manufacturing, various methods used to process orders by others in similar circumstances, the process must be manageable by teams, there may be ways that haven't been invented, and so on.
3. *Identify the relationships and hierarchies*—the big picture is that the work team interfaces with several other parts of the organization (customer service, sales representatives, engineering, manufacturing, and so on), and all should have input as well as a final say in what you select. Outside factors such as the customers and suppliers may or may not come into play.
4. *Identify information sources*—which include: industry associations, employees who perform the work, former employees who are either retired or who work elsewhere, customers, academia, literature searches, consultant services, competition, and others.

5. *Identify multiple sources and recognize the importance of doing so*—for instance, you might find that another company in a similar business has an extremely efficient way to process orders, but may require automated systems that are beyond the scope of your operations, so you will need alternatives with which to compare all options.

6. *Select a strategy*—strategies are discussed later in this chapter, but it might be to attempt to find the information from actual contacts and a consultant directory. This will be based on how much time and resources are available, among other things. The strategy could be as simple as looking closely at the competition, possibly emulating them, or possibly hiring someone away from the competition.

7. *Develop a question list*—which is a subset of strategy, where actual things to do are laid out in advance while you gather information. For example, it might include such questions as how much will it cost? Will new systems be required? How do the potential solutions impact your communication channels? Does it work well in a team environment? Who should be involved in making the decision? This is where the ability to develop both open- and closed-ended questions using the old standby device of who, what, where, when, why, how, and if can help derive probing questions.

8. *Conduct the search*—which would mean making the telephone calls, surfing Web sites, sending e-mails, gathering relevant documents, faxing requests, making observations, or keeping logs to obtain the information. It also means that information must be formatted in ways the researcher and others can easily review.

9. *Authenticate the information*—to determine if it is believable and usable. To continue with our example, does the information come from a bona fide company in a similar business? Were experts involved? How long has it been used? What hidden factors might be involved? This step includes verifying believability, accuracy, completeness, and reliability.

10. *Filter the information while remaining focused*—including identifying how much information within a body of facts is potentially of use; not getting lost in the vast sea of facts, while simultaneously keeping focused on the objective of the search—in this case, selecting an order processing method that will significantly reduce the time now spent in processing orders. This step goes hand-in-hand with step 9 above.

11. *Analyze the information*—which in this case would require reading with varying degrees of comprehension, both scanning and selecting specifics buried within the minutia of the information; sitting back and absorbing what you've learned; asking questions and comprehending responses; using communication methods, such as accommodation networks and telephone systems; possibly using a computer to access bulletin boards of manufacturing operations data; electronic mail to query other organiza-

tions; taking notes. Again, results must be captured in clear, easy-to-use formats for all who will be using the information.

12. *Summarize the information once gathered*—listing the potential knowledge alternatives; sorting out and assigning selection factors to each choice; identifying key decision variables, such as cost, ease of acquisition, impact on others who must interface with the workers in question, and so on.

13. *Select the information that applies*—in this case choosing one alternative and providing enough information for you to answer the questions and provide a feeling of comfort that it's reliable.

14. *Put information into context*—by comparing what you have learned with what was already known, such as comparing suggested actions from outside sources with what other companies are doing for order processing. It could also mean ensuring that the proposed answers are in context with the problem, as opposed to being too little or too much of an action to take. Even if you had a good idea what the solution was before you started, this will give you a much more comfortable feeling about it.

15. *Apply the information*—make a decision and implement the new order processing method. This might also include preparation to ensure that the new method installation will "stick," which could include training, communicating to everyone involved what they must do differently, and so on. Note: See chapter 11 regarding change management. For major changes, a planned change process is mandatory for successful implementation of new ways to do business.

16. *Evaluate the action taken and reenter the process when and where necessary*—follow-up to make sure closure has been achieved, or if further action is required (i.e., more information searches, and so on). Has order processing time been reduced? Have new sources come to mind? Are any hidden effects (positive or negative) now obvious? Are the costs and time frames what you had expected?

Fundamentals of Information Literacy

Fundamentals providing the framework for information literacy have been identified and are reinforced by the scenario just presented and are shown in exhibit 2.1. They include a number of the skills a person ultimately needs to be truly information literate and are used to form the basis for the peripheral skills addressed in later chapters. It's a broad, eclectic list of the challenges faced by those who exercise information literacy at work. All come to bear sooner or later, along with ones not included, when it comes to being information literate. Most of these items will come up again in the context of peripheral skills discussed in subsequent chapters, where they've been gathered into the key information literacy skills.

Exhibit 2.1
Fundamentals of Information Literacy

These fundamental characteristics have been compiled from numerous sources

- Functional literacy (read, write, compute at a basic level)
- Reading and comprehension
- Writing (both with pencil and digits)
- Processing (as a mental activity)
- Determining learning styles and capitalizing on them
- Reasoning
- Note taking
- Summarizing
- Outlining
- Formulating and asking questions (as we've learned from motivational seminars, the five Ws, H, and I—*who, what, where, when, why, how* and *if*)
- Goal orientation
- Goal and objective setting
- Focus on objectives at all times
- Open-mindedness—no prejudging
- Empathy
- Self-esteem—that the job can be done
- Knowing how to solve problems
- Know the difference between means and ends
- Ability to separate the "wheat from the chaff"
- Communicating orally
- Nonverbal communication skills
- Understand and be able to apply relevant Total Quality Management (TQM) principles—e.g., continuous improvement
- Planned change principles and techniques—be able to apply
- Knowing how to make decisions
- Knowing how to listen
- Making comparisons
- Being creative
- Taking risk
- Integrating new information into existing body of knowledge
- Persistence

- Perspicacity
- Exercising patience
- Understanding systems and how they work
- Seeing the big picture
- Determining ways to make systems work for you
- Adept at computer and related use
- Setting priorities
- Identifying key words and phrases

Problems Associated with Literacy

As with virtually anything crucial to life's successes, there are problems associated with literacy in general and information literacy in particular. Information overload is one of the largest, as noted in the first chapter. Another problem is more subtle, and more important. Not all people are ready to deal with information, particularly when there's so much to wade through. We're told by librarian Patricia Breivik, "In fact, most people today are information illiterates, and this is having a significantly negative impact on business and society in general.[5] There's nothing like being competent at something—in this case information literacy—to feel more in control of the situation. Mastery places you in total control.

Yet another problem is that technology is such an intricate part of being information literate. Some would say that technology has a stranglehold on the workplace and all that transpires therein. It causes stress, obsolescence of people skills, and more. Often, it results in large expenditures that end up causing more problems than the technology was to have resolved in the first place. More on this in chapter 6, "Computer Literacy."

HOW THE INFORMATION LITERACY PROCESS WORKS

To better understand the concept of information literacy, a look into the skills that make one so qualified, along with samples of its application and implementation strategies, will help. Fortunately, understanding is assisted by the fact that the concept of gathering information is not new at all, it's something we first learned on a formal basis in elementary school, possibly when we first picked up an encyclopedia or a dictionary.

Examples of Implementation

Three typical workplace information literacy examples will illustrate how information literacy works—actually, how we usually seek, find, and apply information. Each is presented in terms of the expanded sixteen step model.

Minor Example. For this illustration, we'll take the situation of a woman who has been asked to advise her boss about when to have the department picnic. This one is straightforward. As supervisor of the group, she merely asks each group member, perhaps in a meeting where all nine of them are present, when they would like to have the annual picnic. She would make sure to invite her boss as a courtesy. There should be a question or two about who pays for the affair, where to go, and who else should be invited. Exhibit 2.2 shows how this situation fits into the model. Not all the sixteen steps are required to a great extent, but the process, if not followed to a reasonable extent, could result in information leading to bad decisions. A spoiled department picnic can be as detrimental to productivity as a malfunctioning machine—work is as much a part of our social fiber as family, play, and religion (see chapter 10).

Medium Example. For this example, we'll create a situation where the manager in the example above must design and implement a new method for processing orders for the services provided by her group. Perhaps orders have previously been taken care of by one or two individuals, but now they are moving to a team-oriented work environment where everyone will be cross-trained. If the orders have become bogged down when one person gets overloaded, the challenge is greater. If the company and manager in question have had no experience in such matters, then there is a reasonably large information literacy challenge. Everyone in the department will be effected to some extent. There'll certainly be precedent for establishing teams, as other companies and order departments have done in the past. This means there will be extensive information available. Many choices will have to be made, ranging from whether or not to get outside assistance to how much training should be conducted. Information on work teams and team building, as just two examples, will alone overwhelm even the hardiest of researchers. There'll be plenty of sorting, filtering, and analysis. Of particular concern will be the need to make sure the alternatives selected fit within the organization's culture. Exhibit 2.3 shows how this situation fits into the information literacy model.

Major Example. This example will feature a small electronics firm that has developed a great new product, a home use robot. An executive decision to obtain financing and take the product worldwide would mean growing the company from one location to multiple locations and from perhaps a hundred employees to thousands of employees around the world. Whereas the previous problem impacted a department with significant change, this problem impacts people who haven't been hired yet. In fact, a human resources strategy, a major information literacy challenge itself, is but one major element of the overall situation. The executive or consultant in charge of this transition will be delegating numerous information literacy challenges over perhaps a three- or four-year period. Exhibit 2.4 shows this situation being implemented.

Exhibit 2.2
Minor Information Literacy Example

---

1. Establish the need—a look at the calendar shows it's time for the annual picnic.
2. Break the subject down into its parts—key elements of the picnic are place, what to serve, and who'll volunteer to help.
3. Identify the relationships and the hierarchies—they don't apply, as everyone in the department is equal when it comes to social events.
4. Identify information sources—employees are the primary sources.
5. Identify multiple sources—need to get input from everyone in the department.
6. Select a strategy—call a meeting and talk to everyone at the same time.
7. Develop a question list—where do you want to have it?; who'll volunteer to help?
8. Conduct the search—hold the meeting and ask.
9. Authenticate the information—unnecessary.
10. Filter the information while remaining focused—double check the calendar to make sure no critical jobs were planned for the day.
11. Analyze the information—make notes.
12. Summarize the information once gathered—review the decisions with the people while in the meeting.
13. Select the information that applies—only gathered what was necessary.
14. Put information into context—already in context; everyone wants a picnic.
15. Apply the information—reserve the location, give the volunteers money to purchase supplies, and have the picnic.
16. Evaluate the action taken and reenter as necessary—ask everyone if they had a good time.

A Note about the Process

Information literacy has been well established as a set of distinct steps, and this chapter has further broken down the process into additional steps for better understanding. However, when you are hard at work, looking for that last piece of information needed to complete a new business plan, you're not likely to stop and think about each step before doing it—and you may well skip one or more steps, depending on the present situation, time, and so on. In other words, information literacy is a process of distinct steps, but in reality people who are truly information literate don't stop to think about the process—they just do it. Learn the process well, then you won't have to stop and think about it. It best serves you when it's intuitive, natural, and fast.

Relationship to Business Processes

People at work perform a wide variety of processes, ranging from mundane daily tasks to major organizational evolutions. Some processes (such as main-

Exhibit 2.3
Medium Information Literacy Example

1. Establish the need—since team formation, order processing has slowed down; also, orders have increased in number and hiring freezes prevent hiring more people (the reason to go to teams).
2. Break the subject down into its parts—team concept (it's new); cross-training; old way of processing; new way to process (to be developed).
3. Identify the relationship and hierarchies—everyone on the team is equal in position, but not all have same skills; two people on team have order processing experience; customers are involved.
4. Identify information sources—team members; customers; industry association networks; literature of the industry; Internet; company files and library.
5. Identify multiple sources—make note that all sources will have to be used because of the relatively complex nature of the problem.
6. Select a strategy—have a team meeting and assign different information-gathering tasks to appropriate people (e.g., one who is adept at net surfing, one who knows customers well, etc.).
7. Develop a question list—what has worked best for others; what do customers expect when placing an order; what were the good and bad points of the old way; what other similar processes have succeeded when done by teams, etc.
8. Conduct the search—put everyone to work
9. Authenticate the information—ask others what they think, say, of an apparently good Web site article on team order processing; call industry experts for advice on gathered information.
10. Filter the information while remaining focused—set aside any information that is suspect, particularly any that is not authenticated; eliminate solutions that have significant problems.
11. Analyze the information—review the information, gaining input from all team members; play the "devil's advocate" on all key information pieces to make sure it stands up to the toughest scrutiny.
12. Summarize the information once gathered—develop a list of alternative solutions, highlighting those items that are most important to the problem at hand.
13. Select the information that applies—after polling participants and possibly outside experts.
14. Put information into context—walk through the proposed solution as if you had adopted it and see how it holds up to additional scrutiny.
15. Apply the information—implement the new process for team order processing with an open mind for adjusting later.
16. Evaluate the action taken and reenter as necessary—adust as needed and continue to monitor over time. Get feedback from those most closely involved (team members and customers).

Exhibit 2.4
Major Information Literacy Example

1. Establish the need—the desire to become a global competitor clearly generates the need to significantly change the way business is conducted.
2. Break the subject down into its parts—there is need for an overall business plan, which includes major subplans for marketing, finance, distribution, and human resources.
3. Identify the relationships and hierarchies—the company functions as a system, meaning each of the major functions impacted (marketing, human resources, etc.) must be changed, but the changes are all related.
4. Identify information sources—major sources are consultants, including those form others cultures; literature of changes with lessons learned; networking with executives who have had similar changes; university libraries; Internet-related sources; and so on.
5. Identify multiple sources—the nature and magnitude of the problem dictates that only through multiple sources can enough information be gained.
6. Select a strategy—hire a consultant who has taken other companies through similar change processes, with key managers assigned to assist and gather information from a variety of sources.
7. Develop a question list—which will be quite extensive and organized by different elements of the change process.
8. Conduct the search—which may take several weeks, possibly months, even while relying on the expertise of the consultant/change agent.
9. Authenticate the information—relying heavily on outside expertise.
10. Filter the information while remaining focused—by discussing potential solutions in view of your company's culture.
11. Analyze the information—following through on the step above, where key executive discuss the possibilities and ramifications.
12. Summarize the information once gathered—done by the consultant in conjunction with assigned management team and presented to the company.
13. Select the information that applies—hopefully the solutions suggested by the consultant as modified through the above steps—which may be a complete restructuring of the company.
14. Put information into context—of your company's culture and circumstances.
15. Apply the information—implement the change process, using a proven model and evaluating every step of the way.
16. Evaluate the action taken and reenter as necessary—as noted above, at all steps along the way due to the magnitude of the change. For major change, this could easily be a long-term step in itself.

taining employee hours) may be common to most organizations; while others (such as developing new, proprietary life-saving medicines) may be unique to one or a few corporations. They are closely related to the information literacy process because they mostly require acquiring and using information—thus, the sixteen-step model applies across the board to virtually all business processes.

Information Literacy Strategies

Several strategies have been identified for accessing, processing, and evaluating the mountains of information with which the typical person is subjected. These include learning how to perform the following tasks:

- Formulate questions.
- Pinpoint what you really want to know.
- Organize information.
- Plan a search for relevant information.
- Evaluate appropriateness of materials.

These deal more with the mechanics of conducting information searches rather than strategies for the overall process. Complimentary concepts include cognitive processes, educational reform (e.g., interactive learning), critical thinking, assessment, technology policy, and national educational goals. All this is from the educational-library community. For our purposes, we'll develop a more broad discussion of strategy in order to serve the needs of business and organizational applications of information literacy.

A widely used system in schools is the Big6™, which includes the steps of defining the task, determining the information seeking strategy, locating and accessing information, using the information, synthesizing it, and evaluating the product and process.[6] It closely parallels the standard approach outlined in this chapter. The company's resources provide the tools for teachers to implement the process.

Another system used by schools is called START, an acronym for Scope, Treatment, Authority, Relevance, and Timeliness.[7] It's used to evaluate Web material and provides a handy reminder to consider how broad the scope of the effort is, how completely it is treated, how authoritative it is, how relevant it is, and whether or not it's timely.

The University of Buffalo, following the information literacy model, also identifies six steps in the information search process: initiation, selection, exploration, formulation, collection, and presentation. Their model provides a helpful tool for information seekers by superimposing feelings, thoughts, and actions over the six tasks performed. Feelings start with uncertainty, moving to optimism to clarification to either satisfaction or disappointment. Thoughts range from vague at the beginning to focused upon completion, and actions range from exploring to deciding.[8]

A natural conclusion to draw about information search strategy is that whatever you do, it closely follows the information literacy process and implements in one way or another the steps within the process. It comes as no surprise that simply using the information literacy process is a solid, field tested strategy in and of itself.

Factors Impacting Strategy Selection

Several common threads can be identified that impact information strategy and help determine what the specific strategy might be. These include:

- Time available—obviously, if the boss says the information is needed for a two o'clock executive meeting with the board and you were on your way to lunch, time is of the essence.
- Cost—always a factor, since time is money. Also, using computers, telephone lines, and other technology elements have cost attributes attached to them.
- Other resources required—such as telecommunications, facilities, people to assist in the process, technical library staff members, and so on (which are also cost factors).
- Level of importance of the outcome—need for information for the picnic noted in the first case would not be nearly as important as the need for information related to a complete corporate makeover.
- Degree of risk to be taken—which is also a function of level of importance.
- Value of outcome—also a function of level of importance.
- How many people are impacted by the process—using more people in the process might speed it up, but will add to the cost as well as to the potential for distortion in findings.
- Variety, number, and nature of sources—if there are numerous potential sources, there will be more leeway in selecting which ones to access, and some sources are much easier to access than others.
- Reliability of sources—some sources are more reliable—are more authentic, accurate, trustworthy, and so on, which can help determine which ones to use.
- Expertise of the person implementing the information literacy process—an experienced person can take more risks and potential shortcuts than can a less experienced person.
- Filters—can online sources, visual scanning, use of extra people, or other resources be put to use to filter information when there are enormous amounts of it to deal with? This is where careful thought (e.g., identifying key information attributes) at the beginning pays off handsomely.

A Simple, Interim Strategy Approach

Using the criteria above, we can develop a simple method of determining a strategy. Each of the following major categories is to be weighted as to its applicability to a given information literacy process—which will help the decision maker determine the most effective strategy:

Time	This might be the single most important criterion if a competitor is about to announce a product that will better yours.
Cost	Will the expenditure to gain, then use, the information be worth the effort when the long term cost is considered? Time and cost, by the way, are directly related.
Importance	How does this situation stack up to other things under consideration by your organization (i.e., what is its priority)?
Resources	Do you have the resources to first gain the necessary information, then to act positively with it?

Any one, or all, of these categories could easily become the key impetus for selecting a search strategy. The scale ranges from simple exercises to major information literacy evolutions. The primary factors, as noted in the preceding discussion, include: time available, estimated cost, degree of importance, and make-up of the sources. For each criteria, there are a number of questions that can be asked to help determine which criteria is critical. The ultimate choice is based on how much risk can be taken, compared to the degree of criticality of the desired end result. For highly critical situations, such as the major example described above, the risk is greater, and more time, money, and resources are in order. The thinking skills identified in chapter 4 will also be quite useful here.

ASKING QUESTIONS

Socrates said it all about literacy in general and information literacy in particular: "The unexamined life is not worth living."[9] This Greek philosopher (469–399 B.C.) taught us all we need to know about asking questions, and his advice is every bit as valid today as it was over a millennia ago. Unfortunately, his high principles cost him his life, but when so many of us get bogged down in giant-sized mounds of information, perhaps we need a martyr to help us through. It's an amazing, simple concept: if you want to know about something, you ask.

Questioning Techniques

The first rule of how to ask questions is that there's no such thing as a dumb question. However, it does pay to ask the right questions. Track the commission income of successful sales representatives, and you'll find a direct relationship between high commissions and the ability to ask the right questions. One Web site promoting questioning techniques for salespersons listed the following advice: prepare questions in advance; go from general to specific questions; clarify ambiguities; keep questions short, clear, and jargon free; and be careful that your language will be understood, among others.[10]

Questions can be classified in at least two ways: open-closed and direct-indirect. Closed questions require direct, probably simple answers. When you ask the question, "Is this information valid?" you would expect either a yes or no in reply. If you trusted the source, it might work; otherwise you'd be left no better off than before. An open question might start with, "How do you know these were the correct income figures for last year?" would lead to more in-depth responses, and would require additional questions. Open questions will do the most good. They arouse interest, stimulate thinking, keep the questioning process on track, provoke feedback, and get everyone involved. They start with one of these words: *who, what, where, when, why, how,* or *if*—the old faithful five Ws, H and I—just like the good newspaper reporter was taught in journalism school.

Direct-indirect questions might apply when there is more than one person to whom to address the question. You can either toss it out to everyone present, such as in a fact-finding group session, or direct it to a specific individual. When more than one person is present, make sure there's no confusion about who is expected to answer the question. Sometimes you don't expect anyone to answer a question, in which case you'd ask a rhetorical question, one not requiring an answer. Such questions might help you or others think about the issue at hand. A rhetorical question might be, "What do you think the competition is doing about this problem?" in which case it would get everyone in the fact finding session above to thinking about the issue to be resolved before more specific questions are asked.

Look back at the sixteen steps in the expanded information literacy model and review each one. As you do so, think about questioning—what are the odds that the step will require asking one or more questions? how critical is asking questions to successful completion of the step? what kinds of questions might be asked to complete the step?—and you'll get a better picture of the importance of asking questions. Remember, there are no dumb questions, just dumb answers. The information literate person knows how to filter out the dumb answers (and doesn't ask many dumb questions, either).

MEASURING INFORMATION LITERACY

The need for information literacy in the workplace has been identified. Whatever the information literacy skill level now required of any given job or workplace task, it will become more acute in the future as knowledge, competition, and technology continue to dominate work and organizations. One of the challenges is to develop methods of measuring just how information literate a person is. Also, as you get into the following chapters on individual-related skills, there are means of measuring each of the them. The problem is complicated by the fact that there are so many skills needed, and it is difficult for many people to have all of them to the extent of competency, let alone mastery. Think of the overall concept of information literacy as a continuum, one you'll want to continually strive to progress along.

The academic and library communities have pioneered the effort to first define, then measure information literacy as they strive to give students information power. A National Forum on Information Literacy, for example, has been formed. The forum's Web site, www.inforlit.org, provides access to various programs around the country. Several institutions with the California State University system, for instance, have extensive programs to provide information literacy training and measure student information literacy levels.[11] Numerous books and other materials have been generated on the subject, almost exclusively directed toward academic and library instruction. However, they do provide insight into competencies and skills needed, which are virtually identical with those outlined in this book. At the present time, information literacy measurement on the job is essentially how effectively each information-related task is performed. Reviewing the skills identified here, and acquiring them to the best of our abilities, will hopefully make the job of measuring more precise.

CHAPTER 3

Communicating in the Digital Age: Mixing the Old with the New

INTRODUCTION

The more technologically advanced we become, the more important is the simple art of communicating. Yet, it still boils down to one human being communicating with another, albeit with gadgets, wires and wireless, satellites, and more, in our quest to communicate with one another. The unique human capability to communicate continues to play a pivotal role as we evolve, particularly at work. It also grows more complex. First, there's the fact that as we become truly global, the number of languages we're exposed to—written, spoken, gestured, intuited—increases. Also, the more paperless we attempt to become, the more paper we consume. Technology gives us more ways to communicate than we ever dreamed of, perhaps too many. To top it off, we have the technical capability to communicate instantly with virtually anyone, anywhere, anytime we want. This brings more pressure than ever on people in the workplace to be able communicators, in all media, at all times. Throw in workplace teams, committees, and meetings occurring on a regular basis at work, and the challenge is raised to an all-time level. When the meeting is digital, with an audience dispersed around the world, the challenge increases, and increases even more when the participants speak several different languages. In short, the ability to communicate well goes hand-in-glove with information power.

This chapter begins with a basic communication model that fits within the framework of information literacy. It then discusses problems with communication, emphasizing the newer problems related to digital versions; workplace communication; skills required to communicate during the information literacy process; and ending with thoughts on how to acquire the communication skills needed to be information literate.

BACKGROUND

The communication process and its elements are shown in exhibit 3.1. Our concern is with successful communication, where one person sends a message that is acknowledged by another person. Failed attempts occur when we take short cuts, or don't pay enough attention to a particular element. Whatever the type of communication, each of these elements is present in one form or another. It's a familiar process, but a brief review will help put it in perspective for the remainder of the chapter.

First, there's the human angle. Two or more people are involved in the process. This is the simplest way. When more than two people are involved, the de-

Exhibit 3.1
The Elements of Successful Communication

Step A—Start	First person sends a message to another
	Must select a method of delivery
	Must deal with interference
Step B—Interim	Second person receives message
	Must have access to delivery method
	Must also deal with interference
Step C—Completion	Second person acknowledges that message has been received

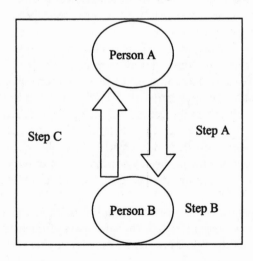

gree of complexity goes up. Considering how we conduct more and more business on a remote basis as well as through teams, this part of the process becomes more complex.

The message recipient must recognize that the message was received. She doesn't necessarily have to guarantee the sender that she'll act on it, and he won't have to provide assurance that the message is fully understood. It's simply a matter of saying yes, the message was received. This is what closes the loop, making it a true communication. As previously noted, e-mail and voice mail take their toll on this last step.

There must be some method to send the information. There are so many to choose from, and some work far better than others.

Interference is the static, or noise, that gets in the way of successful message transmission. This could range everywhere from the recipient having a cold and being unable to hear well (or speak clearly), to *el niño* literally kicking up a storm and wreaking havoc with satellite signals. Seldom do we have the luxury of no interference when it comes to communicating with one another. In addition to these types of interference, others include the following:

- Problems with the method, equipment, and system (e.g., telephone system, computer, connection)
- Compatibility of all parts of the system used
- Mindset or demeanor of each individual involved in the communication, which could include perception, experience, priorities, ego and status, and current mental state
- Cultural or language barriers—or both
- Ability to state things clearly and understandably
- Location of the sender and/or receiver and local conditions for communicating
- Using wrong or impractical medium for the exchange
- Hearing or visual impairment
- Functional illiteracy

Much interference can be attributed to purely human form, as, for example, these:

- A man attaches to an e-mail a voluminous technical report to a colleague who works at home in another region, without bothering to ascertain the type of interconnection, modem speed, or computer the other person has.
- Voice mail is used to send a message of sympathy to a subordinate who's just suffered a personal loss.
- A message admonishing an employee for poor performance is faxed to him at a fax machine serving the entire office staff.

- An urgent message requiring immediate action is sent to a person who receives hundreds of e-mail messages a day.
- A fellow attendee at a video conference is addressed with a personal message over the video conference system.

This is one of those lists that could be endless, as long as people continue to communicate with one another.

RELATIONSHIP TO INFORMATION LITERACY

When these elements are added to the initial steps of the information literacy process, you can see how it can easily get off to a bad start. To put it in a more positive light, the challenge for the information searcher rises dramatically. Exhibit 3.2 lists many of the ways communication manifests itself during the information literacy process. Ranging all the way from jotting down the address of a Web site, to crafting a one hundred-page research report; from telling the librarian you want a book on telecommunications, to explaining to a group of people how telecommunications work; and from listening to directions of where to find the book mentioned above among the stacks, to hearing a speech that was recorded and presented by way of an online video and downloaded from a Web site, the picture is clear. Communication, successful, two-way communications using any and all media, is essential to find and use information effectively.

PROBLEMS WITH COMMUNICATING AT WORK

Problems abound when it comes to humans communicating with one another. "In the workplace, what's the one thing that breaks down more often than the copy machine? Communication. When people communicate poorly in the workplace, they waste time, squander resources, fail to accomplish goals, and sour their relationships."[1] Communication has always been tough; now it's tougher. By identifying and discussing problems, we'll be better able to reduce them. They can be organized into three general groupings: electronic, situational, and cultural. Together, they become an integral part of the information age paradox: an increased emphasis on interpersonal communication and the skills it requires, and the degree of isolation and anonymity of people caused by electronic communications.

Electronic Effects

How do you know you've reached someone at the other end of the communication process? What guarantee is there that a voice mail message will be heard and acted upon by the intended receiver, or even get to the intended person? Some systems will maintain a history of who has and who has not read

Exhibit 3.2
Example of How Communications Relates to Information Literacy

	Write	Speak	Listen	Read
1. Establish need				X
2. Break the subject down	X			X
3. Identify relationships/hierarchies				X
4. Identify information sources			X	X
5. Identify multiple sources			X	X
6. Select a strategy	X	X	X	X
7. Develop a question list	X	X	X	X
8. Conduct the search		X	X	X
9. Authenticate		X	X	X
10. Filter				X
11. Analyze the information			X	X
12. Summarize	X	X		X
13. Select information	X			X
14. Put information into context	X			X
15. Apply information	X	X		X
16. Evaluate and reenter as needed	X	X	X	X

particular pieces of e-mail. But what if the person at the other end, instead of reading the message, simply deletes it sight unseen? A well-known fact is that voice and e-mail make excellent filters for information receivers. One push of the delete button and vast amounts of information are reduced to nothing. It will still register as having been delivered.

Another problem area is that there are still a significant number of people who do not deal well with technology in general and electronics in particular. This either eliminates electronic communications as an option for such people, or makes it a challenge resulting in miscommunication much too often. A part of this problem is the new vocabulary that has sprung up, giving us such terms as URL, ISP, WWW, FAQ, spam, hacker, desktop, right click as opposed to left click, RAM as opposed to ROM, gigabytes as opposed to gigahertz, and more, all seemingly designed to trip us up when trying to carry on a conversation with someone else. (See exhibit 3.3 for definitions.) Even our trusted dictionaries can't keep up with the new lingo, with new words and phrases are being coined daily.

Time and experience will hopefully bridge this gap, but no doubt communication problems will continue for some time. The process will be slowed down by the fact that we have become global in much that we do, and not every place on this globe has become as electronically advanced as we are. Developing nations, such those as in Latin America, strive to make giant leaps forward by adopting wireless communications technology, but this process takes time and money. In this case, time is a problem because of restlessness to move forward, exacerbated by the problem of not enough funding to do it.

Additional problems with electronic, or digital, communications include these:

- Legality—issues related to copyright continue to boil as information spreads rampantly in a manner that at best is difficult to police. An unanswered question is "who owns the rights to specific bits of electronic information?" Throw in free speech concerns and it becomes more interesting.

Exhibit 3.3
Definitions of Selected Terms

- URL is universal resource locator—the unique address given each site on the World Wide Web (WWW).

- ISP is Internet service provider, the organization you send your money to in order to be connected to the Web.

- FAQ is frequently asked questions, which you'll find with news groups and other sites.

- Hacker is the person who breaks into people's and organization's files and destroys and/or steals them.

- Spam is the term used for all those unsolicited and unwanted e-mail messages that clog up your mail slots.

- Desk top is the personal computer that sits on your desk (as opposed the one that fits on your lap or in the palm of your hand).

- Right clicking the mouse will cause some things to happen, while left clicking will cause something different (consult your system's help service or read the manual).

- RAM is random access memory, which is in your computer, while ROM is read only memory, which means you cannot write anything over the data that is in it.

- Gigabytes means large amounts of storage; gigahertz means really fast modems.

- Privacy—closely related to legal issues, and one that will likely become more controversial. Does an employer have the right to eavesdrop on conference calls, e-mail, and employee electronic files? So far, the courts have said yes, because the company owns the system and they are put in place for business purposes. The flip side of this is that people who use PCs most of the time find every move they make monitored, starting from the time they log on the system in the morning and essentially never ending if they tap into them at night or when on the road. Another problem that occurs is information leaks. With hackers able to peek into files supposedly heavily guarded, no wonder organizations are concerned about leaks and disclosures of their trade secrets.

- Control—or lack thereof. Unlike television and radio, where channels are controlled by government agencies, there is far less control of electronic means of communication, and probably for a valid reason—they're world-wide and growing by leaps and bounds, making it difficult to exercise strict control. Agencies are springing up, and existing agencies are gearing up, to track down and prosecute the worst offenders, but this area still remains largely unregulated.

- Quantity of information—which is indescribably vast. Problem is, it's diffi-cult to determine at times the authenticity and origin of certain informa-tion. To say it another way, there is an inordinately large amount of garbage awaiting those who go net surfing through massive databases and Web sites, providing simultaneously excitement, challenge, and a huge burden.

- Quality of information—anyone who wants to can put whatever they desire on the Internet, no holds barred. Authenticity and reliability are up to the recipient to determine. Even prestigious university sites may proffer ambig-uous or otherwise questionable, if not downright bogus, information put forward by students and others having access to the system.

- Permanence—which is to say that often a perfectly good location for mean-ingful information that was here yesterday is gone tomorrow when you try to revisit the site or source (and thus the note at the end of the preface to this book). It's part of the fast-moving nature of electronic media. Such rapid disappearance could well be indicative of the information's original value.

- Systems—which is to say that you must have the wherewithal to communi-cate electronically—PC, modem, telephone line, Internet service provider (ISP), and appropriate software. True, systems have come down in price, but if you have a slow modem and five-year-old processor, you'll be in for long waits for your electronically received information. The growing devel-opment of applications packages designed to help gather, digest, and other-wise deal with information help close the gap, but present their own information dilemma in that they, too, saturate us with more to cope with.

Situational Effects

Situations within which communications occur are as varied as the people and places around the world doing it. A given communication delivery has a lot to do with the mood of the person sending or receiving it. If a sales representative returns to her office after being informed by her boss that she's been promoted and will be immediately transferred to a new office across the country, how much attention will she give awaiting voice mail messages from customers who need help? Or how well received will be the boss's message to work harder and longer when the man to whom it was directed had just learned his child was having school problems again?

Cultural Effects

A few years ago, during a workshop to train literacy and English-as-a-second-language tutors, each member of the audience was asked to tell about themselves and state why they were taking the course. Many of the replies were centered around sincere desires to help adults who couldn't read and write, or perhaps were learning English as a second—or third or fourth—language. One answer, however, was at the heart of much communicating that goes on in the workplace today. The woman, a human resources director of an electronics firm, stated that one day the workforce had taken a poll and realized that on the production floor eight different languages were spoken as a first language and, none of them was English. She was taking the first step towards bringing them all together, through on-the-job training, to be able to work together more effectively.[2] Another example occurred when an informational technology professional traveled from Los Angeles to Hong Kong to help build an online query system. Expecting to work with others sharing his same technical expertise, he found "that there's more to overseas endeavors than meets the eyes. In particular, learning international business practices and customs, communicating clearly and effectively, and planning for the return home are crucial preparations."[3]

Added to this complexity is the fact that, according to Jared Diamond, there are approximately six thousand languages in the world.[4] A U.S. professor working overseas commented that he spoke two versions of English. One was the regular, culturally rich academic English he'd been trained in and that he used in his usual circle of friends and colleagues. The other was a far more simple version applied when speaking with the local students attending the overseas branch.[5] It illustrates what one person did to be sensitive to the needs of others, something that goes a long way toward successful intercultural communication. Remember, too, that it always works both ways.

HOW DO WE COMMUNICATE IN THE WORKPLACE?

How we communicate in the workplace can best be described by simply saying "you name it." The methods of communication are not only many, but the list of ways and means continues to grow, and even the old ones take on nuances. For example, primary methods of communicating can be either formal or informal, and these can include verbal, written, manual, or electronic. Media for communicating includes computers, face-to-face interaction, cell phones, voice phones, fax, signage of various sorts, and others. Some of the ways we communicate at work include the following: one-on-one, in teams, socially, in training sessions, during chat sessions, at the water cooler (real and virtual), with customers, during meetings, with suppliers, while filling out forms, sending e-mail, making public appearances, coaching, and mentoring. We use so many methods to send and receive information, as well as to just pass the time with others. No doubt the equivalent of the old time water cooler chats take place these days over chat rooms and e-mail circuits. Some of this communication is small talk, some perhaps of little consequence, and some that fits into the category of vital to corporate survival (bearing in mind that small talk serves a quite useful social purpose). It's quite a range, and it isn't always possible to determine in advance where on the spectrum of importance the particular communication process lies. Since so much of the time the goal of the process is to obtain information for work rather than merely to say hello to someone, it's vital that we pay close attention to how we communicate. Doing so will greatly enhance our chances of success in implementing the information literacy model.

COMMUNICATION SKILLS

Ability to communicate in the information age adds a second major category of skills. The first is basic skills: reading, writing, and speaking—but we must also add typing for the second category, primarily because of the next category, which is digital communication skills. This includes being able to communicate via electronic mail (e-mail), chat rooms, use (news) groups, and to use search engines.

Basic Communication Skills

Reading. This is about as basic as it can get. Perhaps some of us learned to read by sitting on our mother's lap and seeing the words on the page of the picture book she read from, carefully pointing out the words and pictures and relating them. At work, we must read books, manuals, memos, letters, screens full of information, blueprints, engineering drawings, handwritten pieces of paper, and more, including, at times, between the lines. If there's much to read, then we sometimes find that skimming it, or speed reading it if we've been trained, is essential if we're to get through the material in the limited time available.

Let's compare some of the extremes of reading as related to information literacy. On the simple end of the spectrum, there may be a brief report that contains one fact, say a sales total for one particular year. There would be little chance of misunderstanding what was written. To go farther down the line, however, take the case where the words are part of a lengthy attachment that was quickly put together by a colleague in Brazil whose third language is English, Portuguese being first and Spanish second. Reading and understanding the information, interpreting misspellings and grammar lapses, takes on a whole new meaning. Even the first example could become complex if missing from the communication were needed facts, such as how the sales totals compare with those of last year, or why it's going down. Or perhaps a business unit responsible for a significant portion of last year's sales has spun off into a new company.

Writing. It's quite conceivable that we have come to do far more writing with the advent of computers and telecommunications that we ever did before. In fact, one report notes that "American businesses generate an estimated 30 billion pieces of original writing a year. Workers on average spend one-third of their time on the job writing letters, memos and reports."[6] E-mail and chat rooms reduce traditional conversations to the written word, for example, and they're not included in the above estimate. There are many reasons why we need to write well at work. Some of them are the following:

- The saying about putting it in writing still works and works well. E-mail precludes the need for copies, but this old saw still holds true in the electronic era. It's easy to forget what someone told us to do, but when it is written down (and perhaps has the boss's signature at the bottom), we are much more likely to not only remember to do it, but to do it properly.

- When we take time to write something down, we ordinarily think about it first. This provides a further assurance that we have stated the message as clearly and completely as possible.

- Written forms of communication provide an audit trail that is sometimes essential.

Speaking. Not only do we speak to each other at work, but we speak to the tape recorders found in voice mail and answering machines, to computers, and to other machines to give them instructions. Verbal communication is used often and in many ways during the information literacy process. We ask librarians for assistance, place telephone calls to subject matter experts, discuss information needs in meetings, try out potential solutions over coffee with colleagues, and stand up in meetings to report our findings, all as part of being information literate. Inability to communicate clearly at any step along the way can distract from the validity of the process, if not render it ineffective. The entire chain of the information literacy process must flow smoothly, and communication is the substance that holds it together and gives it momentum. A few rules for speaking, whether to a person you meet in the hallway at work or to an auditorium full of people, are as follows:

- Think before you speak.
- The more you have to say and the more critical the content, the more thinking you need to do beforehand.
- Speak clearly.
- Speak to the audience—all of them, whether one or a hundred.
- Watch your body language—get everything together.
- Keep it simple.
- Keep your speech as jargon free as possible.
- Listen sincerely and continuously, as speaking must be equally balanced with listening before, during, and after.
- Keep your eye on the audience; keep the audience in mind when being filmed.
- Never speak condescendingly—never.
- Mean what you say and show it.
- Stop talking when you're through.

Listening. Sounds are all around us—cars, radios, televisions, computers, airplanes, wind, doors slamming, houses creaking, dogs barking, children yelling, babies crying, and people talking. Much of it we either tune out or ignore as it becomes part of our everyday existence. But which parts of it do we need to hear, and which sounds must be comprehended and responded to? This is something we must be aware of, as listening—hearing, comprehending, responding—is one of the truly critical elements of effective communication leading to effective work performance.

Much of our listening is done for pleasure, providing we have time to devote to rap, rock, or classical music, television, and other audiovisual forms. More serious listening, such as most of what occurs at work (even some of the most casual may be important if we just listen carefully) requires more discernment. The more important a conversation is, the more discriminatory we must be. This is when we may need to ask questions to make sure we understand.

Another form of listening, one that can often make a great difference when two people converse, is active, or emphatic listening. This is where you pay particularly close attention to what's being said. The following are the steps in the process:

1. The sender sends a coded message.
2. Receiver receives the message.
3. Receiver decodes the message.
4. Receiver feeds back what the message is (as it is understood)—nothing more or less and no evaluations.
5. Sender (now a receiver too) either agrees with the receiver's interpretation or starts the message over again.

Active listening offers many advantages, including these:

•   Shows the other person you want to hear what he or she has to say
•   Relieves you of having to have all the answers, as all you've fed back is what you heard, without offering anything else
•   Gets closer to the communicator and creates atmosphere of honest communication
•   Recognizes the feeling part of communication, identifying negative feelings without rancor since there's no judgment
•   Helps to overcome resistance on part of speaker
•   Keeps any problems where they belong—with the speaker
•   Keeps communication going

One more comment needs to be made about listening, and it's an important one. How do you listen to e-mail or to a vigorous chat session? The answer is simple—you listen by reading and carefully interpreting, asking questions about any situation you're not sure about. Listening is equally as important during electronic communication. It's just that it's different, substituting eyes for ears.

Typing. This is a skill many of us take for granted, yet it's the primary way of communicating electronically, as mundane as it may seem. How many people do you know who must labor through a day slaving over a keyboard, using the traditional hunt and peck system of typing? Perhaps you're one of them. One thing that has become perfectly clear with the rise of the PC is the absolute need to have typing skills, even if they're of the two-finger variety. Speed helps, but isn't necessary. Just knowing where the QWERTY keys are located helps tremendously (showing that old-fashioned ideas are still alive and well amidst technology).

Digital Communication Skills

E-mail. One sure thing about electronic mail—e-mail: it comes with plenty of praise and plenty of problems. As for the praise, it gives us so much flexibility, enabling us to talk to someone halfway around the world as well as to communicate with many people at once. *The Wall Street Journal* used this headline to set off a note about e-mail: "An added joy of e-mail: fewer face-to-face meetings."[7] The brief article stated that two-thirds of polled executives say e-mail has cut back on meetings, and that nine of ten say it has reduced need for paperwork and improved overall productivity.

E-mail also can present us with such unwanted scenarios as dozens, possibly hundreds, of messages awaiting you after one day away from the office, not to mention messages so garbled you have no idea what they mean. To add insult to injury, the same *Journal* article noted that companies still have too many meetings. Fortunately, there are rules to follow that can eliminate most, if not all, of the problems, leaving the trimmings we seem to need in this day of instant communications. A search on the World Wide Web for rules and training for e-mail turned up a wealth of information. By going through several sets of rules followed by selected sites, it was possible to derive a general set of rules worthy of consideration:

- Give serious thought to the question, "Does this message really need to be sent?"
- Think it through before sending it.
- Write it down first, particularly if it's a complex or critical message.
- Reread it before sending.
- Remember that it is a permanent record and will be seen by persons you never imagined would see it (and may never disappear, as people have been embarrassed to find out).
- What if someone you didn't want to see the message saw it anyway?
- Remember that there are rules and laws that apply.
- Omit offensive language.
- Follow your organization's rules about using e-mail.
- When in doubt, don't say it or don't send it.
- Send only to those who need it.
- Scrutinize group addressees to make sure too many people aren't being included.
- Make sure the message is readable by all recipients, particularly if they're from other cultures.
- Check out all your resources.
- When including attachments, make sure recipients will be able to receive them properly and in a readable form.

Chat Rooms. Have you talked to your favorite entertainer or sports figure on a chat session? It's becoming more common, and who knows, perhaps it could take the place of personal appearances at some time down the road. After all, through cameras, television monitors, multimedia computers, and the Internet, we can make long-distance communication almost as realistic as being there. Almost.

A chat over the Internet is a real-time conversation. The difference is that participants ordinarily don't see one another as they talk (although the capability exists of adding live video). Also, you can't always predict when one person or another will enter a message. This means that control must be exercised in order to keep the conversation orderly. It isn't uncommon to read the transcript of a chat session to see question number one answered just after question number four is asked. It's also important to provide the guidance necessary to prevent idle messages or discussion irrelevant to the topic at hand. Nonetheless, chat is a popular forum for business. How else, through a toll free number, can you bring people from around the globe together to talk business. The idea that two heads are better than one applies to one of the key benefits of chat room sessions. Is it fair to assume that Socrates would've felt at home leading an online chat session? Assuming the rules were adhered to, the answer is probably yes.

To give an idea of how chat is permeating corporate ranks, it has been reported that Mail Boxes Etc. has decided to use chat to conduct monthly sales meetings with 2,700 franchises. As with e-mail, a search of the World Wide Web also identified numerous sources of rules to following and training to conduct to ensure successful chat sessions. Searching on the topics of "chat protocol," "chat rules," and "chat training" produced numerous lists the procedures necessary to conduct successful chat sessions. The rules range anywhere from avoiding nasty behavior to simply being courteous. Following is a composite of rules that in one form or another will provide users with the guidance needed for good "chatting."[8]

- Terms and conditions—established at the outset
- Language—clean, understandable by all who will receive it; avoiding slang, acronyms, demeaning terms
- Harassment—don't do this under any circumstances
- Overloading the system—nor this
- Impersonation—be yourself
- Legal issues—if in doubt, don't say it or do it
- Flow of the chat—keep it going; give everyone a turn
- Unsolicited information—forbid it
- Reproduction—think of legal ramifications
- Time limits—set them and stick with the time frame

Rules can be laid out to keep chat sessions orderly and productive, including requiring that certain symbols be typed before asking a question, other symbols to signify the end of a statement, and other symbols to take on special meaning, such as a joke.

Use (or News) Groups. Informal groups such as The Dead Poet's Society as depicted in that popular film, grievance support groups, and neighborhood book clubs are quite alive and well, representing one of the greatest aspects of democracy—the right to get together and discuss virtually any topic under the sun. They meet in homes, clubhouses, coffeehouses, libraries, street corners, wherever there's space. One of the greatest benefits of the Internet, however, has been the formation of discussion groups. Participants sit at their PCs wherever they may be and carry on electronically, covering such a variety and depth of topics it's difficult to comprehend their magnitude. These are called various terms such as use groups, news groups, support groups, and perhaps other names, and they provide more opportunity than many people can fathom. The interesting thing is that their topics and reasons for getting together electronically cover the full spectrum of human needs, including groups that discuss poetry, support one another during illnesses and other needs, argue the merits of books and authors, discuss professional topics, and more. Children are particularly quick to take up mouse and keyboard to get together with other kids around the world.[9] Face-to-face meetings have their advantages, but electronic interaction can be lively in its own right.

Usenet news groups abound on the Web. They provide much-needed forums, and plenty of ones that are considered controversial and unneeded. Nevertheless, they're formed quickly and continue to grow with the proliferation of World Wide Web accessibility. Their convenience is obvious, and members don't have to be together at the same time. The discussions simply continue and people contribute as they care to. Because of their growth, and because they are so open, rules are established for participants. A consensus of such rules include these:

- Learn the rules of the particular group before joining it and follow them to the letter.
- As a new participant, monitor the group for a while to get a feel for the group and how it works before jumping in.
- Watch your language.
- Be nice to everyone.
- Be clear with your information and responses; use titles where it will help keep information better organized and more understandable.
- Keep it brief.
- Act as though it was a face-to-face discussion.
- Don't try to be someone else.
- Give credit where it's due.
- Don't be repetitious.
- Keep it legal.

Electronic Bulletin Boards. A subsidiary of these forms of electronic communication methods is the electronic bulletin board. Here, information of possible interest to certain people can be posted for easy access, with responses left on the board or provided through e-mail, for example. This way, people who want and need the information can get it, the rest can ignore it, thus keeping both e-mail and discussion groups from getting clogged up. By the way, there are sites, such as dejanews.com and altavista.com, that will provide help in searching for particular discussion groups. A significant difference between an electronic and the old-fashioned cork board variety is that the former is accessible to people no matter where they are located. Electronic bulletin boards provide an easy way to send messages, ask for help, and exchange information with a large number of people.

Search Engines. Using search engines, which are the software tools that allow us to find what we need from all the great information available on the Web, is part of the overall search process. It takes skills to use them properly, and the skills are quite similar to those that capable researchers already have. It's a matter of becoming acquainted with the engines and learning how to maximize their capabilities. It's also a challenge. "Ask a couple of strangers for street directions and you never know what you'll get. . . . Searching for information on the Web carries the same uncertainty."[10]

We definitely need help, as expressed by the statement that "The vast amount of information on the Internet should be laid out before us like the greatest library ever conceived by man. It's not. For many people, it's like a library that's been hit by a raging twister."[11]

What search engines do for us is make it possible to find information without knowing exactly where it might be located. If this sounds like what a librarian and card catalog system does, you're absolutely right. It's just an electronic library system that searches through the maze of what's available—incredible oceans of information—in a short period of time. A most interesting speculation is how much better an engine might be if they had been organized by a librarian. These software packages perform miracles, it seems, by telling us that a mere 350,647 potential sources of what we needed have been called up for our purview.[12] Of course, when you start scanning through them, you quickly find that many aren't really applicable, some you wonder why were included, several have disappeared, many are trying to sell you something, and then there are those that are exactly what you wanted. Trouble is, you must search through all of them. The key is to know which engine to use and how to use it to its best advantage. Just like in the library, the more you know about what it is you want, the quicker you'll find it.

Generally, using search engines boils down to these primary considerations:

- Selecting the right engine—and there's no right engine, just many choices, some of which work better than others, depending on what you need.

- Learning the rules for using engines in general and the one selected in particular. Fortunately, they usually provide helpful hints about how to make the most of them, and many of the rules (such as putting quotation marks around phrases) apply to engines.
- Selecting a search strategy—try to determine whether the information might best be found from news groups or online libraries, what language it might be in, and so on.
- How to assess information once it is obtained. Some sources are easy to decide upon, others may be less obvious (i.e., they look good but you aren't quite sure).

The Web itself provides extensive information about how to use search engines, and the search engines themselves come complete with instructions. Here's a collection of rules on the general use of search engines:

- Spend time thinking about your information needs before starting out: What key words and phrases apply? Which engines are most likely to yield the desired results? What might you expect to find? (In fact, a quick review of the information literacy model might be of immense help.)
- Study the engine and be familiar with all its capabilities and rules.
- Use quotation marks (most engines require them) for a more precise search (e.g., "search engine skills" will hit on only those with this exact phrase).
- Use a plus sign in front of a word to denote that it must appear (where appropriate).
- Use a minus sign to denote that you do not want that word to appear (where appropriate).
- Use advanced searches applying the plus, minus and other techniques recommended by the engine.
- Take advantage of all the engine has to offer to refine a search and make it more advanced.
- Try more than one engine.
- Experiment and learn every time you have the opportunity and make notes about what you learn about each engine you use.
- Net search to find repositories of the latest information about specific search engines.
- Ask others who might have been there before you.
- Check library and bookstore literature explaining how to use specific engines.

Search engines come and go, mostly come as new ones are continuously developed. Sites include specialized search engines for use of the site. Other search possibilities provide a choice of engines, and others incorporate several engines at the same time (e.g., Beaucoup). A sampling of engines, bearing in mind that there will be excellent new ones making their debut in the future, include:

- Altavista
- Google
- Excite
- Hotbot
- Infoseek
- LookSmart
- Lycos
- Northern Light
- Yahoo!
- Webcrawler

One of the biggest growth areas is in specialization within numerous topical areas, engines which "vary in size, scope, and types of materials they encompass. They cover a cadre of subjects, including employment, computers, family life, medicine, education, news, sports, personal finance and travel."[13] Several examples were given, and two more interesting ones were Invisible Web (www.invisibleweb.com) which contains over ten thousand search engines in eighteen subject categories, and AskJeeves (www.askjeeves.com), where you ask the cyber steward anything you want. The irony of this proliferation of engines is that there's an avalanche of ways to get to the even bigger avalanche of information "out there."

One World Wide Web expert offers these as key skills to find information on the Internet: know how to choose, install, and use software to access the Web: know a variety of ways to navigate through the resources on the Web, know some of the best starting sites for searches, and know how to use a process-oriented approach to gaining information from the Web.

Some additional guidelines are these:

- Have in mind a good place to start.
- Think about the topics and key words and write them down before starting the search—and make sure all the words are spelled correctly.
- Try several search engines.
- Be selective in the information you focus on.
- Be leery of all information you find.
- Take time to authenticate the information that looks promising.
- Use all the tools available (e.g., refined searches, using symbols, and so on).

Experience indicates the need to be concerned about proper Internet etiquette—netiquette, as it's called. It's not only proper, but leads to more efficient use of the Net. A review of the rules for proper usage of e-mail, chat rooms, and other electronic methods identifies several common threads, often referred to as netiquette. These include the following:

- Keep messages short and focused (and easy to download where appropriate).

- Be careful of what you say, using humor sparingly—in other words, be culturally sensitive to others.

- Use your real name, but give out only your e-mail address

- If you're using company time, keep this in mind.

- Avoid confusion by spelling things out and avoiding slang and buzzwords.

- Give credit where it is due, but gain permission where appropriate.

- Be professional and considerate at all times.

- Bear in mind what you do and say is potentially recorded for posterity and readily available for others to see, including people you might not want to see it.

Special Considerations

We know that body language, tones of speech, inflections, cross-communication (e.g., telling a subordinate what a good job he did through clenched teeth), all have a place in our day-to-day communications. But how do we do it electronically? Sometimes we purposely use body language or other methods (e.g., gesturing) to reinforce or provide additional meaning to what we wish to convey to others. Standard symbols have been adopted to depict humor and other feelings when communicating electronically—if you care to use them. Some people swear by them, but others will quickly point out that you still can't see the actual body language to determine the sincerity of the symbols, or the message itself for that matter.

Another issue is privacy and protection of information, which was previously mentioned. On the one hand, people tend to jump into electronic discussion without considering some of the consequences. Whereas private face-to-face meetings may or may not be recorded, electronic meetings are saved for posterity. All the other problems with privacy and who owns data become compounded when the audience becomes diverse, in different countries and part of different cultures. If tourists have problems using the wrong gestures and phrases when traveling abroad, imagine the problems of an electronic communicator who doesn't know who the audience is.

CULTURAL DIVERSITY IMPLICATIONS

Cultural diversity adds a significantly new dimension to the communication process. Diversity permeates the whole spectrum of doing business, searching for information and knowledge, and communicating. The question that arises here is what are the electronic implications?

ACQUIRING THE SKILLS

We're in luck when it comes to communication skills training. This is because people at work have always needed to be successful in all forms of communications. Thus the ongoing demand for trainers who specialize in such training and the training materials with which to do it. The new element is the digital forms of communicating. Without too much speculation, it can be estimated that few people have had the good fortune of being trained in how to send e-mail before they were launched into the process. Perhaps there was training in how to access the program, but little about any rules to follow to make the result attain the desired results. There are many ways to acquire communication skills, depending on time, learning style, location, resources, and how hard you want to work.

Traditional Communication Skills Acquisition

Many avenues exist to improve basic communication skills. The possibilities are so vast, in fact, that no attempt will be made to select out specific ones. Instead, you will simply be directed to a few possibilities, such as these:

Continuing education	Adult education programs (usually inexpensive).
Online	Numerous possibilities exist, but you must filter through them, applying the information literacy process to determine appropriateness.
Media	CD-ROM, video, films.
Books	There are plenty of books available—just check in the library, online, and in bookstores.
Library searches	A search of professional publications will generate numerous articles and related materials written by experts and available free, or perhaps a small copying charge.
Groups	Join discussion groups, speaking groups, book clubs, and others where you can practice all forms of communication and receive constructive criticism for improvement.

There is one exception, however—using the computer keyboard (typing in old-time vernacular). If you've made it this far without acquiring at least rudimentary keyboard skills—meaning the ability to touch type, even if at a slow speed—then it would be to your advantage to do so. In fact, it's virtually mandatory, unless you have a good reason not to want to become a basic typist, if not expert. Granted, voice recognition, scanners and bar codes, and user-friendly systems that allow you to click your way through many applications, all make the job of the computer user easier. However, communicating with others is spontaneous and specific and must be a totally individualized undertaking. Despite all the great technology, for now at least, you'll need to rely heavily on keying in your messages. Fortunately, there are a number of ways to learn keyboard skills:

Formal classes—The old-fashioned, tried and true way: schools, adult education programs, professional providers, and instruction incidental to other computer-related training

Self-study—Requires perseverance, but is readily available and is advertised as the best way today to acquire keyboard skills; also can use CD-ROM, books, and television courses

Electronic Communication Skills Acquisition

Acquiring, then improving upon, electronic communication skills is a two-step process:

(1) Learn the rules for properly using the communication means (e.g., chat or e-mail), and (2) start doing it.

There are plenty of opportunities available. The Web, for instance, is loaded with opportunities to join discussions, both live and otherwise. You'll quickly find more people to communicate with than you'd ever imagined. The key is to observe, then practice (this precise order is important to learn the proper way to do it, as well as to make yourself more acceptable to the group you join). What works and what doesn't work? What happens when people don't follow the rules? Through practice and paying attention to protocol, you soon will become adept at electronic communication. You'll need to be a good, conventional communicator as well, one who can clearly express thoughts in writing. It won't be long before you recognize that digital communication requires virtually all the traditional ways as well. A sampling of ways to learn to type, as an example, are listed in exhibit 3.4.

Exhibit 3.4
A Sampling of Software Programs for Keyboard Training

SupterType V9 for Windows—developed for schools and colleges; designed by teachers; teaches standard QWERTY key positions along with computer special characters

Accu-Type—typing tutor that adjusts to your learning rate and states you can learn in as little as twelve hours

Fingers for Windows

Mavis Beacon Teaches Typing—for helping children learn keyboard skill

Source: Various Web sites and computer-related publications.

CHAPTER 4

Thinking and Action-Taking Skills: Exercising Information Power

INTRODUCTION

Making decisions is the bottom line of information power. From a workplace perspective, we seek information for one reason—to use it to make business decisions. *Business* means what organizations of all types do on a daily basis to carry out their missions. It might be but the first of a series of decisions, each one leading to the next, making it all the more critical to be information literate. The decisions may run anywhere from determining the best place to order office supplies to where to expand into world markets. Good decisions are based on sound information. They're also made quickly in this day and age, meaning the search might be of extremely short duration. It's the ABCs of business, yet made much more complex and demanding because of technology, competitiveness, and the press of change.

We come into life with little ability to make decisions on our own, but we're wired for it and learn quickly. By the time we enter school, we've learned to use some sort of decision-making process. This is the key: that decision making can be learned, which is good news to organizations requiring managers who can not only make decisions, but make solid ones contributing to organizational success. Closely related to decision making are the concepts of strategic thinking, critical thinking and problem solving. Together, they form the fundamental thinking skills set. Sound decisions are reached when priorities have been established and the less useful information has been eliminated. As for problem solving, there are many who view management as one continuous challenge of solving problems. Thus the quartet—strategic thinking, critical thinking, problem solving, and decision making—are closely intertwined, and have everything to do with being information literate. Equally as important as being learnable skills, they can be continuously improved upon. This chapter begins with a discussion of how we think, providing key definitions. The primary types of thinking—strategic thinking, critical thinking, problem solving, and decision making—are reviewed, along with the skills people need to be successful thinkers during the process of becoming information literate. Numerous tools for thinking are identified.

THE THINKING PROCESS

We think, then we act. Sometimes the subconscious mind does the thinking for us. Either way, the results determine how well we have performed our jobs and, ultimately, how well our organizations have performed. Thinking skills are fundamental building blocks for information literacy. Thinking critically, logically, and forcefully, and sometimes pragmatically is required at every step on the way from quest to final action to applying the newly acquired information. We've been told that the key factor in determining whether a manager succeeds or fails is the "ability to analyze a situation and come up with the right answer, quickly."[1]

The following assumptions are made regarding thinking and decision making:

- Is based on accurate, useful information (at times the biggest challenge)
- Uses a proven, systematic model to arrive at the final conclusion (though a bit of luck now and then is greatly appreciated)
- Is done in a timely manner (which sometimes means yesterday, and almost always as soon as possible—ASAP)
- Is done by a person who has been trained or otherwise gained the experience needed to do these things

It's this last item that causes the glitch in what sounds like a straightforward situation. Not everyone who needs to make decisions based on gathered information has the proper tools to do so.

DEFINITIONS

When we think, we're using our brains to sort through information, recall items from our past, compare what we just saw or heard to what we already know, and otherwise exercise the muscle that has been developed to the state that sets humans apart from other species. Speaking of species, one observer noted that in a learning laboratory to determine if orangutans could think, the proof being used was whether or not there was evidence of images, intentions, and flexibility.[2] This is essentially what humans do when we have our thinking caps on. There are many types of thinking and many ways to think. The types we're concerned with here are thinking strategically and thinking critically.

Strategic Thinking

Businesses aiming to grab a share of the world marketplace and hang onto it for any length of time must be driven by strategy. In fact, strategic planning has made a comeback in recent years. As a *Business Week* article stated, "strategy gurus with visions of new prospects are in."[3] Laying out a strategy based on sometimes lofty values and goals is no guarantee of competitive success, but is an integral part of those that do make it. The reason is simple. Luck can't consistently do what carefully laid out events can—which is to beat the competition. As mentioned previously, we get the same effect with nonprofit organizations as they strive for survival as the competition for public funds and donations continues to heat up. The result is that thinking must first of all be strategic, meaning strategy and strategic thinking are integral parts of information literacy.

Strategic thinking is "a process of reasoning about complex problems or systems to achieve a goal."[4] The process includes a variety of mental skill types and techniques, whatever habits and attitudes we have accumulated, all in the context of gathering and sorting through data to solve problems and to make decisions. Strategy pulls everything together in a meaningful way, providing the guideline for our minds to follow in striving to meet organizational goals. Considering that the information isn't always clear-cut and easy to obtain, strategy-driven decisions can become quite challenging, and strategic and related decisions are usually made by the highest levels of organizational decision makers, although some organizations have succeeded in pushing this responsibility to lower echelons of their employees.

Today's strategic thinking comes with a new twist from past practice. It has taken a turn toward the unconventional. As one author has stated, "you may survive, but you will not thrive with 'me-too' strategies and hypercautious management decisions."[5] This less conventional, riskier approach is referred to as "leap frogging." More on this in chapter 5, "Creativity, Innovation, and Risk Taking." To stress the importance of developing strong thinking skills, particularly strategic thinking, consider these examples:

- Proctor and Gamble increased its profit margins by almost 12 percent.
- Hewlett-Packard brings its managers together with customers and suppliers to create new market opportunities.
- J. M. Smucker created a strategy that will potentially double its revenues over a five-year period.
- Nokia, through its well-developed strategies, is exploding at a 70 percent a year growth rate.[6]

A word about tactics. Organizations differentiate between the long term and short term by using the term *strategy* for the longer term and *tactics* for the shorter. For a military commander, the strategy might be to place an embargo on all goods coming and going from a foreign power; the tactic might be to set up a naval blockade to help achieve the longer-term objective. A pharmaceutical company's strategy might be to open new markets in South America; one tactic toward achieving this end could be to test market a new drug in Brazil. Businesses often conduct strategic planning for the next ten years, whereas operational, or tactical, planning lays out what needs to happen during the next twelve months to achieve the strategic objective. The types of thinking are similar; the time periods are different. For this reason, the discussion has been limited to strategy although the types of thinking and processes would be essentially the same for either one.

One last thought on strategy. Organizations that maintain successful operations within their marketplaces don't hesitate to rethink and make midcourse corrections to strategy when it's necessary.

Critical Thinking

Critical thinking is a process of evaluation resulting in conclusions that are sound and acceptable. This could mean different things to different people, but generally issues and problems are viewed analytically and objectively, thus yielding unbiased and acceptable conclusions that most people would consider reasonable. Classical music lovers think critically when listening to a concert, comparing what they hear with the way they know the sonata should be played. Sports fans think critically while watching a championship match, perhaps trying to determine what game strategy the teams are using, but our concern is for thinking critically within the model of information literacy we have defined.

For a comparison, students have been taught how to think critically through frames that include explaining, categorizing, comparing and contrasting, evaluating, interpreting, justifying with reasons, applying principles, and deriving propositions. These frames not only help to define what is meant by critical thinking, but show that it can be learned. Each of these takes the mind far beyond merely stating the problem.[7]

The importance of critical thinking is illustrated by the declaration that "critical thinking skills are the foundations on which all other organizational improvement practices and theories rest."[8] The process includes the ability to appraise situations, analyze problems and solutions, and determine potential problems and solutions. Yet another definition implies that critical thinking is the ability to think about how you think, and includes such basic thought elements as purpose, questions, information, assumptions, interpretations, concepts, implementation, and point of view.[9]

We're also informed that critical thinking consists of these components:

- Systematic approach to reasoning
- Asking questions to evaluate
- Understanding what others have to say
- Picking out the fallacious arguments
- Developing our own rational arguments[10]

Note the similarities in these assorted explanations of critical thinking. Note also how closely the concept follows the information literacy process. Critical thinking is a "built-in" component of information literacy.

Problem Solving

Problem solving is thinking in a way that leads to a solution to the problem, which sounds simple but can be extremely complex. Perhaps it would be better to use the concept of dealing with challenges, as not everyone thinks of situations as problems, but rather opportunities in which to excel. Either way, it's the requirement to confront and master each situation in the working environment where information is key, and coming out with the problem resolved to the best of our ability. The desired end result is that the organization run more smoothly, make more profit, cut costs, overcome hurdles standing in the way of developing a new product, provide better services, or simply get better at what the organization does for its corporate living—and do so on a regular basis. In a sense, problem solving is all elements of the thinking process rolled into one. If we think of problems in the broadest sense of the word, it's what leads to having to make decisions.

Decision Making

We have noted that the purpose of information literacy is to support the decision-making process. We certainly don't go through all those steps for the sheer fun of seeking out, sorting through, and selecting information. We do it because we need to derive information in order to make a business decision. The same holds true for personal, social, and other decisions outside the organizational environment. One way or the other, the effort must contribute to the broad definition of the bottom line. Decisions are actions, usually coming after choosing from one or more alternatives that have been derived from the information literacy process.

Think about actions you take in your personal life. They're based on decisions, some of which you made a long time ago, and each time the particular situation arises, the decision is made automatically. For example, you have a set of personal values by which you live. If you find a wallet stuffed with money, your immediate decision would be to find the owner. No hesitation, no doubt of the action. The only information you need is inside the wallet, a name, address, and telephone number. At other times, such as purchasing a new automobile, you may find yourself exercising all sixteen steps in the information literacy process before coming to a decision. In this case you can see how information is gathered from multiple sources, all of which are essential to the ultimate decision of what to purchase. In short, we make decisions all the time, many of which go virtually unnoticed, but we also make plenty of significant ones all the time.

KEY ELEMENTS OF THE THINKING PROCESS

Strategic thinking, critical thinking, problem solving, and decision making—are these acts we commit at random? Must we choose which of the parts we want to use? Are they unrelated? The answer is that a fine line separates this array of thinking elements so essential to information literacy. Actually, they're virtually inseparable, together comprising the way a truly information literate person must think. Acting in the strategic interest of the organization mandates that strategic thinking be applied. Getting the best information is a critical process, thus demanding critical thinking at all times. The bottom line is a combination of problems and decisions that needs to be made, usually quickly and, hopefully, flawlessly. There are different ways to approach each of these, which provides opportunities to acquire and enhance thinking skills. For this reason we've separated them for discussion purposes, though in real life, they work closely together.

One of the most fascinating aspects of thinking is that it is a fundamental form of communication—the way we communicate with ourselves. It's all those things going on continually in our heads, even as we sleep. Images are formed that allow us to reason and solve problems and to be information literate. This is where mental images, ideas, and concepts come into play. Sometimes we think divergently, coming up with many possibly solutions to a given situation, and sometimes convergently, bringing a possible solution to a single situation.

A simple model to show this interrelationship is shown in exhibit 4.1. Thinking and acting—being information literate—is a dynamic process. There is neither time nor need to stop and be conscious about where within the model you might be at any given time. You are involved in a natural chain of events, and the more information literate you are, the easier it flows. Each element of thinking and action flows directly from the other, and the fact that we must continually repeat the process means that all elements are being exercised often. Not all decisions and problems are so lofty as to require deep thought, yet in most situations where information leads to business ends, thinking strategically and critically, then deciding, are in order.

Basic to thinking is the process of reasoning. Greek philosophers set the stage for others through the ages who wrote about logic and other aspects of reasoning, such as deductive (conclusions following premises), inductive (de-

Exhibit 4.1
A Thinking and Action Model as It Applies to Information Literacy

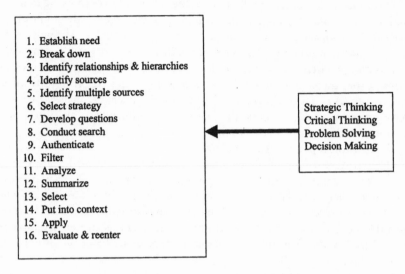

1. Establish need
2. Break down
3. Identify relationships & hierarchies
4. Identify sources
5. Identify multiple sources
6. Select strategy
7. Develop questions
8. Conduct search
9. Authenticate
10. Filter
11. Analyze
12. Summarize
13. Select
14. Put into context
15. Apply
16. Evaluate & reenter

Strategic Thinking
Critical Thinking
Problem Solving
Decision Making

riving from facts), stating hypotheses, using statistical methods, and variations of these. From such processes, we arrive at solutions to problems and decisions.

Another consideration about thinking processes is that there are old ways of thinking and new ways. The old ways include such methods as gaining agreement, using established formulas, addressing multiple realities, and using conflict as the basis of thought. This has been called bounded thinking. The new type of thinking, then, is "unbounded" thinking, which is to say, removing all barriers and old constraints.[11] This will be discussed in more detail in the next chapter. The traditional thinking process requires having some or all of the following elements in place to be properly carried out:

- Relevant facts (gained from information searches)
- Application of reasoning (where all parties involved may or may not agree on what is reasonable, but discussion is based on so-called universal reasoning)
- Application of opinions (potentially as varied as for reasoning)
- Gaining of consensus where appropriate
- Identifying personal prejudices (such as stereotypes)
- Removal of as much bias as possible
- Other parts of the overall system involved

Then, there is the statement by Kaufman that perhaps says it best: "Life used to be much simpler than it is now."[12]

Relationship to Information Literacy

Throughout the foregoing discussion, the relationship of thinking to information literacy has been apparent—thinking is what we do throughout the process. Some of the commonalities are shown in exhibit 4.2. All apply to the thinking and action-taking process required of and used as a result of information literacy practice. Many of these elements can be arranged into hierarchies, showing that there are different levels of thinking required, with some information literacy situations requiring all of them. For instance, analysis may lead to reflection, which leads to synthesization and ultimately to hypothesis formulation, with many possible combinations.

The relationship of thinking and action-taking skills to information literacy has been made throughout this chapter. To summarize, exhibit 4.3 shows how the model of thinking and action applies to an information literacy process. You can see that these skills are at the heart of it. Think of it this way: thinking is a skill that is exercised every step along the way, not just at the end. So, too, must decisions be made all up and down the line. This is another example of how critical are the skills for information literacy, as well as how systems oriented is the process.

THINKING SKILLS

Studies continue to show the value of thinking skills. A two-year study in the United Kingdom identifies visioning and strategic thinking skills as two of the most relevant skills needed by top executives. The study also shows that business leaders have shortcomings in these areas.[13] The insurance industry has determined that chief information officers who want to become chief executive officers must be able to think strategically. The CIO who can think strategically adds the power of technology strategy to overall business strategy.[14] Also, Sears has used a revised strategic planning process to help it regain its former place as the leading U.S. retailer.[15] Boeing has, through revised strategic

Exhibit 4.2
Commonalities of Critical Thinking and Action Taking

Analyzing	Validating	Formulating hypotheses	Sorting
Interpreting	Focusing	Generating ideas	Sequencing
Inferring	Reflecting	Selecting criteria	Imaging
Evaluating	Resolving	Conceptualizing	Framing
Explaining	Clarifying	Integrating	Screening
Synthesizing	Contrasting	Reflecting	Visioning
Questioning	Verifying	Finding critical paths	Comparing

Exhibit 4.3
Information Literacy and the Thinking Process

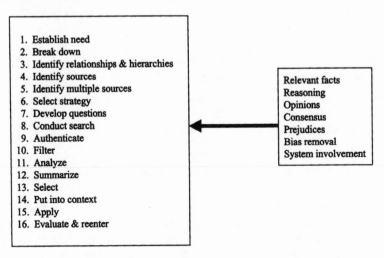

1. Establish need
2. Break down
3. Identify relationships & hierarchies
4. Identify sources
5. Identify multiple sources
6. Select strategy
7. Develop questions
8. Conduct search
9. Authenticate
10. Filter
11. Analyze
12. Summarize
13. Select
14. Put into context
15. Apply
16. Evaluate & reenter

Relevant facts
Reasoning
Opinions
Consensus
Prejudices
Bias removal
System involvement

processes, forged new alliances with leading airlines.[16] These are but a few more examples of the value of developing and using thinking skills in organizations.

General

One author has identified five skills required for leaders:

- Situation review—being able to clear the fog
- Cause analysis—being able to get to the root cause of the current situation
- Decision making—being able to determine the appropriate action to take
- Plan analysis—being able to determine how well the action fits the overall plan
- Innovation—being able to improve upon the action taken[17]

These overlap with some of the other characteristics of thinking we have seen and give us further insight into what types of skills are required for a person to become information literacy thinkers. The commonalities identified previously will be useful in stating skills and determining how to acquire them.

Problem-Solving Skills

Strategic and critical thinking skills lead to the solution of problems. Problem-solving skills provide the basis for moving up to these more advanced thinking skills. There's one skill worth discussion here, actually one that's already been addressed. Ask the right questions and you'll not only get the right answers, you'll come up with the best solution to the given problem—just about every time. As you're solving a problem, here are four situations when asking questions is important:

When you are trying to define or uncover a problem. In business, as in medicine, symptoms can often hide the real disease;

When you are collecting relevant information. In any situation you have to work with available information. Therefore, you should acquire as much as possible and questioning is a major way of doing that;

When gathering ideas that may lead to possible solutions;

When evaluating ideas in order to select a possible solution.[18]

How many questions do you ask during the course of a work day? Sometimes we ask a question because it's part of the job—How may I help you? Sometimes it's to avoid problems in the first place—Do you think it's time we called on our number one customer? And often the questions are intended to resolve a problem—What can we do to provide better service to that number one customer and fend off the competition who's breathing down our necks?

Strategic Thinking Skills

One source has identified an extensive list of strategic management skills, which is to say, strategic thinking skills.[19] A review of these and others provides us with a composite list:

• Finding strategic information
• Analyzing industries
• Analyzing markets
• Analyzing economic conditions and indicators
• Conducting strategic analysis
• Synthesizing results of all the above
• Identifying contingencies
• Developing alternative plans
• Developing strategic plans
• Writing reports
• Presenting reports on results

This list indicates how broad and comprehensive the required skills are. Though a lengthy list, it illustrates two key points: (1) the skills are interrelated to other aspects of thinking, and (2) they can be acquired through experience, coaching, and training.

Critical thinking should remain focused on one key point: the organization's mission. This could be as grand as becoming the world leader in its industry, to achieving one work group's minor objective. Regardless, the ultimate focus is on the overall reason for the organization's being. Everything ultimately comes back to this.

One strategic thinking model uses the acronym BACHA, for Blindspots, Assumptions, Complacency, Habits, and Attitude. The objective of the analysis is to help organizations "eliminate blindspots, question assumptions, reduce complacency, identify unproductive work habits and induce a positive attitude to take action for strategic change."[20] Using this or some other model helps provide the degree of orderliness and thoroughness needed for strategic thinking. Two final points are: (1) strategic thinking needs to be a recurring activity, not one to be conducted every year or so, and (2) it is driven by the organization's mission and values. The need for accurate and current information for the process becomes readily apparent.

Critical Thinking Skills

One view of critical thinking is that it is composed of five activities:

- Assessing complex situations
- Solving problems
- Making decisions
- Identifying potential problems
- Identifying potential opportunities

Notice the overlap between these factors and the overall thinking process. This follows a common model of improvement, which is encouraging in that it usually works.

Developing employee critical thinking skills has a payoff. "Critical thinking's effectiveness," for example, "has been observed among Chrysler Corp. employees whose problem-solving skills increased after they joined problem-solving groups."[21] The process used by many organizations who choose to teach thinking skills to their employees is straightforward. The skills are taught and then the people are expected to put them into action right away. It's okay if they fail, which is discussed in the next chapter, as long as they try. As the Chrysler case noted, "Start—and keep—your people thinking."[22]

Kuhlthau has identified quite specific skills related to critical thinking as it relates to information literacy, which allow us to see more clearly what is meant by the concept:

- Distinguishing between verifiable facts and value claims
- Determining reliability of a source

- Determining the factual accuracy of a statement
- Distinguishing relevant from irrelevant information, claims, or reasons
- Detecting bias
- Identifying unstated assumptions
- Identifying ambiguous or equivocal claims or arguments
- Recognizing logical inconsistencies or fallacies in a line of reasoning
- Distinguishing between warranted or unwarranted claims
- Determining the strength of an argument

These skills are directly related to information literacy—in fact, they could easily be redesignated as information literacy skills. Key skills, they are essential to overall information literacy success.

Distinguishing between Verifiable Facts and Value Claims. We already recognize this as one of the main challenges of information literacy. With so much information available, how on earth can you figure out which piece is good and which isn't? Even when it may all be okay, there's still the challenge of dealing with so much of it.

Determining Reliability of a Source. Much like the challenge above, some sources are more reliable than others. Then there is that great Web site that had that excellent list of facts, but when we went back to retrieve them a few days later the site had disappeared. It's possible to determine reliability, however, and the following lists a few check points for this and the verifiability challenge:

- What is the source? Is it a university, research institute, library, or other well-known organization that takes credit for the information?
- Is complete information provided about the source, including how to contact it?
- Who is the person who's responsible for the information? Is he or she someone you can check up on? Same questions as above.
- Are references cited?
- Is there an audit trail provided where you can trace the information to its original source?
- If an electronic source, can it also be found through a library or other reliable database?
- Is the source dated? When was it last updated?
- What is the message provided—is it written from a perspective of personal opinion, sales promotion intent, or does it appear to be an unbiased, professional presentation?

- What is the level of detail provided? Is it quite short, exceptionally long, or does it otherwise appear to be at a reasonable level of detail?

- Are there other sources with which to compare and validate the source?

- Can you contact the organization and/or individual directly to verify or gain further information?

Determining the Factual Accuracy of a Statement. This is fine tuning the problem of verifiability of a statement and can be one of the greatest problems when the data comes from a Web site or obscure print source. Verbal statements often fall into this category.

Distinguishing Relevant from Irrelevant Information, Claims, or Reasons. This is one of the most common problems. With so much information, which is relevant and which isn't? We all have the experience of believing that an article or statement is just the quotation or fact we are looking for, only to discover later, after more careful perusal, that it isn't so hot after all.

Detecting Bias. We all have our biases, even when it comes to facts: findings can be interpreted in many different ways. Being able to detect biases often depends on how good a writer (or speaker) the presenter of the information was. Good communicators can hide their biases quite nicely and, indeed, may attempt to do so either out of the sheer conviction that they are right or to literally cover up their biases. The challenge is to get through all the subterfuge and see the bare truth of the matter—or at least as close to it as possible.

Identifying Unstated Assumptions. This is perhaps the subtlest challenge of all. Think of times you prepared a position of a matter, thinking you were talking about one thing, when the final result makes it obvious that you had something else in mind when you generated it. It's vital to know all the assumptions behind a piece of information, stated or otherwise.

Identifying Ambiguous or Equivocal Claims or Arguments. The Internet has provided one of the greatest shields for people who don't have their facts quite right, or who want to present their own claims without conducting the required detailed research, or who simply want to leave out the other side's argument, valid or not. Times change, and we do equivocate, but when it comes to expressing the result of an information search, we must be able to make our positions without equivocation or ambiguity. This is the litmus test. Fortunately, ferreting out these largely unusable claims and arguments can use the same principles devoted to authenticity, reliability, and so on.

Recognizing Logical Inconsistencies or Fallacies in a Line of Reasoning. Here is where our logic training comes into play. We must take on the role of detective—sometimes master detective—to make certain that we discover all the illogical aspects of the inquiry. This is exactly what the efficient information literate person wishes to avoid when pursuing ends and means, but must wade through all that was created by others. This is one of the many problems challenging the cause of information literacy.

Distinguishing between Warranted or Unwarranted Claims. This gets into the realm of conclusions, which are the prerogative of the person doing the research. Yet they may clash with the accuracy of the information we need. In fact, it is safe to say that all claims and conclusions that we use during and as the result of the information literacy process must be fully warranted. This follows closely with considerations we would make for how logical a statement is. If a claim is warranted, then the logic followed in arriving at it should stand the test.

Determining the Strength of an Argument. Does it stand on its own merit, or does it require biases, unstated assumptions, and other vagaries to make its point? Will it stand up to tests of time and other expert opinion, not to mention other background information that will undoubtedly turn up after you have made your statement using the argument? These are but a few of the questions that must be answered to give a decision or problem solution, or even an element of one or the other, the support it needs to stand alone.

The best way to develop the skills needed for thinking and action-taking is to practice them. Take every opportunity to think about and act on a variety of levels of problems, preferably similar to the ones that you will encounter at work. One source has identified some of the things to do to develop critical thinking (which means essentially all the elements of thinking and acting).[23] It starts with creating an environment for acting critically. When people's actions are supported and affirmed, people are more apt to develop the necessary skills. People new to the process of thinking and acting need to quickly be able to see the value of creating order out of chaos—the first challenge of thinking and acting—and then learning how to break a problem down into its elements, followed by learning how to graphically or otherwise view a situation and, finally, being exposed to a structure for problem solving and decision making. This is a formula that works, particularly with students, and applies equally to the workplace.

Another source identifies a number of questions to ask when it's necessary to exercise critical thinking in the information-seeking process. They include questions related to who the author is (point of view, reputation); is it fact or opinion (or both) and is there potential bias; currency; what isn't being told; and so forth.[24] It shows how the communication skill of being able to ask good questions carries over to the skill of critical thinking.

Not all the experts agree that there must be structure and models. Successful thinkers often choose nonstandard ways to solve problems, and usually with success. Other elements for successful critical thinkers that have been identified include the following:

- Having a wide range of interests and fields
- Taking multiple perspectives to a problem
- Viewing the world as relative rather than absolute

- Frequently using trial and error
- Focusing on the future
- Being self-confident

Keep these thoughts in mind while reading the next chapter as well.

TOOLS FOR THINKING AND TAKING ACTION

Following are several items to consider when attempting to determine how critical a piece of information might be to a particular decision. Certain factors can be applied, though they might vary between given situations:

- Safety factors—is personal safety a consideration?
- Financial factors—how much is at stake?
- Competition—is it a do-or-die situation?
- Time—how long do you have to take care of the matter?
- People—how many are affected?
- Support—how much assistance and support is required, and is it available?
- Information—how accurate is the information upon which the decision must be made?
- Ethics—are there ethical considerations to be made; are there to be winners and losers?
- Personal—how personally involved are the interested parties and how much do these ties matter?
- Organizational mission—how related to the organization's mission, goals, and objectives is the situation?
- Strategy—how related to the organization's strategy is the matter?
- Amount of information—how much can you filter out?
- Duplication—did you find the same information in more than one source?

These quickly get to the meat of the situation by addressing the key elements for which most organizational decisions must be made.

Kaufman's Model

A reliable model for problem solving is presented by Kaufman.[25] Its strength is in its simplicity. The five steps, which are quite similar to those used by scientists, engineers, logicians, and others are as follows:

1. Identify the problem based on the need.

2. Determine the solution requirements and identify solution alternatives.
3. Select solution strategies.
4. Implement the solution.
5. Determine the effectiveness of the solution.

This model contains the basic elements you would expect: needs assessment, analysis, selection from alternatives, implementation, and follow-up. It's also quite similar to the information literacy model, further illustrating how inter-related all these concepts, processes, and skills are. You've probably noticed their close resemblance to engineering and scientific problem solving ap-proaches as well. Only when we get into the next chapter and discuss other ways of thinking will we think about challenging these effective allies.

Focus Groups

Since focus groups delve into the more creative aspects of thinking, they will be briefly addressed here, then treated in more detail in the following chapter. Focus groups are where a group of people, usually with expertise in the areas needed to deal with the problem at hand, get together—literally put their heads together—to come up with a solution based on their collective thoughts and inputs. There are variations, but this tool is an excellent one for a number of reasons. Looking back to the list of critical thinking skills competencies, you can quickly see where several people dealing with a problem will be more likely to collectively have most, if not all, of these skills. We know how much can be accomplished by passing along something that has us stumped to another who is not so engrossed with the issue. Fresh opinions are always welcome and most often helpful. Teams in particular are good for thinking and taking action and is recommended by many experts in the field.

Role of Brainstorming

Brainstorming falls into the same category as focus groups—it's a tactic that leads to creative solutions. However, it is still a mechanism that two or more people can use to deal with information, particularly when making the final de-cision. As such, it can be a valuable tool for the information literate person. The topic will be addressed in more detail in the next chapter.

Subject Matter Experts

Complex issues can be resolved by calling in subject matter experts (SMEs). What faster way to resolve an issue about information related to, say, aviation, than to ask an experienced pilot or Federal Aviation Administration executive? How often have we heard the saying that two heads are better than one, particularly when the second head belongs to a person who knows more than most people about the subject at hand? Asking the question, "What did Ms. X have to say about the subject?" or "How would Mr. Y have acted in this situation?" are excellent ways to ensure the best results to thinking and taking action.

Software

Software packages are available to help pave the way toward thinking skills success. Popular game software has been offered as a way to learn to think critically. One Web site identified several programs that serve as strategic tools:

- Situation Assessment Advisor—expert tool to help determine your current position and establish goals
- Business Planning Advisor—models business alternatives
- Product Planning Advisor—helps quantify what customers want
- Business Insight—planning tool that integrates established business concepts
- Alcar Strategic Financial Planning System—analyzes data and makes best strategic decisions using value-based metrics[26]

In addition, there are expert systems that literally capture what experts have to say and do in given situations, ranging from trouble shooting electronics problems to making complex surgical decisions (more on this in chapter 9, "On-the-Job Help"). This is literally capturing the ideas of the master thinkers.

Pulling It All Together

Several key concepts emerge from our discussion of strategic thinking, critical thinking, problem solving, and decision making. Included in this list of key concepts are elements common to many of the theorist and management chroniclers who provide the background for studying thinking and action taking.

Visioning. This involves keeping in mind the organization's mission, the guiding light for all that transpires in the organization. Great thinkers can somehow see "down the road," to where the organization should be, to where the pending decision should lead, and so on. It is the future that matters. The organization thinks and acts in order to be competitive for the long haul.

Maintaining a Systems Aspect. This means keeping in mind the big picture (see chapter 11, "The Future"), which is closely related to the item above. Thought and action must support the entire system, not just one aspect of it at the potential expense of other parts. It is the total organization that competes and succeeds in the long run.

Asking Probing Questions. It's still an effective method, recognizing that one decision will often lead to having to make several more. Socrates taught us how to do this, and it has been an invaluable aid to thinkers and action takers ever since.

Using Available Expertise. Use it to maximum extent possible. As the saying goes, why reinvent the wheel, when someone else has already done it. Relying on experts can save inordinate amounts of time and money, and successful thinkers and doers know this, and know whom to ask.

Keeping within the Context of Organizational Strategy. This is similar to visioning, and doing so will also help to send up a flag when strategy needs to be modified. Strategy is everything these days, and it is fully integrated throughout the information literacy and decision making processes.

Driven to Seek Successful Outcomes. Do this always, because it's what competition, survival, and success are all about. Good thinkers and action takers are passionate about what they do, and for good reason—it is what separates them from their less successful counterparts.

One researcher has provided us with a list of the characteristics of problem solvers. First, they have a positive attitude. Next, they are concerned about accuracy. They also have the ability to break the problem into smaller parts. Along the way, they exercise restraint by not making guesses, and in the long run, they are active in the problem-solving process.[27] These elements can be added to the list above to paint an accurate picture of the successful thinker and action taker when it comes to being information literate.

CHAPTER 5

Creativity, Innovation, and Risk Taking: Taking the Extra Step to Action

INTRODUCTION

Competition is the greatest thing that ever happened to creativity. When it reached a global scale, it became the catalyst that organizations needed to be creative, so they could compete profitably in the world marketplace. Often, the only way to beat the competition is to outthink them, to come up with something better, faster, cheaper, more appealing, or all the above. Warren Bennis shares this view about how important creativity is: "The importance of leadership to an organization's success is probably overrated. Collaborative work groups that encourage creativity and risk-taking are just as important as good leaders."[1] Creativity has been known to work well, used anywhere from solving daily problems to giving new life to public sector organizations.

Fortunately, creativity can be learned, the just as decision making and all other elements of information literacy can be learned and improved upon. Certainly there have been geniuses such as Walt Disney and Steven Speilberg who were born with their unbounded ability to electrify us with their genius, not to mention J. K. Rowling and Leonardo da Vinci. We can be thankful for that. However, by practicing exercises designed to bring out the creative juices in all of us—studying, attending courses, surfing the Web for creative opportunities, accepting new challenges, and setting our minds to it—we all can contribute to "better, faster, cheaper, and whatever it takes" to improve productivity and effectiveness. This is true whether doing so for enhancing our own lives or that of our organization, an exciting prospect.

What is creativity? One author calls it "an act of deviance," noting that "creative people are deviant."[2] Creativity researcher Mihaly Csikszentmihalyi notes that "creativity is a central source of meaning in our lives," stating that it's what separates humans from other primates and more importantly, it gives us the feeling of living more fully.[3]

This chapter defines the role of creativity in the information literacy process (as well as at work in general), provides definitions of its elements, then describes what happens during the creative process. A number of ways to be creative, innovative, and amenable to risk taking are described, along with ways to enhance the process. Creativity, innovation, and risk taking lead to decisions the same as problem solving, critical thinking, and strategic thinking. Think of this chapter as a more exotic way to get to action that keeps an organization on top. It's the path to more apectacular results that are needed so often today.

THE ROLE OF CREATIVITY

"Innovate or evaporate."[4] This is what one person had to say about whether or not corporations and the people who work in them should be creative. Stated in such unequivocal terms, the decision of which one to choose is easy to make. No doubt, innovation is a popular term not just in corporate America, but in the global arena as well. It means that innovation and creativity are heavily involved in gathering the information needed to make companies viable for the twenty-first century.

How important is creativity to the process of turning knowledge into organizational gain? The great historian Daniel Boorstin provides one answer. "My hero," he tells us, "is Man the Discoverer. Only against the forgotten backdrop of the received common sense and mythos of other times," he went on to say in *The Discoverers*, "can we begin to sense the courage, the rashness, the heroic and imaginative thrusts of the great discoverers."[5] It is these discoverers who turn ordinary events into epic ones. From our more modest information literacy viewpoint, the discoverers—men and women who are creative and continually seek knowledge—turn ordinary information and decisions based on it into significant achievements and knowledge that enhances organizational success.

Some of the concepts related to creativity are innovation (which is used virtually interchangeably with the term *creativity*), improvisation, imagination, ingenuity, inventiveness, inspiration, insight, and risk taking. These are provocative concepts that make being information literate more that just being able to do a good job of research, or find a possible solution or answer in the quickest time. The payoff is definite. One report confirming this idea comes from the United Kingdom. A company that used Edward de Bono's lateral thinking techniques (more on this later in the chapter) to improve meetings, found that the length of meeting was reduced by 75 percent.[6] When you think how much time people spend in meetings, that's a truly significant improvement, one equating to a significant cost savings.

Creativity covers a lot of territory, ranging from the evolution of Disneyland from an idea into an entity that continually astounds people as it grows and gets better with age, to a single idea thought up by a clerk to improve upon a simple work task. Walt Disney said early on that "Disneyland will never be completed as long as there is imagination left in the world."[7] Yet it doesn't have to be all grandeur, magic, and events of epic proportions. Take the example of an American Association of Retired Persons (AARP) newsletter. An issue from a few years ago bore the title "Beyond Creative Thinking."[8] The title implied articles filled with new and different ways for organizations to compete and succeed. The issue instead was a listing of documents available from AARP to help organizations find the people needed to be competitive and successful. It wasn't a major new idea, and you can anticipate what the simple message was: hire more older workers. At a time when many older workers find themselves likely to become unemployed because they tend to have higher salaries and benefits costs, and have wished otherwise, hiring older workers to fill the gap in skilled jobs is, indeed, an innovative idea worth exploring. As we'll discuss in chapter 8, "Learning How to Learn," the learning process—and thus the creative process as well—never stops. The growing number of senior citizens becoming net surfers is testimony to this.

There's another way to view creativity. It has to do with orthodoxy, or, rather, the lack of it. Most of the time, humans are predictable in how they do any given thing. Some people rise early and stay up late, some do the opposite, but whatever the pattern, it usually follows a familiar series of events. So it is, too, with how we seek out information, make decisions, and solve problems at work. Humans are creatures of habit. Yet there are those of us who dare to be different. For them, the "old" way—read traditional, expected, usual, or predictable way—is shunned for the unexpected, perhaps totally unorthodox way. For example, does Hewlett-Packard wait until a competitor comes out with a better printer, then react by announcing a bigger and better model? It has been reported that H-P actually has but one competitor—themselves.[9] If they can come out with a better product, then that product takes over, even if it's another H-P model. The key thought here is that creativity can easily be just doing things in a different way, not following the textbook and by-the-numbers methods of the past.

Finally, we can address the criticality of creativity in the workplace and tie it in with the other concepts previously discussed. As an introduction into the desire of many organizations to increase their creativity quotient, Warren Bennis's statement that "To a large degree, our growing recognition of the need for a new, more collaborative form of leadership results from the emergence of intellectual capital as the most important element in organizational success,"[10] tells us a lot about the importance of creativity. Everything—leadership, intellectual capital, information literacy, and creativity are brought together to form the nucleus of the type of organization that is today successful in maintaining its place in the sun.

RELATIONSHIP TO INFORMATION LITERACY

On the surface, it might appear that creative thinking has little to do with being information literate. After all, isn't information literacy the ability to acquire and use information? It's achieved through a step-by-step, well organized process, and creativity is anything but. Information literacy is that, but much more, and the key is thought. Thinking, as discussed in the previous chapter, is required at all steps along the way from information need to its application for problem solving and decision making. In fact, being creative and innovative can tremendously enhance the overall process—and do so at all sixteen steps of the way. This is shown in exhibit 5.1. Truly creative people and organizations allow new ideas and innovative thinking to actually drive the information process. Continuously coming up with great ideas may well dictate the information needed.

Being creative when, say, you're considering alternative solutions to a problem (the alternatives resulting from an information search), may produce far better results than taking a more traditional thinking approach. The innovative approach to selection could well land you the most surprising and profitable result possible. Always doing things that are totally predictable may be more comfortable, but meanwhile the competition is overtaking you by applying the very innovations you need to make. One of the messages coming through

Exhibit 5.1
Application of Creativity to the Sixteen-Step Model

---

1. Establish the need—continually searching for new ideas may well dictate the need.
2. Break the subject down into parts—thinking outside the box may identify parts not otherwise found.
3. Identify the relationships and hierarchies—a creative approach may turn up far more relationships than otherwise possible.
4. Identify information sources—as in item 3, using different perspectives and thinking processes may identify sources not otherwise thought of.
5. Identify multiple sources—the more sources the better.
6. Select a strategy—which is where being creative begins to really come into its own.
7. Develop a question list—which is something creative people are quite good at, often asking unexpected questions.
8. Conduct the search—which may take on new avenues because of thinking in different patterns and being unpredictable.

9. Authenticate the information—sometimes, such as with a nebulous Web site or obscure written document, being creative is the only way to determine the authenticity.

10. Filter the information while remaining focused—the act of being creative automatically ensures a fresh approach at each and every step.

11. Analyze the information—again, being creative helps ensure an open mind without bias, which will help lead to the best information available.

12. Summarize the information once gathered—being creative will help provide new and innovative ways to view the results of the information search.

13. Select the information that applies—the process continues as new approaches help guide the entire process, helping select the most appropriate information within a framework of taking different slants towards solutions and decisions.

14. Put information into context—which is to say, within the context of the more creative approach to the end results.

15. Apply the information—where being creative all the way through may well require a creative approach to using the information to solve problems and make decisions—and as noted in step 1, creativity may well have led to the need for the information in the first place.

16. Evaluate the action taken and reenter a necessary—which means closing the loop on the creativity process, as well as starting at the beginning when necessary.

loud and clear during the information literacy process as it is addressed in this chapter is that competition drives the need for being innovative and creative.

THE CREATIVE PROCESS

Textbooks, teachers, and creative persons themselves have identified the creative process as having five distinct steps (exhibit 5.2):

Step 1   Intake (recognition)—an opportunity or problem presents itself. This could be by accident, or it could be the result of a serious problem that arises, possibly with meetings held to try to determine what to do about it. This is the conscious registration of the opportunity or problem. Solutions may occasionally present themselves when we didn't know there was a problem in the first place, but most of the time this step must be taken. It's important that the real nature of the problem—and the real problem—be recognized, and that the effort is aimed at the wrong problem.

Step 2   Immersion—deep thinking about the problem or opportunity, including research if needed. This step could go on for some time as you absorb and contemplate, and it may require intense concentration, perhaps consultation with experts, to get all the materials

Exhibit 5.2
The Creative Process

Step 1 - Intake: Our Widget sales are down.

Step 2 - Gather information: From sales, customers, competitors, other departments, and so on.

Step 3 - Incubate: Digest the information, implement creative techniques to look for alternatives.

Step 4: AHA! After watching a PBS program on e-commerce, the next morning in the shower the idea comes -- sell Widgets on your Web site.

Step 5 - Apply - Get a domain name, build a Web page, and start taking orders.

needed inside the brain in order to take the next step. This could be so extensive as to parallel a full-blown information literacy process. This is where the steps in the information literacy process related to gathering information are used extensively.

Step 3   Incubation—which is when the thinking becomes part of the sub-conscious mind. The reaction to the problem or opportunity, based on immersion, is literally hatching within the brain. For all outward appearances, the person who is incubating the idea is con-cerned with something, anything, entirely different. This, too, could take a long time. An often heard recommendation at this stage is to put the problem in the back of your mind and go on about your business. When you wake up in the middle of the night with an idea, or arrive at a profound insight while taking a shower, you know that incubation is working.

Step 4   Insight—which is the "aha," the time when the solution or idea comes out into the open. This is just as apt to happen while taking a shower as it is upon awakening in the morning. In other words, there is no predictable method, other than letting it go into the subconscious that will cause it to come out sooner. Quite possibly the quicker it's allowed to fall into the subconscious, the faster will come the "aha." It may require a lot of patience, which may be ex-acerbated by the crunch of time, so have faith that it will happen.

Step 5   Application—checking out the solution or idea to make sure it will be okay, then actually using it however it should be applied. There's no use thinking up good ideas or solutions to problems—perhaps great ones—unless you're going to use them. This is where the rubber literally hits the road—and the question of whether or not the idea will work is determined.

Other models may show a different number of steps, but all five functions are needed. Either way, these are the events that occur when a new idea is being hatched, whether it be large or small. Sometimes the time lapse between steps is minuscule; sometimes it might take days for things to fall into place in the subconscious before erupting into being. Some scientists and other great thinkers may well spend years searching for their "aha," while an advertisement copy writer may have minutes to come up with the winning slogan before the commercial goes on the air.

The conventional approach also uses a step-by-step procedure. The major difference is that it will likely lead to a predictable solution or idea, which may have been the culprit in the first place. Being creative allows the subconscious to become involved and brings out the best of people's minds, and it's what sets apart the truly successful people and organizations.

WAYS TO THINK AND ACT CREATIVELY

There are many ways to think and act creatively. This section addresses several of the more widely accepted methods, including brainstorming, mind mapping, lateral thinking, outdoor programs, brain dominance theory, risk taking, unblocking, changing perspective, and exercising all domains of the mind. All are forms of what has been called "thinking outside the box," meaning to think in some way different from the traditional (inside the box), by-the-numbers method.

Brainstorming

We've all gone through variations of brainstorming, if only during party games. The process is straightforward. A group of people get together and are assigned a problem to solve, the task of creating something, coming up with a new idea, or something similar. For example, the challenge could be to identify a way to enhance a product that is a computer application software package for publishing newsletters. The following rules are set:

- All ideas will be recorded.
- No judgments will be made at this time regarding any idea—all will be accepted.
- People are encouraged to come up with as many ideas as possible.
- Screening and selection will come later.

The process then begins. One of the developments that quickly becomes obvious is that having several people involved in the process will cause a synergistic reaction; what others say will stimulate everyone to be more creative and prolific with their ideas (e.g., if each of the three participants come up with five ideas each, for a total of fifteen, together they could easily come up with fifty, perhaps more). The result of the process is a list of ideas (one person must act as recorder, preferably by writing them down on a board or newsprint so they are visible during the process). Following our example of the software enhancement, the list might contain such ideas as expanding the available fonts, adding other languages, adding color, adding fancy clip art, simplifying how material from other files are imported, developing versions for different size systems, developing systems for other countries and languages, and so on. Once a list of ideas has been made, the next step might be to refine it. At this time, the rules may be changed to eliminate certain ideas because of major stumbling blocks such as time required or exorbitant cost. In our example, adding other languages might be too costly, and adding fancy clip art might use up too much disk space.

Brainstorming has many uses and applies to any given business, situation, problem, or process. It's a simple tool that forces thinking outside the box and results in viable ideas that might not otherwise be generated. Individuals can brainstorm on their own, but adding other people provides a multiplier effect to not only the number of ideas generated, but the level of innovation as well.

Mind Mapping

Mind mapping is a form of brainstorming and works well when several people are involved (although it does lend itself to individual use). Another term that has been used, in fact, is visual brainstorming, where the results are diagrammed much like the mind works in generating variables to problems and ideas. As in the brainstorming process, the starting point is a problem that must be solved or need that must be fulfilled. This idea becomes the focus of the exercise. The process requires that participants generate key words and thoughts, everything and anything that flows from the collected minds regarding the central idea. From the primary focus, subtopics are identified and linked to the center. Circles are drawn around the central focus and subtopics. From here, branches to subtopics can also be made. The result might be quite complex but will pictorially show the ideas generated and likely be a more extensive list, as well as one identifying additional variables for ideas. A sample visual brainstorm or mind map is shown in exhibit 5.3. The result of this process need not be a perfect picture. The key is to record all thoughts regardless of whether or not they fit nicely into the picture.

Exhibit 5.3
Sample Visual Brainstorming (Mindmapping Exercise)

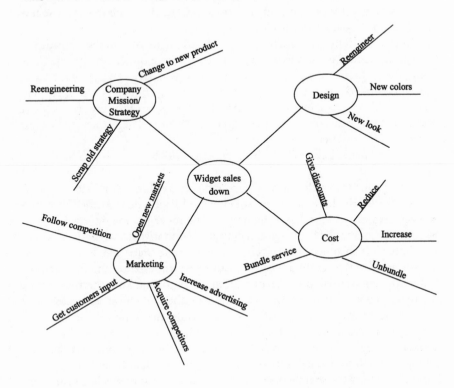

Lateral Thinking

According to Edward de Bono, one of our foremost experts on creative thinking, lateral thinking "is concerned with the generation of new ideas" and the "breaking out of the concept prison of old ideas."[11] It's a deliberate process, one where you think in ways you might not have done before. Some of the ideas behind the concept of lateral thinking include changing patterns in how you think; being nonjudgmental; avoiding putting labels on things; exploring the least likely avenues; being provocative; and making giant leaps forward with your thinking. De Bono tells us that "when ideas lead information rather than lag behind progress is rapid."[12] This is a profound statement, indicating that by continually being creative we will actually generate the information we need, rather than having to go looking for it.

Brain Dominance Theory

Are you right brained or left brained? Or do you even remember which side controls which function? In everyday usage, the brain, of course, uses both sides. In fact, that's what brain dominance theory (and creativity, for that matter) is about—using all parts of the brain to their fullest. Estimates range anywhere from 1 to 99 percent, but the consensus seems to be that we use less than half our actual brain capacity.

Left brain—right brain theory simply stated is that we use the left side for everyday functioning, and that the right side is where our creativity lies. Generally, the left brain is credited with such functions as logic, facts, planning, organization—all the things that make administrators, engineers, and managers function within well-defined boundaries. The right side of the brain is credited with emotions, intuition, holistic concepts, and other related concepts that are prized by artists, writers, and others who are more creatively oriented. Blended together and making the most of both generally yields the most productive results.

Ned Herrmann, a well-known figure in the field of brain dominance theory, further divides the brain into four quadrants.[13] Each side is divided into two hemispheres, the cerebral and the limbic. The more pragmatic left side thus consists of the cerebral left (logic, analytical, quantitative, fact-based concepts) and limbic left (planned, organized, detailed, sequential). The more creative right consists of the cerebral (holistic, intuitive, synthesizing, and integrating) and limbic (emotional, interpersonal, feeling-based, and kinesthetic). From a creativity viewpoint, this allows us to stimulate the brain more accurately. For instance, activities can be developed to both bring out our best integrative reasoning, as well as make use of our feelings to help develop new and different ideas. For the most effective overall result, using the whole brain works best, calling upon all four quadrants that Herrmann has identified. The more we know about how the brain works, the better we can ensure maximum application of its vast capabilities, particularly when it comes to being more creative. The more the brain's potential is tapped, the greater the opportunity for creativity. The fascinating thing about all this is that what we have is the brain literally learning about itself.

Outdoor Training

Training in the great out-of-doors has become a staple for many organizations who want to promote independence, risk taking, and survival to their employees. The extreme version is that experienced by military pilots who are given a few items such as string and knife and turned loose in the wilderness to learn how to survive off the land. Some of the more tame versions may find attendees passing their classmates through the air, hand to hand, or perhaps passing hula hoops around a circle of people linked together with intertwined arms and legs. The intent is to help people take the risk of depending totally on teammates for their well-being and do things they might not ordinarily do. Studies have shown that outdoor management education improves attributes such as attitude, motivation, knowledge, and organizational commitment.

One particular study clearly showed that people who attended this type of training showed more favorable attitudes toward risk taking, as have other similar studies.[14] The idea is that taking responsibility for teammates through risky endeavors will lead to more open thinking and trust, and ultimately to more creativity at work. Such training has also been used to help improve organizational visioning and implementing the vision.[15] One of the reasons is that it helps people communicate better. Such companies as Oracle, Abbey National (UK), and Red Lion Hotels have used it extensively.[16] An Australian outdoor training provider boasts of clients in Australia, Asia, Europe, and North America.[17] (A note: outdoor training doesn't come without problems. People have been injured, creating tremendous problems for everyone concerned.)[18]

Hewlett-Packard is no slouch when it comes to outdoor training. Taking a new twist a few years ago, they sent nine managers to Equatorial Africa who "were given the task of finding local business sponsors for young Ugandans to participate in conservation and community schemes."[19] H-P believed the payoff for the managers to take risks would be that the managers could then contribute to the company's maintaining its competitive position.

Risk Taking

Taking risks brings to mind such concepts as betting everything on one spin of the wheel at a Las Vegas roulette table or running with the bulls in Pamplona. Indeed, those do represent a highly risky and, with the bulls, a most dangerous situation. The type of risk we're talking about regarding creativity and innovation is quite different. It does mean sticking your neck out, doing things you might not otherwise do, but danger to health and fortune are not part of the risk-taking equation here.

As one Web site put it, "Today's changing business environment challenges us to make highly risky decisions more quickly than ever before."[20] A workshop advertised on the site is reported to help attendees learn to take intelligent risks. The concept of risk taking is often associated with the concept of being an entrepreneur, which is logical because people who are entrepreneurial must take risks if they're to succeed in a highly competitive world, where more new businesses fail than succeed. A corollary to risk taking is that the path to reaping large returns is often directly related to taking large risks. If you follow investment funds, you know that the more conservative the fund (e.g., less risky), the lower is the rate of return.

Intel, one of the fast-moving, pack-leading companies in recent years, encourages its employees to take "informed risks." A quotation of a senior manager on their Web page notes that "We are doing things that have never been done before."[21] Another company, Trilogy Software, holds a three-month boot camp for recruits. One of the three major thrusts of these intensive sessions is to make sure their employees take chances (along with creative teamwork and meeting customer demands).[22]

Unblocking

Writers are often accused of suffering from writer's block, the inability to transfer words from brain to fingers to keyboard, or to pencil and pad of paper as the case might be. It's an easy malady to fall prey to, and so it is with being creative. You don't have to be a writer. Artists, engineers, anyone who would be creative can come down with this affliction. It's often easier to do it the old way, or not do it at all. However, ways have been discovered to help the mind unblock, to unleash all those creative powers. The nice thing about them is that they work. Here's a composite list of those recommended by experts in how to be creative and innovative, by unblocking the mind:

- Take a position that is exactly opposite from that which would ordinarily be taken—for example, if you're having trouble getting spare parts from vendors, think of how you could make them yourself, or use something different in place of the parts.

- Break the rules, particularly if you're having difficulty thinking of new and different ways to do something—for example, disregard the rules that may be established about how much to spend on solving a problem, or how long to take.

- Be totally negative, such as thinking only of ways to solve a problem that you know will not work—sometimes it loosens up the mind and gets you focused on what will work.

- Clear your mind, such as putting the issue aside and doing something irrelevant and relaxing, such as going to a movie, meditating, or taking a shower (where "ahas" often occur)—getting rid of the cobwebs and other mental images that interfere with being creative is necessary and most helpful.

- Turn it into a fun situation, particularly if you're getting nowhere with being creative—such making the issue into a joke, with funny or ridiculous solutions.

- Make checklists, which might unloose other ideas and get you started on the right path to creativity—you never know how many of the items on your seemingly frivolous and useless list might be good solutions.

- Force relationships, such as ones that shouldn't work—such as using engineering solutions on marketing problems, or vice versa.

Changing Perspective

Perspective seems to always be getting in the way of being information literate. Sometimes it may lead us right to the exact piece of information, and decision, we were looking for. But it can also hinder finding fresh ideas and ones that provide those leaps forward we sometimes need.

Perception is the process of using our senses to acquire information. We see things and immediately have an idea of what they may or may not be. We see, hear, smell, touch, and mentally process information that comes to us. Each person views a given object or event differently, all because of a difference in perception. Some people can see an object and instantly know what it is because they are spatially oriented, such as artists. The significance is that our perceptions either point us in the right direction regarding a piece of information or action, or quite possibly in a somewhat skewed direction. In other words, perception guides how we intake information and is thus extremely important.

The key is to recognize that our perceptions can be broadened by many of the same techniques previously discussed. By thinking in different ways, for instance, we may see an object as being useful, perhaps valuable, whereas otherwise we might have dismissed it in hand. The need here is to avoid biases that may taint our judgment. The broader our interpretations are, the greater the chance for reaching more creative ends.

Exercising All Domains of the Mind

In chapter 8, "Learning How to Learn," learning domains will be discussed. Briefly, the three paths to learning are cognitive, psychomotor, and affective, representing knowledge, physical skills, and behavior, respectively. In addition, Howard Gardner has identified several ways of learning, including spatial, musical, kinesthetic, interpersonal, intrapersonal, linguistic, logical, and nature. These and other learning concepts will be discussed in more detail in chapter 8. They do, however, have an important bearing on creativity: we each learn differently, and our ways of learning may vary as well as we learn different things and operate in different environments. The same holds true for how we become creative, and by keeping all avenues of thought open, we are far more certain to exercise our full creative powers. In other words, our thoughts, feelings, and physical presence, stimulated by any and all of the eight ways we learn, should be opened full throttle to be the most creative.

THE CREATIVE PAYOFF

Many organizations are discovering the payoff from being creative. They establish environments where employees can be creative, take risks, go off in directions others might shudder to think of as too nontraditional, and otherwise jump onto the innovation bandwagon. One study indicated that training improved creative problem finding and solving.[23] In fact, researchers have found that employees can learn to develop (and not waste) their innate creative and critical thinking abilities. Examples of creative payoff are all around us. For instance, 48 percent of companies surveyed in a study indicated they provided creativity training for their employees.[24] Such training ranges everywhere from metaphoric thinking, six hats (six different ways to think from de Bono), lateral thinking, performance engineering, and more. The reason they do it is because creative people create new products, new ways to make dollars stretch farther, and contribute directly to the organization's well being.

One particularly excellent study that's already been mentioned is that offered by Collins and Porras in their book *Built to Last*. They studied eighteen companies that valued creative, innovative employees. For example, 3M encourages its employees to take risks and creates an environment where failure is okay as long as you're trying to create new products and generate new ideas. Hewlett-Packard, we've already seen, attempts to be its own biggest competitor. (More on these companies later in the chapter.)

Starbucks is another example of creativity and risk taking in action, action that continues to pay off handsomely for the company. Their values include such statements as "Care more than others think wise. Risk more than others think safe. Dream more than others think practical. Expect more than others think possible."[25] The book chronicling Starbucks rise to success is liberally interwoven with terms such as using imagination, being people oriented, reinventing oneself and the company, taking risks, and avoiding being a cookie cutter company.

An international example is the Matsushita Company. The founder, Konosuke Matsushita, started in 1906 against the odds. As reported by John Kotter of Harvard, Matsushita had to use unconventional strategies as a small startup company in a land where the only successful relations were between the government and gigantic corporations.[26] Today the company successfully competes internationally with numerous companies and products.

Yet another source noted these examples of corporations striving to make the most of the creativity of is employees:

- Frito-Lay is reported to have used creative problem solving to save more than $500 million during a six-year period.
- Dupont formed a creativity group within the company, which has taken on a wide variety of activities to promote creativity, including extensive training.
- Texas Instruments applies creativity techniques to improve quality.[27]

Creativity and Competition

Progressive, competitive companies are both promoting creativity among employees and seeking as new talent those who are creative and willing to take risks. And what is the payoff for the potentially creative employee? When it comes to chief information officers (CIOs), it pays exceptionally well. "The new-wave CIOs are young, extremely business-savvy, creative," and so we are told, "have interesting life outside the office." Because they are responsible for increasing strategic technology for their firms and providing vision, they are quite well paid. One example—a CIO who went in to resign from a $175,000 per year job to take a CIO position elsewhere for $250,000, only to have his boss give him a raise to $350,000.[28] Creative people help push their organizations forward.

More on Corporate Creativity

It's helpful to look carefully at organizations—and not all of them are for-profit (e.g., a government agency facing severe budget cuts may have to be creative or simply not be)—that take being creative and innovative seriously. By doing so, greater insight into what it takes for individuals to be creative and innovative can be gained. This in turn provides tools to be used during the information literacy process to gain better information make better and decisions.

One approach identifies six factors that contribute to corporate creativity:

- Alignment with corporate goals—which will guide the creative and all processes.
- Self-initiated activity—corporation motivates people appropriately.
- Unofficial activity—people use their own initiative to act and be creative, and do not wait for someone to tell them to do so.
- Serendipity—circumstances are created where fortunate accidents occur, to the good of the corporation.
- Diverse stimuli—outside sources of stimulation are encouraged.
- Communication—internal interactions are promoted, people communicate well with one another.[29]

From these we can see similarities with many of the other elements of creativity discussed in this chapter. These same authors have identified what they call truths about creativity in organizations:

- Creativity is not always what you might expect—it comes by accident and from unexpected sources.
- Rewards do more harm than good for creativity—they take the position that people should be creative for intrinsic reasons, that they simply want to be creative and are rewarded by the simple fact that a new idea happens.
- Systems with follow-through go a long way—accentuating what we've already seen, that creative organizations must create an atmosphere where creativity is welcomed.

Another author has identified what he calls the seven secrets of innovative corporations, which are to have a strategy of innovation, form teams (two heads are better than one), reward creativity and innovation, allow mistakes, provide training in creativity, and create new opportunities.[30] Companies such as General Electric, Rubbermaid, Apple Computer, Campbell Soup, 3M, and other companies are cited as examples of companies who have discovered these so-called seven secrets of innovation.[31]

This latter study identified similar events that occur during new product development: preproject research, identification and screening of new product possibilities, project initiation and coalition building, project outcome evaluation, and project transfer to production. Five activities that occur during the new product development process include these:

- Idea generation—done through creative staff people and primarily teams
- Entrepreneurship or championing—recognizing that someone has to back the project
- Project leadership—recognizing that someone qualified must take charge of the project and see it through to completion
- Gatekeeping—paying attention to the project as it develops
- Sponsorship or coaching—recognizing that people working on the project must be continually encouraged and given direction when needed[32]

Companies That Were *Built to Last*

Collins and Porras studied eighteen companies that they determined to be visionary organizations that had withstood the test of time (e.g., the newest is Wal-Mart, started in 1945, the oldest Citicorp started in 1902). This study indicated these common traits, with creativity and innovation being at the heart of their success over the years:

- Organizational culture, which is strongly innovation oriented, is continually instilled in employees, starting before they are hired.
- Organizational structure is fluid.
- Innovative compensation packages, which are usually generous, are used, including dual-track pay and promotion systems where technical staff can earn more without having to become managers.
- Innovation and creativity are promoted in individuals.
- Training and developing all employees is an essential part of the success story.
- Such catch phrases as "empowerment" and "participatory management" are fundamental practices, and have been since the beginning (long before such phrases became popular in their own right).
- They are driven by strong, clear values.

Companies in the study were 3M, American Express, Boeing, Citicorp, Ford, General Electric, Hewlett-Packard, IBM, Johnson & Johnson, Marriott, Merck, Motorola, Nordstrom, Philip Morris, Proctor & Gamble, Sony, Wal-Mart, and Walt Disney. They are "people" oriented, meaning they value their staff highly and do everything they can to provide an environment where they will contribute positively to the company mission. Numerous examples of "accidents" from these companies illustrate how creativity comes about: Post-It Notes, Band-Aids, Johnson Baby Powder, and Traveler's Checks are some of the items that came about by accident, yet live today as flagship products of these companies. They happened because of the devotion to creativity on the part of employees.

Common Traits of Creative Organizations

From these and other studies, several common traits of creative organizations—and thus the people within them—can be determined. Three common, overall traits include making creativity a top priority, providing the environment where it can occur, and promoting continued creative effort.

Making Creativity a Top Priority. This starts with the organization's mission statement and emanates from the top. This includes an organizational mission that demands creativity as an integral part of long-term growth and competition. This mission, and goals and objectives that accompany it, must be continually renewed and disseminated to employees. It has been noted that "More companies than ever recognize the advantage of having creative people," and they act accordingly.[33]

Providing an Environment Where Creativity thrives. This is an integral part of the organization's culture that is clear to all and continually emphasized. This includes allowing, even encouraging, people to make mistakes. *Empowerment* is one of the premier terms of this decade, and it works to the advantage of innovative organizations who not only expect people to act on their own, but prepare them to do so through training, coaching, and general encouragement. 3M provides a great example by allowing its employees to spend 15 percent of their time being creative through work on individual research projects, and Hewlett-Packard has a similar program for its scientists. New employees are selected based partly on how creative they will be—how well they will fit within the creative culture of the company. Check Web sites and literature of these companies, and you will see the emphasis on people and innovation.

Promoting Continued Creative Effort. This is done through rewards, training, and results. Appraisal systems must seek out creative performance and publicize and praise it when it occurs. Reward systems must be in place that pay people to be creative. Some organizations provide two tiers of advancement as noted above, one for managers and one for engineers, scientists, and other creative staff members. This way people can continue to be creative and still have hope of moving forward. Careers for creative people must be recognized, and continuing education and training programs conducted that allow people to continue to develop their skills and learn new ones. Forming teams is a popular method of getting people together to become more innovative than individuals might be.

ENHANCING CREATIVITY

One thing is clear from the foregoing discussion—people can acquire the skills needed to be creative, innovative, intuitive, and so on. Organizations send their valued employees to training sessions and otherwise create environments where they can be creative. What seems to work best is a combination that includes continuous training and individual focus on thinking outside the box when it will add value to the results, all the while in an atmosphere where taking risks and generating with new ideas is encouraged and rewarded.

Sources for enhancing creativity skills are plentiful, ranging from books full of exercises to Web pages to formal training courses and institutes for creativity. Exhibit 5.4 provides a sampling. Resources are as nearby as a Web search, the corner bookstore, and organizations specializing in providing skills training. Though much has been recorded about how companies enhance creativity, it isn't difficult to adapt it to individual use. Here's one example of what individuals can do, turning reported organizational mandates for creativity into individual ones:

- Build an idea bank.
- Be aware of what's "over the horizon."
- Think about how knowledge can be translated into technology and new or improved process.
- Think about applying technology, including that which is under development.
- Make creativity your personal culture.

Creativity works for individuals and groups. Both ways contribute generously to organizational creativity. If individual creativity is fostered, then the group process is enhanced accordingly. If two heads are, indeed, better than one, then certainly two creative heads will be far more creative. To reinforce the preceding discussion of how to bring about creativity in an organization, here are some tips offered to executives in association management: "develop a relaxing environment to allow members to think freely, prepare them to think creatively from the start by focusing only on the task at hand, conduct an ice-breaker activity to cultivate out-of-the-box thinking, and use open-ended questions not related to the problem subject." The tips go on to say that members should "be open to risk-taking and break the thinking gridlock by asking members to temporarily follow one way of thinking."[34] Examples of how to enhance creativity are shown in exhibit 5.4.

Exhibit 5.4
A Sampling of Ways to Enhance Creativity

Following are sample activities from a variety of sources to both give some idea of what can be done as well as illustrate the vast array of resources available (these are by no means the most recommended resources or the best—merely representative of those that can be used).

From *A Whack on the Side of the Head* by R. von Oech:[35]
Ask and answer the following "what if" questions to get your imagination going:

What if animals became more intelligent than people?

What if human life expectancy were two hundred years?

What if when you looked in the mirror there became two of you?

What if people didn't need to sleep?

From *Creativity* by Mihaly Csikszentmihalyi:[36]
Selected tips on how to enhance your personal creativity:

Try to be surprised by something every day and try to surprise at least one person.

Wake up in the morning with a specific goal.

Make time for reflection and relaxation.

Develop what you lack.

Look at problems from as many viewpoints as possible.

From "Managing Your Career" by H. Lancaster in *The Wall Street Journal:*[37]
Get yourself in a frame of mind to be creative by doing the following:

Bear in mind that creativity isn't a sometimes thing.

Build your tolerance for bad ideas.

Think big.

Seek out diverse friends.

Discipline your creative urges.

From *de Bono's Thinking Course revised edition,* by E. de Bono:[38]
Find the easy alternatives by imagining a glass full of water standing on a table. How would empty the water without damaging or tilting the glass? Some of the possible answers:

Siphon or suck the water out.

Blow it out.

Bubble out with detergent.

Boil it out.

Freeze it and lift it out.

Displace the water with objects.

Capillary action such as a rag.

Sponge it out.

From *Thinkertoys* by M. Michalko:[39]

How to break old habits—start by making a list of your habits. Try to consciously change each of the habits, such as:

Take a different route to work.

Change your sleeping hours.

Listen to a different radio station each day.

Read a different newspaper.

Make new friends.

Try different recipes.

Change the type of restaurants you go to.

Change your reading habits.

From *The Magic of Your Mind* by S. Parnes:[40]

In generating ideas, use these idea-spurring categories to expand the list:

Magnify—enlarge multiply, add, increase, exaggerate, and so on.

Minify—subtract, divide, eliminate, shorten, simplify, and so on.

Rearange—reverse, turn around, combine, substitute, scatter, and so on.

From *Brain Power* by Karl Albrecht:[41]

Use hypothesizing to develop your association skills by hypothesizing about the following:

A car approaching you on the freeway has its lights on in the middle of the day. Why?

One cow is standing alone in the pasture, one-hundred feet from the rest of the herd. Why?

You don't receive any mail for three days. Why?

Someone who has been very unpleasant to you for a long time suddenly begins treating you very pleasantly. Why?

From http://www.selfgrowth.com/creativity.html, Self Improvement Online's Creativity Training[42] related Web sites:

This site has the following categories of online Web sites:

Sponsor Web sites

Articles online

Additional websites

From "Discovering and Developing Creativity," The American Society for Training and Development *Info-Line* series, S. G. Bulruille, editor:[43]

Use the following idea propellers instead of idea stoppers:

It's OK.

I don't know much about that. Tell me more.

I was not aware that . . . ?

What are the options?

Could you give me some ideas for this?

Are there other ways we can do this?

What if . . . ?

CHAPTER 6

Computer Literacy: Information Literacy's Shadow

INTRODUCTION

Only a generation ago, an organization's computer literacy resided in one or two, possibly a handful, of employees. They worked in what might have been called data processing, or perhaps the computer center. Whatever it was called and wherever it was located, its threshold was crossed by the few and the different. Everyone else stayed away. Distributed processing delivered by the PC, complete with powerful applications software, changed all that. Changed it in a big way, and continues to change it as things get faster, smaller, more powerful—and more complicated. To describe it more accurately, it had a multiplier effect that quickly forced most, if not all, employees to acquire those esoteric skills previously known only to a select few. The newest challenge is to find people who know how to use all this technology most effectively. It isn't easy, which underlies the criticality of being computer literate as it applies to being information literate. As an example, in order to fill the void in information technology jobs, placement firms are turning to high schools for talent. Entry-level salaries for the teenagers who become certified after training are as large as $26,000 a year.[1] Not bad for a high school student, and it illustrates the great demand for computer-related skills. It also has had a tremendous impact on information power. The amount pales when placed alongside the salary of a dot.com electronic commerce business data miner, the person who gathers all that information about shoppers, or the salary of a Microsoft software design engineer. But it's a lot more than most high school graduates make the day after receiving their diploma.

A challenge with the term *computer literacy* is how to define it. How literate is literate? Is it enough to simply know where the on/off switch is located, then let the software and mouse do the rest? Or does it require the extensive expertise of the computer "guru" who can do practically anything with a computer? The best answer is, it depends. It depends on what work the computer is expected to do, the nature of the configuration, which applications are needed, and so on. In other words, computer literacy could run a wide gamut of capabilities and skills, depending on the particular situation. It could range from writing a memo to developing a fully automated, multicolor, animated presentation, or perhaps setting up the household or business budget on a spreadsheet; from developing customized software packages to sending e-mail. For information literacy purposes, however, it's expedient to assume that the skills needed for computers lie at the high end of the spectrum. This chapter will first look at how critical computer skills are to computer literacy. Following this, computer literacy will be discussed, including a working definition for information literacy purposes, and a detailed review of the components of computer literacy. The chapter ends with techniques and advice on how to enhance computer literacy skills.

IMPORTANCE OF BEING COMPUTER LITERATE

Even though technology changes rapidly, principles of how to use it stay relatively constant—a big boost for being computer literate. Computers must be bootstrapped, word processors all have similar capabilities, and relational database functions are quite similar. Primary differences are how specific capabilities are implemented, and some are almost identical. Being truly computer literate thus means being able to move from one brand of application package to another, and from one system to another.

A National Bureau of Economic Research study showed that from 1984 to 1993, the number of workers operating keyboards almost doubled, and that these workers who were college graduates earned as much as 30 to 50 percent more than their noncomputer literate colleagues. Another study showed that three of four executives surveyed agree that computer literacy skills "have a major impact on their companies' overall operations,"[2] but interestingly enough, most didn't offer computer literacy training. On the other hand, the American Society for Training and Development (ASTD) has reported that 91 percent of the companies they surveyed indicated they do, indeed, offer courses in computer literacy and applications.[3] The difference is perhaps one of degree.

Adults hear so much about turning to their children and grandchildren to learn about computers. But how valid is this? A report from California notes that "Education has always been the corner-stone of our children's future, but there are cracks in its foundation," and goes on to say that for a variety of reasons, technology isn't being "integrated into our educational system."[4] On the other hand, there's *The Monster under the Bed,* by Davis and Botkin. It tells the story of a five-year-old who used her computer to get rid of the monster under her bed and then shared the story over the Internet (with a graphics program, she drew a picture of the monster and put it under her brother's bed). "Megan did not yet know how to write, but she knew how to use a computer. She learned to use it at home, with the help of the computer itself."[5] This is the spectrum of the ability of children, who will grow up and enter the workforce, to use computers—a crying need in many schools on one end and total competency from five-year-olds who learn at home. There definitely is no consistency, and there is evidently a need for more technology in the classroom.

An article directed to the insurance industry carries a message for everyone: "Would you buy a piano and not take lessons?" or "purchase a car without knowing how to drive?"[6] The article goes on to note that business acquires technology, but doesn't acquire the training needed to make it work. One of the biggest user knowledge gaps occurs at the organizational top. "Most middle and senior managers rely on their subordinates to operate their computers and electronic mails," one reporter has boldly stated.[7] Even if this is only partly true, the need for computer literacy at the top is great. If this scenario is anywhere near accurate, you'd have to wonder how things get done. It's interesting to think that CEOs who make multimillion dollar decisions to purchase technology, don't use it themselves. Kelly Services finds that "Jobs such as spreadsheet preparation are now being assigned to secretaries rather [than] being done by management."[8] Of course, there's an argument that some jobs should be passed down the line, freeing busy managers for more critical decisions—but there seems to be enough evidence to warrant managers being more conscious of computer usage. This question, whether a six-figure-earning executive should be spending time on a laptop while traveling to an international corporate conference is a valid use of his or her time, will not be answered soon, and some executives will continue to delegate technology usage while others will take it up avidly.

Then there's the statement that "The skills of the digitally literate are becoming as necessary as a driver's license."[9] It's most interesting that the author, whose book is actually about becoming competent in using the Internet, identifies such core competencies as making informed judgment about what you find, thinking critically, and developing search skills. Ford Motor Company showed how it feels about being computer literate for its employees by "providing each of its 350,000 employees worldwide—from loading dock to the boardroom—with a home computer, a color printer, and unlimited access to the Internet for about $5 a month."[10] It cost Ford $300 million to "leap the digital divide" to make its people computer literate.

Computer skills are disarmingly obvious. Either a person can use the thing or not. Testing is thus relatively easy, which brings up a key point—computer literacy can be measured through tests designed for the purpose, or simply performing various tasks on actual systems. This, in turn, leads us to an important consideration—just what skills do we mean when we say computer literacy. One excellent way to determine this is to look at what computer skills employers expect from the college graduates they hire. Exhibit 6.1 shows what one study noted to be the case.

RELATIONSHIP TO INFORMATION LITERACY

For a person who works almost exclusively with computers—and there are a lot of folks who do—the terms are virtually one and the same. However, for most of us who deal with information on a regular basis, not all information is available digitally. At least, not yet. Much of it is, however, and more is coming online all the time, thus behooving all information literate practitioners to be as adept as possible at using the computer and all the digital capabilities it brings. Exhibit 6.2 provides examples of how being computer literate might not only be directly related to the elements of information literacy, but enhance the process considerably.

There's another important consideration regarding the digital and technological aspects of information literacy. It has to do with duplication, or perhaps *parallelism* is a better word. Since information literacy requires so many technological skills, technology has become integrally related with information literacy. This isn't always the case, but no doubt technology in general and computer literacy in particular have become essential elements in the quest for information and knowledge. An intriguing fallout is that much of the informa-

Exhibit 6.1
Computer Skills Expected of College Graduates

The following is adapted from a study conducted by the Cornell University Library designed to determine what computer skills were required by employers.[11] An overriding finding was that computer skills were essential.

Skills Required	Level Expected
Word processors	Intermediate
Desktop publishing	Not relevant
Presentations	Basic
Create Internet documents	Not relevant
Install and upgrade software	Basic
Create or modify programs/macros	Basic
Database editing	Basic
Create commercial software	Not relevant
Spreadsheet	Basic to intermediate
Computer network skills	No level stated

Exhibit 6.2
How Computer Literacy Relates to the Information Literacy Process

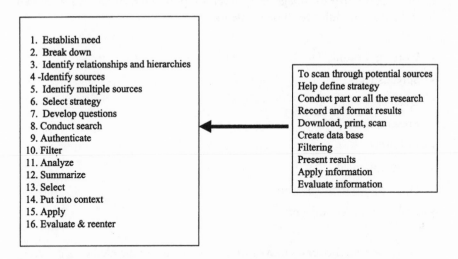

1. Establish need
2. Break down
3. Identify relationships and hierarchies
4 -Identify sources
5. Identify multiple sources
6. Select strategy
7. Develop questions
8. Conduct search
9. Authenticate
10. Filter
11. Analyze
12. Summarize
13. Select
14. Put into context
15. Apply
16. Evaluate & reenter

To scan through potential sources
Help define strategy
Conduct part or all the research
Record and format results
Download, print, scan
Create data base
Filtering
Present results
Apply information
Evaluate information

tion we seek is about technology. We use technology to acquire more information about it.

One last thought before examining the elements of computer literacy: the computer is a tool, albeit a crucial one, to help in getting work done. The user controls it just the same as if it were a drill press or food processor. The more computer literate a person is, the more in control of the tool he or she will be.

ELEMENTS OF COMPUTER LITERACY

Overview

Is computer literacy the ability to turn on a computer and set about playing a game, or perhaps sending an e-mail message to a friend? Or does it mean the ability to write programs in C++, using the full power of the computer and networks? The real issue here is the same as that for information literacy—there's a broad spectrum of skills, and the higher up you are on that spectrum, the better off you'll be. It doesn't mean you need to learn how to write code (unless your job calls for it). But it does mean that the more useful work you can coax out of the machine, the more successful you'll be, the higher up on the information literacy spectrum of skills as well. This, as so many other aspects of information literacy, sounds much like the topic itself. Another person has said that it's about mastering ideas, not keystrokes, which puts it in the proper perspective.[12]

There are many elements that could be included and many skill levels that could be addressed. For our purposes of what it means to be information literate, and facing the reality of the growing needs of the workplace, computer literacy requires having expertise in systems operating software and components, applications programs, Internet, electronic communications, and digital learning. A number of college entry-level computer literacy curricula included introductory modules to these elements:

- Word processing
- Spreadsheets
- Databases
- Presentations
- Internet
- Electronic mail
- Operating system software
- Basic computer concepts

Intermediate-level courses moved on to actually using the elements to create letters, presentations, perform specific Internet tasks, and so on. This particular program covers the key elements you need to be computer literate. For comparison, additional computer literacy programs are briefly discussed at the end of the chapter. An interesting sidelight: one study has shown that organizations, for whatever reason, don't necessarily spend as much money making their employees computer literate as they should.[13] A puzzling situation, but it shows that people need to take control of their own computer literacy needs, taking it upon themselves to improve performance.

Specific software applications are not recommended here as it's beyond the scope of the book. As a matter of fact, to become truly computer literate, it's a good idea to learn principles (as noted at the beginning of the chapter) so that you can move easily from one word processor to another, or from one spreadsheet to another. Different employers may have different tastes, and if you're a contingency worker, you'll need as many different packages in your skill set as possible.

To further validate the selection of computer literacy components, a review of the table of contents of a standard book on the subject comes in handy.[14] The introduction discusses Windows, and the next chapters, in order, address hardware, software, communications, Internet, word processing, spreadsheets, and databases. Then there's a chapter on graphics, sound, multimedia, and presentations. The final three chapters deal with different types of programming. At least there's some general agreement on what constitutes being computer literate.

For our purposes, the elements noted above will be used as the basis of computer literacy (exhibit 6.3) with the addition of administrative software. The latter includes calendars, scheduling, and other office-type applications. Es-

Exhibit 6.3
Elements of Computer Literacy

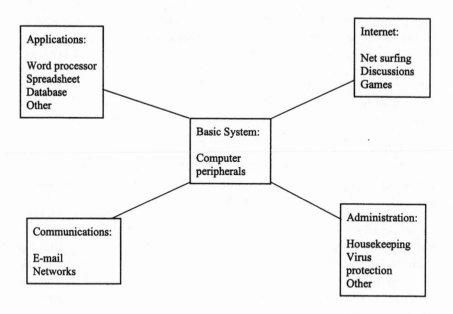

sential utility programs such as virus protectors are also included in this latter category.

Operating System Knowledge

The operating system software bridges the gap between human and machine. By turning the computer on, the user gains access to the operating system, which is literally the doorway to the digital, online world. Operating systems come in a number of varieties, with Microsoft Windows being the most widely used. Others include the Apple operating system, UNIX, OS-2, and Linux, all providing the capability to access the power of the computer and the software applications that go with it.

The computer literate person is comfortable with viewing, for example, a Windows 2000 screen and getting from there to whatever work is needed to be done on the way to acquiring information. Fortunately, vendors have the end-user in mind (at least they attempt to) when designing and issuing new operating systems, which helps the cause of the user. However, new capabilities are continually added, and it is to the user's advantage to learn to use much of the power of the system offered. New versions of any type software often add new capabilities to keep end users on their toes.

Application Programs

This covers the bulk of the software provided in the name of information literacy—and application programs have many other uses, as well. It is the software that brings value to the end-user because these applications do the work for them. They go hand-in-hand with hardware because as software packages become larger and more powerful, they require the higher end of hardware components in order to function properly. For instance, they occupy large chunks of memory and have sophisticated routines that require speed and power in order to compute in a reasonably short time span. They also cover a multitude of possibilities. Note: For the following discussion, specific programs will not be used—rather, the application types will be treated as generic for purposes of our discussion.

Word Processors. Information must be recorded, organized, and stored in a manner other users can easily view and understand, and be communicated to others. This includes letters, reports, memos, cover sheets, tables, charts—virtually any way information can be recorded. Therefore, the information literate person must be computer literate enough to use much of the capability of a word processor program. The most advanced form of this would be a desktop publishing application, which adds other capabilities such as graphics, formatting, and other things that allow the end-user to prepare sophisticated documents such as newsletters, technical publications, and brochures. Templates are usually available for the more common documents.

Spreadsheets. Much of the information we find and need is numerical. It must also be organized and categorized, making the spreadsheet an excellent candidate as an information gathering tool. The ability to quickly lay out a set of newly gathered information into a format that can be easily accessed and used at a later time is invaluable, meaning computer literacy includes at least fundamental knowledge of how to use one or more of the available spreadsheet applications. Like many other types of application software, predesigned formats are often provided to help novice users. These templates can greatly simplify usage as well as open access to less qualified end-users.

One study showed that the majority of users have basic skills of simple data entry, data retrieval and storage, cell connectivity, and presentation graphics. A handful had the skills of linking worksheets and database creation. None in the study could do the most advanced skills of using specialized functions, automation, and customization, which showed the need for this training.[15] Another report showed that accountants didn't use spreadsheets to their full potential, which is critical since "Spreadsheet software is to an accountant what a hammer is to a carpenter."[16]

Database Programs. In a like manner, database programs provide the means to store information in a way that is not only logical and easy to use, but can be accessed at will and in such a variety of formats. In fact, much of the information that seekers search for is stored in some form of database program, whether it be off-the-shelf or custom-designed. The ability to capture and record detailed information into a database program facilitates all stages of the information literacy process. Everything from inventories of equipment and supplies, to personnel skills, to marketing files can be stored in a relational database for easy retrieval and manipulation of data for analysis, making it a powerful organizational tool.

Presentations and Graphics. Though these programs may be separate packages, many times they're included as part of a basic presentations program. They provide the ability to graphically present information, with standardized charts and graphics styles as well as customized ones. The PC has become a digital photographic system through these packages and digital cameras. When the information is ready for others to see, it can be provided in dazzling color, full-motion, sound presentations that might include video, photography, and more. Such presentations can be stored and provide an excellent means of reviewing digested and organized information at a later date.

Internet. This covers a multitude of things, as it provides access to the incredible amount of information accumulating on the Internet. Access may be in a number of ways, including:

- File transfer protocol (FTP)—used to move files from place to place
- World Wide Web—which is the fastest growing segment
- Gopher—used by universities to provide information
- Telnet—a way organizations (e.g., a university) can provide access to the Web for its constituents
- Use net—discussion groups, also referred to as news groups, which cover about any topic you might imagine (and some you probably would never have thought of, let alone have heard of)
- Net surfing—using search engines to find information on the Web; see chapter 3 regarding electronic communications for more details on search engines
- Bulletin boards—electronic versions of the ones in the hallway, where announcements and notes are posted

It's possible to have the information you're interested in come to you automatically.

Media Literacy

Educators are familiar with the term *media literacy*. A Washington state educational support organization defines the term as "the ability to access, analyze, evaluate and produce both print and electronic media."[17] In a more narrow context, media literacy focuses on helping children become more discerning about the television they watch. Not a bad idea, considering that the "daily use of TV in all types of American households averages 7 1/5 hours a day" and runs a bit higher in homes with teenagers under eighteen.[18] A main purpose of media literacy programs in schools is "To help students become critical consumers of information . . . an experiential process that teaches both 'about' and 'through' media."[19] It incorporates many of the same principles as the broader concept of information literacy and applies as well to work-related information processes. The point is that, with so much information in so many different media, we all need to be more discerning in what we select and take in. We learn better when we see, read, sense, hear, and feel information—the more forms the better, making media a good way to learn and gather information. It's the type of thing that gets our attention.

Another aspect is that we can expand the concept, and use the term to mean all types of media, and there are certainly multiple forms. CD-ROM, MP-3, downloaded animation and video, audio, and other devices may be encountered by today's information seeker. As well, these devices may be part of the output format you choose to store, present, or apply the results of a search—thus the potential need to be familiar with part or all of it. You may even have to know how to use a computer projector to output a presentation from your computer. Then there's the expectation that new devices will come along to replace the old ones as technology continues to rocket forward.

Digital Communications

Primarily, this means using electronic mail, although we also communicate digitally in other ways, such as:

- Discussion groups (see above)
- Web pages (Internet and intranet—see chapter 9 regarding online help)
- Electronic bulletin boards and other forms of postings
- Chat rooms

As a reminder, additional materials on electronic communication are found in chapter 3. Exhibit 6.4 identifies and locates these materials.

Digital Learning

This topic is discussed in more detail in chapter 8, "Learning How to Learn." Digital learning is one of the easiest methods of quickly learning new skills and acquiring knowledge needed to maintain a high level of information literacy. It's also a way of using the medium itself—the computer—to learn about it first hand. Online help and user-friendly software design can go a long way toward making a person computer literate.

Exhibit 6.4
Communication-Related Computer Literacy Skills Appearing in Chapter 3

Item	Page
Digital communication skills (e-mail, chat rooms, use groups, search engines; description)	52
Electronic communication skills acquisition	61
E-mail rules	52
Chat room rules	54
Usenet rules	55
Using search engines	56
Search engine sampling	57
Search engine guides composite	57
General electronic communication rules	59
Keyboard software training sampling (exhibit 3.3)	62

Other Components

One thing about technology. It never lets you alone, and it never ceases to add more elements for us to deal with at work. Multimedia, for instance, discussed above, and its accompanying elements such as graphics, video, digital video, music, films, and more, are reshaping the way we're presented with information and entertainment. Then there are facets of the Internet and World Wide Web, including Web publishing and building and maintaining Web pages. Intranets are the internal versions of the Internet, where only designated people can access the sites. More and more organizations require their employees to navigate the home site for critical work information, documentation, work schedules, and personnel related information, among other topics.

Then there's groupware such as Lotus Notes that are required usage for certain organizations. Groupware "applies to software that businesses can use to promote collaboration," which includes mail and scheduling functions.[20] Even though the Internet and intranets are increasing by being used to connect people within organizations, there are still plenty of groupware installations around.

Next comes programming, which is usually left for professional staff programmers or contractors. Yet there are high-level packages for building Web pages, for instance, and some people may be programming and not be aware of it. All these components could potentially fall within the realm of being computer literate, even though they're on the more advanced end of the spectrum.

Transferability of Skills

Computer literate persons have discovered that it isn't enough to learn a particular application package, particularly when it comes to word processing.

Because of job changing, doing independent work for many different organizations, and other reasons, it may be necessary to go back and forth between
two or even three different word processing packages (or spreadsheets, for that
matter). The key is to know the principles of word processing (e.g., that you
can move files around, format pages, use macros to edit, and so on). This will
ake it easier to go from one package to another with the minimum of read -
justment. One interesting approach to computer literacy is that it can be used
to teach basic literacy to those who are low performers, thus combining the acquisition of both sets of skills.

Principles of Computer Literacy

Analyzing the components of computer literacy identifies several principles
that will help to fully understand the concept, thus leading to a higher level of
literacy:

Operating—the system in general and various hardware elements, such as the
    CPU, printer, and other peripherals. This principle indicates the
    hands-on nature of being computer literate. It's a skill that requires
    knowledge, ability to think on your feet, and manipulate devices. The
    term implies hardware, but may include operating software that gives the
    machines their power.

Importing—files from your own and other systems, ranging anywhere from
    photos from back home to entire software packages. Through down-
    loading from the Web and electronic mail, we gain access to far more in-
    formation than we can imagine. Importing is also used extensively to
    enhance desktop publishing, such as to bring in photographs. Informa-
    tion literacy and information power are all about being able to move in-
    formation around from place to place.

Attaching—is the way files are imported, by attaching them to e-mail messages
    and sending them to people anywhere there is a respondent system.
    Mixing and matching information provides flexibility to use attachments
    in many different ways.

Translating—covers a wide variety of possibilities, ranging from translating a
    text file into the language of a word processor, to converting newly de-
    veloped Web pages into the language acceptable by the Web.

Processing—refers to the applications we use, such as processing a document
    typed into a word processor, computing accounting data from a spread-
    sheet, searching for data on a database, building and upgrading Web
    pages, and more. Sometimes processing involves the simple act of click-
    ing on an icon; at others it requires several steps, each of which may have
    complicated substeps. It's what your mind is doing constantly while

dealing with information and leads to the acquisition of information power.

Backing up— is what we should do daily, particularly when important new files have been created or old ones have been updated. Backing up can be as simple as copying critical files onto a floppy disk or as elaborate as using a tape back-up system to copy every file and program on a large system.

Surfing—the World Wide Web and its increasing millions of sites is just a click away. Unlike our counterpart surfers on the beach, however, the net surfer is able to control the variables. In a sense, surfing is what we do when we're scanning a list of information sources from the library, a telephone book or yellow pages, or anywhere else there's more than one item to look at.

Communicating—is now often done through electronic mail, live chat rooms, news groups and related ways to exchange information and ideas, attachments, information and messages posted on bulletin boards and Web pages, and so on. It happens continuously and must happen effectively if the process of obtaining and using information is to succeed.

Learning—will be discussed further in chapter 7. More and more learning is taking place electronically, ranging from receiving needed information from a friend via e-mail to taking a degree program via a university's on-line courses. In its simplest form, it means striving to improve performance and enhance skills as we use systems and applications.

Connecting— is what happens through the methods of communicating noted above. The World Wide Web has provided a way for the world to literally be connected digitally. Connecting occurs everywhere, and with everyone from kindergartners to senior citizens. The world has never been so connected. You'll find that even your connections have connections, providing a seemingly never-ending chain of information. Knowing when to stop the connection sometimes comes in handy.

Maintaining—refers to such tasks as tidying up files, cleaning out information and files no longer needed, checking for viruses, updating programs, adding capabilities, and so on. It's part of the backing-up process, as well as part of what you must do with your personal information and computer literacy skills—keep them updated.

Playing—on the computer, as many people have discovered, is simplified through Web access and through a growing host of CD-ROMs. Games, puzzles, film previews, mysteries, music, live events, radio stations, entertainment and more are available online. However, as noted in the following discussion of computer-related problems, there's such thing as too much playing, particularly at work and particularly where management has made strict rules forbidding it.

PROBLEMS WITH COMPUTER LITERACY

Being computer literate has its problems. Just think of how long it took you to find a piece of information recently surfing the Web, when a librarian could've found it for you in a few minutes. No doubt a lot of time is wasted by looking for a great site that was there last week but gone today, trying to figure out how to put together the best refined search, and so on. Then comes the aching back, wrists, head, brains, posteriors, and other parts of the human body that result from too much time in front of the monitor. Ergonomic chairs or not, it can become quite tiresome to force the human body to do something it was not evolved to do naturally. A question going around today is whether or not the furniture and layouts used by people who work at home would pass OSHA standards, and whether or not employers would be liable for home-developed problems from repetitive work.

Then there's the problem of worker privacy. The owner of the computer system knows virtually everything the user is doing when connected to it through a keyboard, communication device, voice-activated system, or whatever means is being used to access it. Surveillance, monitoring of e-mail, and censorship are three critical areas of concern. Advanced software packages have been developed to monitor what people do on both the computer via the Internet and what they say in their e-mail. People have been terminated for using systems for personal use. All this brings forth the legal ramifications and privacy issues of digital literacy and all that go with it.

There's also the question of what's available on the Web, what types of groups you might join to discuss topics of interest to you, and how much of what you do might be considered frivolous. There's pornography that's readily available, games that can take up more time than it would ever take to get a work task done, and discussion groups that could easily be subversive to your job. There's also the question of avoiding direct social contact. Robert Putnam paints a frightening picture of how socially isolated we've become in the past five decades in his book *Bowling Alone*.[21] Part of it is generational, but part is also the using the computer and watching television, activities done best alone.

Dan Tapscott informs us that children are *Growing Up Digital*,[22] but we might question whether or not it's okay to assume other identities and participate in a discussion group. It's one thing to be a natural computer user as a subteen, but if it means acting like someone you're not, the question arises about how you present yourself when you're a working adult and must be yourself with coworkers. Perhaps Megan, the five-year-old mentioned earlier in the chapter, is an anomaly, perhaps not.

One of the issues of most concern regarding the move toward total digitization is that of honesty, as noted above. Sven Birkets in his book *The Gutenberg Elegies* has expressed concern about the impact of digital means on such basic skills as writing and reading.[23] Little editing, and sometimes little thought, goes into much of what we communicate digitally. Bill Henderson founded an organization known as the Lead Pencil Club, whose members believe in living contraption free in a computerized world. As a result of the digital revolution, he believes, "We won't have to write letters to friends because we won't have any friends."[24] These arguments aren't entirely tongue-in-cheek.

Ownership of information is also a question. It's so easy to grab a file that belongs to someone else, as we've seen with the teen hackers who break into Defense Department sites and bank files and wreak havoc. There's also the question of who owns intellectual data, as well as one about copyright law, which is in turmoil along with music ownership. These and other problems will not go away anytime soon. In fact, they'll likely grow and become more confusing, which is a factor to be considered when becoming computer literate and exercising information power.

INFORMATION TECHNOLOGY

Computer literate professionals often deal with the area known as information technology (IT). Because of its impact on the workplace, it will be briefly discussed here, recognizing that most people need not be as professional and skilled at information technology as the professionals. They inhabit the highest end of computer literacy. Information technology (IT) consists of these components:

- Computer (PC in most instances, though mainframes are still widely used)
- Telecommunications (which includes a variety of forms, from satellites and fully interactive systems to conference telephone calls)
- Workstations (which may be PCs)
- Information sources

Another component (that may be included in either telecommunications or information sources) is a network. These range from a few PCs tied together with a local area network, to worldwide hookups. They range from commercial applications to broad based networks and provide access to information sources.

You get IT when you combine and interlink these components to create a system ready to tackle applications. The number of applications is limited only by the creativity (and resources) of the builders and users of IT. Some general applications, according to Dr. Peter G. W. Keen of the International Center for Information Technology (ICIT) include:

- Online transaction processing
- Electronic mail
- Video conferencing

- Personal computing
- Executive information systems
- Interorganizational electronic data interchange
- Publishing
- Expert systems[25]

When applications for academia and nonprofit (which are included in the same general applications above) are added, and each is mapped into more specific examples, the list grows. This expanding list is surprisingly similar to the list of skills defining computer literacy for everyone in the workplace, not just computer or IT professionals. This similarity further stresses the vital need to become computer literate—in the name of information literacy.

IT provides an essential tool to create what Keen calls the relational organization (as opposed to the traditional, structured organization). This new organization, built around knowledge-based teams, is the one destined to succeed in the evolving global community. Other futurists, by the way, agree with Keen. Thus it becomes critical that the people using IT to achieve these newer organizational forms become completely information literate.

ENHANCING COMPUTER LITERACY SKILLS

Perhaps the best place to acquire computer literacy skills is in school. For example, one study showed that students could perform better on a computer literacy test than industrial labor workers. The lesson to be learned is that computer skills should start to be acquired as early in life as possible and then continuously be reinforced and expanded (bearing in mind all the way through that the computer is a tool). For those who went to school before the Information Age, here is a representative list of where one can go to acquire computer skills:

- Libraries (one of the best places to go despite sometimes as shortage of systems and staff due to funding cuts)
- Online libraries, which will also give you practice using the system you're mastering—but remember that real-life librarians can provide extensive assistance to your learning process
- Computer dealers
- Schools (from elementary to university, and in particular community colleges, who often are called upon by organizations to provide formal training)
- Adult education programs (including senior centers)
- Books (but be prepared to spend some time screening through the many that are available, and make sure it's the latest edition)

- Magazines, which you can read online, in the library, or subscribe to them
- Videos and CD-ROMs
- Television courses
- Online help and manuals that come with programs
- Newspapers (including some who have provided special computer sections)
- Internet and Web pages
- Sampler programs available through a variety of means
- A formal tutor whom you hire to help
- A family member or friend who's willing to sit down with you
- Others at work
- Simply looking over the shoulder of people who are doing different types of computer work
- User groups, where one person "found that membership in and advice from members of a user group improved both her computer and leadership skills," where she became proficient with desktop computing, word processing, and producing a newsletter.[26]

Despite all these methods, far and away the best way to acquire computters skills is hands-on experience. Reading and watching have their place, but pushing the buttons and watching the results has no substitute as far as the learning process is concerned.

A review of what organizations are doing about gaining and maintaining computer literacy for their staff will provide further insight as well as validate discussion to this point. According to *Crain's New York Business:*

- Eagle Electric Manufacturing's director of information technology says that "computer training is a key to maximizing our investment in people and in the utilization of technology," and that "it's absolutely necessary. . . to take a leadership role in our industry." The company contracted with an outside provider to give instruction on Microsoft Office applications and the Internet.
- A Booz, Allen, & Hamilton partner stated that "In this day and age, it's essential for most, if not all, managers to be computer literate." The company specializes in information technology and therefore must stay on top of the knowledge associated with it.
- Chase Manhattan Bank uses a combination of learning labs, where employees use CD-ROM and audiovisual materials, with outside trainers to provide flexibility for busy executives.
- Nynex has fourteen multimedia centers in New York "to teach managers everything from PC basics to sophisticated programming languages like C++. The telecom company spends about $80 million on professional

training annually." The company also uses local university computer education courses.[27]

Perhaps the best approach is to explore what's readily available to you and make a list, weighing the pros and cons of each. Also, assess your learning style (see chapter 8, "Learning How to Learn") and make a selection based on how you learn best. Usually, multiple sources can work, although paying the price to take a professionally prepared course is possibly the best way for most: there's some guarantee you'll come away with good skills. Keep these considerations in mind before deciding on the method by which you will become more computer literate:

- Check out the course first and ask lots of questions, such as how many others have used the course, and so on.

- Talk to others who've taken the course or participated in the learning process for the method in question.

- Ask people you know who are computer literate how they learned.

- Be sure there's plenty of hands-on experience.

- Make sure the system, applications, operating system, and so on are compatible with the system you'll be using after you've completed training.

- All components should be the latest version.

- Compare costs. Will the price you pay be worth it?

- If in doubt, try out the most readily accessible and least expensive first; then you'll have a better idea of what to do next and likely get more out of the more expensive approaches.

Note the cardinal rule for becoming computer literate: people will likely never become too computer literate in the workplace, now or in the future. Take advantage of every opportunity to learn new applications or expert systems. Following are several representative computer literacy course contents:

Franklin University of Columbus, Ohio (www.cs.franklin.edu/Syllabus/comp085/syllabus.shtml):
- Windows essentials
- E-mail
- Internet
- Word processing
- Computer basics and hardware
- System software, application software, ethics

Regent University of Virgina Beach, Virgina (www.regent.edu/acad/schcom/phd/cplit.html):

- Personal computer
- Word processing
- Installing and configuring common software
- Using a computer modem
- E-mail
- Upload and download computer files
- Print from the computer
- Net browsing

York County Vo-Tech School of York, Pennsylvania (www.lhup.edu/ablenet/abeliteracy.sue1.htm):

- Basic computer and its functions and use
- Creating and using a word processor document
- Creating and using a database
- Creating and editing a desktop publishing document

CHAPTER 7

Subject Matter Literacy: Knowing the Territory

Harold Hill was the salesman made famous in the *The Music Man*. His fellow peddlers claimed, in rousing song, that he didn't know the territory—no one in their right minds would try to sell musical instruments where they weren't wanted. But Mr. Hill evidently knew something, if you recall the show's happy ending, where the kids marched down the streets in their band uniforms and playing "Seventy-Six Trombones" on their newly acquired band instruments. Nevertheless it's a wise message: you've got to know the territory you're working in or else fall short of success. Being literate in your job, profession, or trade is every bit as critical as being information literate.

Being literate in your profession has several side aspects that need to be addressed. Acquiring of basic literacy (the so-called three R's) was discussed in chapter 1, and is the first major step towards gaining any other form of literacy. Then there's the fact that our workplace has become extremely diversified. With so many differences in language, culture, customs, habits, and manners of expression, the impact on all forms of literacy is tremendous. Organizations worldwide are doing everything they can to deal with this fact of global life, and, in fact, to turn diversity into gain. Fortunately, many are having success in this area.

This chapter will look into workplace and cultural literacy before embarking on the exploration of precise subject-matter literacy. We will use business literacy, science and math literary, and other literacies as examples, recognizing that there are as many specific literacies as there are professions, industries, specialties, and ways of earning a living. Further, the key success components of networking and personal development will be discussed as well as the concept of emotional intelligence.

WORKPLACE LITERACY

One of the greatest mysteries of our time is how, on one end of the work spectrum, we demand such highly information literate people, yet on the other end have such a significant number of people who don't possess the basic literacy skills required for entry-level work. It's the problem of functional illiteracy mentioned in the first chapter. The divide is enormous and presents one of our greatest obstacles in giving people information power. "Research indicates that employees' lack of basic skills is causing Corporate America to lose over $60 billion annually in productivity, yet a mere 2.2% of all organizations furnish training in basic reading, writing, mathematics and English language skills."[1]

Workplace literacy problems know no boundaries. In Third World and developing nations, in fact, the problems are more severe. These communities can expect that the gap will widen. The impact on workplace literacy is that, as we become more global, many potential partners will not have the literacy levels needed to compete. It's a compounded loss in that it makes it difficult for such communities to participate fully in the global economy.

Relationship to Information Literacy

An effective comparison can be made by first looking at the skill set for information literacy identified in these chapters.

Communication. Basic skills such reading, writing, and speaking are required to begin the information literacy process. So much of the effort begins by simply reading, even if it's just the instructions for turning on a machine or recognizing the characters to dial a telephone. Writing also plays a vital role. Sending a simple e-mail, or responding to one, requires the ability to write. These same skills are essential for virtually all the other information literacy skills, and they're certainly needed to be subject matter literate, since language is a key element of any given subject, industry, or profession.

Thinking. Illiterate people are as capable of thinking as anyone else but haven't the breadth of knowledge a literate person would have to expand the process into everything it could be. New thinking methods are slow in coming if a person can't read to learn more about them or write to express ideas. Thinking is an essential stop on the way to acquiring any kind of literacy.

Decision Making. Again, does the person have the best available information upon which to make sound business decisions. Intuition, as we'll see later in the chapter, matters, but with a literacy foundation, it goes much farther. The ability to make decisions is key to achieving subject matter literacy as well.

Computer Literacy. Perhaps with icons and easy to use menus, basic skills could suffice for using computers, but then there comes the part about communicating electronically and keying in words upon which to search, and all the other tasks people do when on the computer. Computer literacy becomes even more important when it comes to using standard application packages.

Continuous Learning/Learning How to Learn. Without the basics, there's little growth, as many illiterate people have found out. Then they have gone on to take adult literacy classes and blossom into learned adults.

Basic skills provide the starting place for people to continue to learn throughout their lives. It's as simple as that. There's another simple test. Look back at the sixteen steps in the information literacy process and go through first the small problem and imagine the level of difficulty in completing the abbreviated process if you locked basic skills in reading, writing, or computing. Then do the same for the more complex problems. As the task becomes more challenging, the ability to successfully complete an information search process becomes virtually impossible without basic literacy skills.

What Employers Are Looking For

Several studies in recent years regarding what employers are looking for in their newly hired human resources management professionals reveal a common denominator: they all want these college graduates to know the business—to know, appreciate, and support the bottom line. This same concern can be tracked across the board, for whatever is the mission of a given organization and whatever the discipline of the individuals forming it. "Business literacy," we're informed, "is not a luxury, it is a necessity."[2]

Successful Approaches to Providing Literacy

Here's a sampling of what companies, colleges, and communities are doing to combat illiteracy:

- Canada has extensive programs, including a workplace literacy program at High Liner Foods in Nova Scotia that uses tutors for reading and writing. The purpose of the program is to "give fisheries workers the education and skills to adapt within or outside the industry; to help employed and laid-off workers with basic education needs." Computers are used, providing additional skill training. Attendance in the workshops and tutoring programs has been high.[3]

- The state of Ohio gives Ohio Workplace Excellence Awards to organizations who excel at promoting workforce excellence through training and related practices. Winners over the years, who must have demonstrated investment in developing employee work skills and promoted lifelong learning, have included organizations of all sizes and types. Ohio State

University's Department of Spanish and Portuguese offers a program linking Spanish majors and businesses, an example of an advanced workplace
literacy program.[4]

- Sacramento Area Literacy Coalition promotes literacy through the central
  valley of California. Its Web site offers search options by county and types of
  service provided, with appropriate links. The topics are extensive.[5]

- The state of Delaware offers a survey to determine whether or not an organization has a literacy problem by asking questions about poor product
  quality, high turnover, lack of promotable people, job orders frequently
  misinterpreted, frequent failed equipment, and others.[6]

- Palm Beach County has a literacy coalition that "seeks to promote and
  achieve literacy to improve the quality of life in our county." It, in turn, is a
  member of the Florida Literacy Coalition and the National Alliance of Ur-
  ban Literacy Coalitions, to give an idea of the national magnitude of such
  programs.[7]

- Michigan State University's workplace literacy program teaches "reading,
  writing, and math skills as a means of improving both the work and personal
  lives of employees of participating companies." Its goals include retooling,
  retraining, retaining, increasing productivity, decreasing work accidents,
  improving product quality, and reducing lost management time, making it
  a program targeted to the precise needs of organizations.[8]

Successful examples abound, as this brief survey of selected Web sites indicates. The remarkable thing about workplace literacy is that it doesn't cost
much. Many organizations using volunteer tutors offer services, such as the
Literacy Volunteers of America and Laubach Literacy programs. Many communities, through their literacy coalitions, community colleges, and adult
learning programs offer help as well.

Some words of wisdom gleaned for successful workplace literacy programs
include these:

- Use existing sources wherever possible. They're professionals at providing
  such training, and it's different than regular job related skills training.
  There's no need to start from scratch.

- Be careful in assessing needs. People are sensitive to their literacy levels, usually fully believing they are better at the skills than they actually are. For example, "Sometimes people think they're at a higher reading or math level
  than they really are."[9] More on this following.

- Gear the materials to the job at hand. If reading skills development training
  is being conducted and the attendees are required to read blueprints on the
  job, incorporate blueprints into the curriculum. Otherwise, the training
  will be far less effective, people must relate the training to something that

will directly benefit them. Potential for job success is a tremendous stimulant.

- Because of the above, be conscious of the potential need to do some customizing, even if the material is provided by outsiders—off-the-shelf may be the place to start; then build on it as necessary for specific needs.

- Let results speak for the training, which should help draw in people who need the training but who stay away at first. Resistance to change is a typical reaction, so patience is mandatory.

- Focus on performance improvement, which should appeal to all. If a person believes he or she will earn more because of the training, then there's a much greater chance of first-time acceptance.

One source has focused on the problem of people's sensitivity to needing literacy training. "Most experts agree one-on-one tutoring sessions are most effective."[10] Reasons stated are that illiteracy is a private shame; people read, write, and compute on different levels; and people need special attention to learning such basics.

There's another aspect worthy of mention. It's estimated that 10 percent of our population has a learning disability. This statistic can be added to the number of people who can't read, write, or calculate. There are programs to help persons with learning disabilities to bring them up to the level necessary to go on toward gaining information power. When you include the estimated 20 percent who are functionally illiterate, and the percentage of those who speak little, if any, English, the number becomes startling—and has a great impact on the workplace.

Empowerment, Teams, and Literacy

Two of the most popular business innovations things of the past two or three decades is forming work teams and empowering workers. Of course, organizations have been doing these for years, it's just that they suddenly became popular practices, the kind that get written up in the management literature and studied in business schools. Actually, there's a good reason such concepts as these, trendy or not, are implemented—they produce positive results. It is not enough for individuals to be literate; teams must be information literate and have information power as well. Being part of a team is empowering, since individuals, left to do things on their own often do not check with anyone until the job is completed.

One of the best places to go for a definition is a textbook. According to Professor Robbins, empowerment is "increasing the decision making discretion of workers."[11] It's the process of pushing decision making down into the organization, as discussed in the first chapter. When you consider how many middle management positions have been eliminated over the past several years, and when you consider how many people work on their own at home and elsewhere, it's no wonder empowerment is vital. Whether you call it empowerment, participatory management, Theory Y, or just plain common sense, encourging employees to make decision is a way to get more mileage from all workers, provided they're given the wherewithal to be self-directed. Information literacy provides the power to perform as a decision maker.

The same can be said of self-directed work teams, which is but one term that describes people organized into groups for work. A self-managed work team, another term, is defined by Robbins as "a vertically integrated team that is given almost complete autonomy in determining how a task will be done."[12] In a sense, work teams are groups of people who are empowered. Every member must be information literate, as members are often cross-trained, and all must deal with information.

Impact of Being Career Self-Directed

Whether we like it or not, or whether we even are aware of it, we've become a workforce of people who are responsible for our own fates. No longer are there companies and government agencies to take us in and not let us out until we can safely retire. Lay-off notices arrive; businesses close their doors; institutions scale back; careers become obsolete or fail to work out; hard-earned skills are rendered useless by technology; divorce or death pushes a now-single wage earner onto the street, possibly unprepared and with a family to support; short-term profits take precedence over long-term jobs as the measure of corporate success. Or perhaps people simply are drawn to the idea of being on their own. Suddenly there are more people searching than there are immediate job openings, or long-term openings, for that matter. Earnings fall, frustrations rise, and hopes dim as our economy "reengineers" itself for the global, technological, diverse, highly competitive run into the 2000's. As the subtitle to a *Fortune* article on careers stated, "Let's face it. At some point in our business lives, we're all likely to end up stomped, crunched, and pureed."[13] The shock effect of having to start over, to recreate oneself, has taken its place high on the list of twenty-first century psychological baggage.

One of the most interesting and potentially exciting results is that many people find themselves self-employed. The number runs into the millions, and continues to grow regardless of how strong the economy is. Over 430,000 jobs were cut in 1997, which was considered an improvement over previous years, yet the process is heating up again.[14] Add to this the fact that temporary jobs are the ones in greatest demand, and the picture becomes clearer. The problem doesn't stop here, either. As government cuts back, private sector businesses that depended on it, such as defense firms, health care providers, and telecommunications companies, to name a few, lose their source of income, which means another round of cutbacks. Job security is rapidly becoming a thing of the past.

The gist of all this is that, regardless of the reason, we need, to take control of our own destinies, which may mean managing our own professional development, despite the fact that organizations still spend a lot of money on training. The relationship to information literacy is clear: we've got to locate, extract, and implement information for our own knowledge, whether as a contingent worker, an employee, or a job seeker.

Relationship to the Learning Organization

The learning organization concept was identified in chapter 1 and is discussed in chapter 8, "Learning How to Learn." Since it follows closely the principles of passing responsibility down further within the organization, it is mentioned in that context here. As a reminder, a learning organization is one where the "employees share knowledge, allowing deeper understanding and a more thorough approach to problem-solving. As a result, the organization is able to grow and change in keeping with its environment."[15] Because so many organizations view themselves as fitting this description, it's imperative that the people within them have information power if the organization is, indeed, to learn.

CULTURAL LITERACY

Today's Workplace

The impact of diversity on the workplace was addressed in chapter 1, and it's a significant impact. It also creates an enormous challenge, and in some cases downright problems, for literacy in general and information literacy in particular. Culture today means literally "all the above." The old definitions that were restricted to skin color, language, and country of origin don't hold true anymore. Even people of the same race, if they have lived in different parts of the country and in different economic situations, and have received quite different educations, would find one another strangers and culturally diverse. Dealing directly and positively with diversity is essential in today's global economy. "As companies establish international operations it's important for managers to cultivate cultural self-awareness," is one view of just how critical the need is.[16] Another source notes that "Culture will matter more, not less. Contrary to conventional wisdom, technology isn't eliminating cultural barriers. While the ability to communicate with people far and wide at increasingly rapid speeds and in innovative ways may be breaking down geographic and economic barriers, cultural boundaries are holding fast."[17] Diversity brings this sampling of elements that impact literacy:

- Language, which makes a person who doesn't speak English functionally illiterate, even if she is fluent in three languages other than English.

- Customs, which cause people to interpret the same thing in different ways.
- Learning style, which means that a person from Asia, for instance, might expect a learning situation to be one where the teacher is regarded as a venerable expert and does all the talking. In Asia students do not ask questions without risk of insulting the teacher, which in turn skews sharing information and knowledge.
- Education level, which has a fundamental effect on sharing information and knowledge, particularly when people have completely different bases of understanding from which they start the information process.

Elements of Diversity

Several dimensions of diversity have been used over time to differentiate between cultures. Some things are obvious, such as what we wear, and how we sound when we speak. But there are many other factors, such as beliefs, customs, rituals, family, and symbols that aren't so easy to see. They may require a long time to become acquainted with, or else one can learn about the culture through study. Exhibit 7.1 shows some of the more common elements of diversity with examples of the extremes.

Relationship to Information Literacy

The relationship to information literacy is the same as for workplace literacy in general. Cultural differences may interfere with becoming literate in the official language of the land. They also stand in the way of gathering and using information. Cultural diversity must be accounted for in the workplace in order to facilitate, first, basic literacy, then information literacy. The primary snag is language, since English is the international language of business. Even highly educated people who speak another language as their primary one must be able to have a reasonably good grasp of English, along with the nuances, body language, and added customs, to be able to properly deal with much of the information encountered at work.

How to Approach It

Sample programs for workplace literacy were described at the beginning of this section. In addition, chapter 8, "Learning How to Learn," will also discuss learning situations where workplace literacy topics can be the basis of the training and learning. Federal funding for such English-language programs has ceased, putting the onus on other sources to come up with the needed training.[18] Here's a sampling of programs that have worked:

- Worksmart, a workplace literacy curricula developed through a partnership between Barber Foods and the Casco Bay Partnership for Workplace

Exhibit 7.1
Dimensions of Difference

Time	The classic example of differences in time perception is the United States businessman who goes to Mexico or Saudi Arabia and has a two o'clock appointment. The U.S. man is incensed when the person he is to meet arrives an hour late. The point is that the punctual person should have known in advance the differences in time dimensions and been prepared to deal with it, just as the Mexican or Saudi Arabian should be aware of the regard for punctuality in the U.S.
Urgency	Using the same example, the U.S. businessman may have a strong desire to get the business over with and return home. However, in some cultures, it is considered impolite to not have a social visit prior to talking business, and perhaps a day or two might pass in between.
Formality	This has to do with the degree of formality with which business is conducted. Highly formal cultures place a great deal of value on ceremony and protocol, whereas an informal culture is more comfortable dispensing with such formality.
Gender	Some cultures are highly masculine, and women are placed in a more subjugated role. Although this attitude is considered sexist in many cultures, it still exists. For example, some languages clearly recognize the differences.
Power distance	Power distance refers to how well accepted is the existence of hierarchy and the power to make decisions within it. High power distance means that people accept the fact that someone higher in the organization will make all important decisions.
Risk taking	Some cultures prefer the status quo and will avoid taking risk unless certain there is a reasonable degree of control over the outcome. Other cultures, particularly in ones where high technology companies thrive, except employees to take risks.
Future view	This is literally how far into the future a company looks. In long-term oriented cultures such as Japan, companies will often look many years down the road and not be terribly concerned with short-term dips in the economy. Short-term orientations, such as that exhibited by many U.S. companies in enhancing quarterly reports to be more profitable, look no more than three months down the road.

Learning at the University of Southern Maine. Courses offered include reading, writing, math, science, business communication, and computer skills, though the main objective was learning English.[19]

- Clackamas Oregon Community College is one of the many sources accessible via the Internet offering solutions to cultural diversity needs. As their site states, "Employees now reflect a diversity of ages, genders, races, cultural perspectives, ethnic backgrounds, education, and physical abilities," noting that "diversity is here to stay."[20]

- College of DuPage (Illinois) offers a workplace literacy program including English as a Second Language (ESL) and foreign languages that can be either on-site or on campus.[21]

ELEMENTS OF SUBJECT-MATTER LITERACY

Background

Everyone is subject-matter literate in something. We all have to know how to perform our jobs in order to earn a living. Our expertise, business or professional literacy, comes in many forms. First, there's business literacy, which looks a lot like workplace literacy, or basic literacy. Then there's professional literacy, such as what a physician or x-ray technician must know in order to tend to our health or the lawyer to prepare our living trust. There's also industrial literacy, which people in the electronics, electrical, or other manufacturing industries must know to stay on top of their products and markets. Similarly, there's trade literacy, which means being up-to-date on particular trades, such as carpenters, artisans, metalworkers, and the like. Commerce also has its nitch, since people dealing in a particular area must know the market and economy driving it. Many job specialties, professions, and trades have associations and other organizations (e.g., unions) to help them keep updated on what they do for a living. Whatever the area, the need for the person involved in one or more of these areas to be as literate as possible is mandatory for short term success, let alone long-term progress within the field.

Science and Math Literacy

One of the hottest topics in recent times, actually starting back several decades ago with Russia's Sputnik space launch and continuing to crop up as a critical educational need, is science and math literacy. High technology companies bemoan the fact that they need more and smarter people to continue our quest for greater scientific and technological discoveries. We even import high technology people from other countries in higher than normal immigration numbers in an effort to take up the supposed deficit of qualified people. An interesting sidelight to this need is that an American Management Association survey in 1998 showed that only 40 percent of the respondents perform well on basic literacy or math skills tests.[22]

Schools, as well as businesses, are vitally concerned about science and math literacy. One example of what is being done to increase math and science literacy is the Teaching for Tomorrow program in Providence, Rhode Island, elementary schools. Several local universities, colleges, and medical facilities allocated $1 million to program in an effort to improve achievement in math and literacy.[23] Another effort was a science literacy public-private partnership started by Bayer Corp. in Allegheny, Pennsylvania, to provide a hands-on approach to learning science.[24] These programs illustrate how the workplace and schools can come together to resolve literacy problems and provide stronger backgrounds, in this case, in science and math literacy. A debate surrounds any effort to bolster one area of learning because it means some other area must be reduced; there's a limit to how many special programs can be implemented at once. For instance, one critic states, "Extensive portrayals of science as fun and easy to assimilate could have negative influences on science literacy by misleading beginners, who become disillusioned when faced with the complicated nature of the discipline."[25] Yet there are businesses and other organizations willing to promote programs like the one in Providence. Another concern is how much art, music, driver's education, vocational education, and other practical courses are giving way to science and math.

A good way to tell how important science and math literacy are is to look for related Web sites (as well as publications and associations). Exhibit 7. 2 lists a sampling of such sites. These are simply a few gathered from people who follow the topic.

Business Literacy

How often has it happened that a conscientious worker has spent long painful hours at a workstation, sending faxes around the globe, trying to locate illusive information needed for a decision, when the answer literally sat ten feet away in the next office in the form of a coworker who was a walking company encyclopedia? Or could have been learned through an e-mail to the East Coast division. Any organization that has been around a while has developed a core of people who, between them, have a tremendous amount of corporate knowledge. These are the people who can often be called upon to provide the knowledge so vital to the on-going operations of any organization. This example serves to illustrate two key points: that often the information we need is stored in someone's head, and that corporate knowledge, business literacy, is a fundamental requisite of anyone working for that organization. This latter concept is brought home by more and more companies requiring that those who join their ranks know something about the business.

Another crucial thing to keep in mind, remembering the discussion above about being self-employed, is that there's growing chance that more of us will become contingent workers at some time in the future. Here's what we mean by contingent worker:

- Temporary worker, which could also mean permanent temporary for companies who keep a temporary person in some jobs on virtually a permanent basis
- Seasonal hire

Exhibit 7.2
A Sampling of Science Literacy Web Sites

Building Websites for Science Literacy
    www.library.uscb.edu/istl/00-winter/article.html
Exploration of the factors in the dimensions of scientific literacy
    www.sasked.gov.sk.ca/docs/midlsci/scilmsce/html
Scientific Literacy Skills for Non-Science Librarians
    www.library.ucsb.edu/istl/99-fall/article3.html
ERIC Digest, Teaching Science through Inquiry
    www.ed.gov/databases/ERIC_Digests/ed359048.html
Book Reviews, Linking Science Teaching with Literacy Development
    www.ncrel.org/mands/docs/5-9.htm
The Sorry State of Scientific Literacy
    www.ctt.bc.ca/LQ/summer98/1.html
Toward an Understanding of Scientific Literacy
    ehrweb.aaas.org/ehr/forum/bybee/html
Women and Scientific Literacy, Building Two-Way Streets
    www.aacu-edu.org/intiatives/scilitrhodeisl.html
Electronic Fieldtrips: Student Explorations of the Great Rift Valley
    www.coe.uh.edu/insite/elec_pub/HTML1997/sc_cove.htm
Statements from Various Science Organizations on Scientific Literacy
    horizons.sb2.pdx/edu/!fem-sci-lit/defn.html
Science Literacy for All, An Achievable Goal
    www.project2061.org/newsinfo/research/articles/opa.htm

- Leased worker
- Contract worker
- Consultant
- Part-time worker, which could also be permanent or temporary
- Shared job

What this means to the organization is that the person filling the position will by definition know less about the organization and its line of business, and not know any of the other staff members with whom he or she will work, which might become a problem if a team effort is required. It's an added challenge for information literacy, as it's difficult for a contingent worker to come with the information power needed to get the job done, usually in a short period of time. Thus, it's absolutely necessary that contingent workers have vast business literacy if they expect to move in and quickly help solve problems before moving on to the next assignment.

Business literacy actually comes in three layers: the various elements of the organization itself (e.g., departments, work teams), the organization as a whole entity, and the industry or realm within which the organization operates (e.g., electronics, military, and so on). It is clear that business literacy is as deep as it is broad, and vitally important. Think of it this way: all information, to the greatest extent possible, should ultimately result in improving the effectiveness of the individual and the organization.

Art Michaels has laid down a number of steps for moving up in the corporate world. Several of the steps are directly related to business literacy. The selected recommendations include: "get to know intimately the instrument with which your company or division determines revenue, expenses and profit; improve personal computer skills; get an education in your organization's other areas; network; take charge of all your training and professional growth; and be a problem-solver."[26]

Business Literacy 2000 is a most interesting consortium living up to its name—promoting business literacy. It's a group of business book publishers "brought together by a desire to redefine the term Business literacy, broadening it to include not only understanding of the financial aspects of business, but also the capacity to utilize the theories and practices that will take successful people and organizations into the new millennium."[27] It's an old-fashioned reading group, slanted exclusively toward learning more about how to improve the way business is conducted. By searching online, in libraries and bookstores, and contacting discussion groups, you will find numerous sources for acquiring business literacy.

MAKING CONNECTIONS

There's another side to subject-matter literacy that at times could be more important than anything else you do. It's called networking, smoozing, or perhaps just sharing a few words with others in your line of work. Two positive results occur from having good connections: (1) you can readily obtain filtered, usable information, and (2) the network is available for future use. Networking may often be your best and fastest source of information. Who knows better than the professional member of your society who's many times solved the problem you're facing for the first time? Or the colleague you met at a company marketing meeting who's willing to share information? If the person you contact doesn't have the information you need, chances are he'll know where you can find it. It gives the information seeker an often needed feeling of security that the information is valid and useful. People love to talk about what they do for a living, so why not take advantage of it? The advantages of maintaining a group with which you network are as follows:

- You can share information with them.
- You can share ideas with them, and they can help get you off ground center when you're stuck on a problem.

- They provide all sorts of opportunities.
- They're there for you when you need them—and vice versa.

It's also a great way to keep career paths open.

The potential answer to a tough question may lie as close as a use group or bulletin board, where all you have to do is post it. Perhaps the best way to maintain relationships is to use as many ways as possible, including telephone and personal meetings from time to time. The payoff for business and information literacy is unlimited through sharing with others. There's nothing like having help when wielding information power. More on this in chapter 9, "On-the-Job Help."

Professional Development

Chapter 8, "Learning How to Learn," deals with professional development. It's mentioned here as a reminder that business literacy, like anything else we do, requires continuous maintenance just to keep up and possibly lots of work to get ahead.

EMOTIONAL INTELLIGENCE

People have long known that good, old fashioned common sense, interwoven with a dose of maturity and experience, is better than so-called book learning when it comes to being successful in life's work. These days, of course, we refer to these two fundamental concepts as emotional intelligence and intelligence quotient (IQ). Research is catching up to what we've already known intuitively. For instance, it's been reported that much of our success, "by many estimates, upwards of 75 percent—has to do with emotional intelligence."[28] Emotional intelligence has been defined as an "array of non-cognitive skills, capabilities and competencies that influence a person's ability to cope with environmental demands and resources."[29] In other words, it's the ability to marshal our emotions so common sense and experience can prevail. As one reporter noted, "Everyone has it. Everyone should use it."[30] And as another report headlined: "Some have it, others can learn."[31] There's nothing new here, as "Successful leaders have always been attuned to human interaction and their decisions were imbued with emotional sensitivity." [32]

The five elements of emotional intelligence have been identified as follows:

- Self-awareness
- Self-reflection
- Motivation
- Empathy
- Social skills

Hendrie Weisinger identifies the four building blocks of emotional intelligence as:

1. The ability to accurately perceive, appraise, and express emotion
2. The ability to access or generate feelings on demand when they can facilitate understanding of yourself or another person
3. The ability to understand emotion and the knowledge that derives from them
4. The ability to regulate emotions to promote emotional and intellectual growth.[33]

Put all this together and you're in business. As Daniel Goleman notes, "The rules for work are changing"[34] regarding emotional intelligence. Workers are judged not only by how smart they are, but also by how well they handle themselves (control their emotions). Organizational success, in fact, has been tied to the level of emotional intelligence of the members of the organization. To bear this out, Cooper and Sawaf state that "If the driving force of intelligence in twentieth-century business has been IQ, then—according to growing evidence—in the dawning twenty-first century it will be EQ, and related forms of practical and creative intelligence."[35] Similar to the other descriptions, their cornerstones include emotional: literacy, fitness, depth, and alchemy. These are basically social skills. Think how often we must deal with people. It's easy to let social interaction slide with so much information at our fingertips, but if we're not successful in dealing with people, then it does not matter how much information power we have, especially if we're in a leadership position.

Two examples will further illustrate this. One is the report by a military trainer who uses "his knowledge of EI skills to fine tune training programs," improving on overall training results. EI is the focus for selection and hiring, building high profile teams, career development, and restructuring and workplace planning decisions.[36] Similarly, an insurance company uses the emotional intelligence focus to screen out pessimists after determining that optimists were better at selling their products (which was an example of them exercising their own emotional intelligence). Their results proved the value of their decision. To put this in context with information literacy, think how important being level headed and objective is to each of the sixteen steps in the information literacy process. The contents of a workshop designed to develop emotional intelligence in organizations included such topics as identifying and managing emotions, empathy, social skills, motivation, keeping distress from interfering with thinking, and hope and optimism.[37]

Another example is Parms & Co., a Columbus, Ohio, CPA firm which uses on-going emotional quotient (EQ) assessment. It's a company "aware of the importance of emotional intelligence," and, in using it, experiences "the greatest success and steadiest growth."[38] Assessment shows a person where he or she stands regarding emotional intelligence level, so he or she can make necessary improvements. Input for the assessment comes from as many as nine people with whom the person being assessed interacts. The firm evidently feels this effort is worth the time and cost.

A brief review of the literature—Web sites, business news, and other sources of current business practices—finds that conscious efforts to bridge emotional intelligence gaps within an organization is widespread, just as the examples above do. Following is a sampling of emotional intelligence Web sites:

- The Emotional Intelligence Home Page—general information on emotional intelligence, resources, bibliography, and information about their emotional intelligence test (www.virtent.com/eq.htm)

- Emotion and Emotional Intelligence—online bibliography on emotional intelligence; current research findings and notes (trochim.human.cornell.edu/gallery/young/emotion.htm)

- Emotional Literacy—lists of words expressing feelings identifying emotional intelligence quotient; communications (eqi.org/elit.htm)

- The 90% Factor—emotional intelligence and the new workplace; article in an online magazine (www.canadaone.com/magazine/eq050198.html)

BLENDING THE LITERACIES

There's a definite hierarchy of literacy, starting with the basics of reading, writing, and numeracy, moving on to the skills leading to becoming information literate, and ending with information power. The workplace environment that embraces knowledge and success must advocate all the literacies and help people to achieve needed levels of each. Author John Case has provided an excellent melding of the literacies and competencies necessary for people and organizations to succeed. His book *Open Book Management* recognizes that more people have to get into the act of running a business.[39] His open book management style includes some familiar items, starting with what he calls the first principle, "Information Please," and continuing with a discussion of the power of information. The other principles are business literacy, empowerment, and a stake in success.

CHAPTER 8

Learning How to Learn: A Foundation for Information Power

INTRODUCTION

The human brain is a remarkable muscle. We've learned a lot about how it works, including how people learn and think and act—literally the brain learning about itself. The more we learn about how to learn, the better job of learning we can do in the future, a truly exciting prospect. Considering how quickly we pick up information, and knowledge, from schools, newspapers, books, conversations, television, and all those other sources so readily available to us, it's amazing how equally fast that information can become obsolete. But the brain continues to acquire new information and new skills to keep us up-to-date and competitive in the workplace. People who use and develop their brain power directly enhance their information power.

This is no accident. There's no letup in the demand for people exercising their brains to perform at ever greater levels. Everything discussed to this point—globalization, competition, technology, and others—continue to stir up the pot and keep us ever learning. The need is great, and we respond to it, overall, successfully. It's a lot of hard work, but worth every minute of it.

Technology offers a two-edged sword for learning. It's one of the main reasons why we must keep learning continuously, yet it offers one of the most remarkable solutions. It's revolutionizing education, training, and learning. As one person noted, "The current boom in computer-based teaching products fuels hope that technology has finally reached a point where it can make a difference to education."[1] Libraries have blended electronic resources into their other data sources to make available more information for learning than ever before.

To help understand how we learn, this chapter looks at such topics as adult learning principles, levels of learning, new ways of learning, the concept of the learning organization, the concept of self-employment, and other related areas to help us prepare to continue to learn in the most efficient way—and certainly to be ready to go with the right skills when we need them.

LEARNING AS A LIFETIME ENDEAVOR

In his twenty-year study of the Harvard MBA class of 1974, Professor John Kotter identified rules for success at work based on how members of the class fared in their work lives. It's significant that the last of the rules is "Never stop trying to grow; lifelong learning is increasingly necessary for success."[2] Another writer has identified four components of a program to increase continuous learning: develop a work ethic dedicated to pride and mastery; keep pushing the envelope of learning by exploring other experiences and competencies; set high goals (also noted by Kotter); and make professional development your first loyalty.[3] Executives are expected to continue learning about new products by using them themselves.

Continuous learning means, according to one statement, that "The marketplace for learning is being redefined dramatically from K–12 to K–80, or lifelong learning, whose major segments are customers, employers, and students, in that order." Davis and Botkin in *The Monster under the Bed* further state that, "In the information economy, the rapid pace of technological change means that education must be updated throughout our working lives. People have to increase their learning power to sustain their earning power."[4] Lifelong learning has become the norm. You only need to look as far as the proliferation of senior citizen learning opportunities—classes, field trips, workshops, service projects, and more—to confirm this. Senior citizens are taking to computers in large numbers, proving the adage that it's never too late to learn and grow.

Organizational spending for training employees in the U.S. hit the $54 billion level in 1999, with almost 60 million employees receiving training. Types of training range from the three Rs to leadership and information technology. It's all delivered in a wide variety of ways, from old fashioned classrooms to fully online vehicles, and shows no sign of letting up. These organizations are putting their money where it counts, leading the way for continuous learning and growth. This data, reported for the past nineteen years by *Training* magazine and appearing in the October issue each year, clearly shows that organizations are indeed serious about keeping the learning process going.[5]

Relationship to Information Literacy

Continuous learning and information literacy are major elements of working life today, and unquestionably in the future. Their interrelationships are so many and so complete, it becomes difficult to separate them other than for discussion purposes. One relies heavily on the other. In order to continue learning throughout our lifetimes, we must be information literate. Information literacy demands that we continue to learn in order to maintain a high level of literacy. Suffice it to say that both are critical to workplace success. To put it another way, neither one can get along without the other. The following comparisons of information literacy and learning further show that the two are actually inseparable:

- Both require a high degree of motivation.
- Both require essentially the same skills.
- Both require application of multiple intelligences and modalities.
- Both require a continuing process of skill improvement and knowledge acquisition (from competency through mastery).
- Both are essential to workplace success, not to mention life in general.

These concepts of learning are discussed on the following pages. A look at the sixteen steps in the information literacy process indicates that each one requires not only a high skill level but, because of changes in both information and technology, continuous learning is essential.

HOW WE LEARN

We learn in many ways. Stories of high-school dropouts who make it big are not uncommon, and people who do so must have learned the tricks of success in some way. There's no mystery about learning. We learn in school, through experiences, through relationships with families and friends, and otherwise through going about our daily living—earning our daily bread, shopping for it, as well as sharing it with others. The shift to lifelong learning has brought with it a body of knowledge about how adults learn, as opposed to how children in the typical classroom setting learn. Naturally, there's much overlap, and principles governing one way cross over into the other.

Motivation plays a major part in any type of learning. Students are motivated by grades and scholarships; workers are motivated by the prospect of promotions and pay raises when they acquire new skills. Some people are motivated by the sheer joy of learning. There are as many motivators as there are people being motivated, all the theories ranging from behavior modification to Maslow's hierarchy of needs (self-actualization, the highest and most difficult to achieve; esteem; belongingness and love; safety; and physiological comfort, the most basic human need) apply in one way or the other.[6] Even the thought that learning must continue in order to keep a job can be the only motivator needed at certain times. People generally know what does and does not motivate them. Continuous learning thus has motivational concepts embedded within it.

People with learning disabilities provide a great inspiration for continuous, lifelong learning—and proving wrong the stereotypes—on their way to success in life. Dyslexic persons overcome their reading problems by learning and performing through other means, such as visual, auditory, or verbal. They learn by watching media and other people, or by listening to books on tape. The motivation to succeed becomes so great that barriers fall away as skills and knowledge are acquired in alternative ways. The following sections address multimodality and multiple ways of learning. For now, it's sufficient to say that just about anybody can learn and grow given the right opportunity—or any opportunity at all.

Adult Learning Principles

One of the primary differences between adult and child learning is that adults participate in the process to a greater extent although this has changed significantly in recent times as public education programs stress more classroom involvement by the children. Adults usually know what it is they want to learn and go after it, regardless of what it takes or how difficult it might be to acquire. Sixteen learning principles, seven from adult theory and the remaining nine from general learning theory, have been identified and are discussed in the following paragraphs. As noted, "Chances are you're familiar with most, if not all, of them"[7] because they're what make the difference in how you learn.

Adults learn by doing; they want to be involved. Don't demonstrate, let an adult learner do it for you. Adults want to experience and perform the skill they are learning. For example, if they're learning how to use a computer graphics program, they want to actually take the mouse and keyboard in hand and do it themselves rather than have someone else do it for them. If they're learning how to apply one of the problem-solving solutions discussed in chapter 4, they want to actually put the process into effect to learn about it. Nothing beats doing it yourself.

Real life must be reflected and relevant to learners and the learning. Adults don't learn nearly as well if abstract examples and ideas are used. What good is the learning if we can't use it in real life? Some degree of abstraction might work, but not much. This further reflects the hands-on nature of adult learning.

Adults relate their learning to what they already know, sometimes in a pronounced way. This is a natural reaction. We have a certain understanding of things, and we use these as a standard against which we compare everything else.

Informal environments work best. People simply learn better when the atmosphere is more relaxed. For an adult learning computers for the first time, there's enough tension in the air without creating more.

Trainers, mentors, and others involved should serve as facilitators because we're all adults and we're all equal. Learners are most likely accomplished in whatever it is they do, just like the professional. Telling was okay, perhaps, in high schools, but not in adult learning. At times, in fact, the facilitator is wise to step back and let learning happen.

Variety is the spice of life as you'll see during the remainder of this chapter. Learning is no different, so the more ways that are presented to learn new skills and knowledge, the better.

Remove the fear factor, which is similar to the principle of creating an informal setting, but this is something adults are sensitive to if they haven't been graded on performance in a learning situation for a few decades. Praise and as near a win-win situation as possible works best. This is particularly true for people reentering the workforce after a prolonged absence.

Learning objectives. Make sure you know them. This is the road map for all the learning you'll do, so precise, measurable ones are essential.

Practice makes perfect, an adage which applies to everything. It leads to mastery, and, for those who can't achieve mastery, it leads to at least enough of the skill to perform the job. This is how skills become second, intuitive nature.

Guidance and prompting, is what the facilitator or mentor should do when one is involved in the learning process. Insist on receiving guidance if it isn't forthcoming because it will eliminate much wasted learning time.

Feedback is essential. It should come often, and certainly after every significant milestone during the learning process. Again, if it isn't forthcoming, ask for it, even if—perhaps moreso—if you suspect things aren't going well. Wasted time makes the situation worse.

Transfer of training, is a long-time learning principle. One aspect of learning builds on another, such as the ability to add and subtract transfers to being able to balance a checkbook. Knowing how the learning taking place will transfer into other endeavors helps validate the effort, keeps it on track, and provides further motivation.

Learning objectives. Adults want to know where they're going and to make sure they are learning what they want and need to learn. They are quite goal oriented, particularly when it comes to workplace and life success, so make sure you always know what the objectives are, where you stand toward achieving them, and make changes where necessary. Keep them in front of you at all times.

Good first impressions go a long way. This is true for the facilitator, and the learner has the responsibility to going all out to be every bit as prepared as the facilitator. Facilitators frown on the learner who comes in, leans back in the chair, and says, "Okay teach me." When you impress the facilitator, you'll get more out of the learning.

Enthusiasm rubs off. If the facilitator or others around you aren't enthusiastic, increase yours to try to pump them up. If you're learning on your own, enthusiasm is mandatory to get through the training.

Invoke the three Rs, repetition, reiteration, and rote. It's as true today learning how to use a word processor program as it was learning the multiplication tables all those years ago.

Obviously, there's nothing new here. It's what we know about how we learn. Some may be more important than others, but all have a bearing in some way. They also could easily be superimposed over the information literacy process since as we go through the steps as we do our daily jobs, we're continuously learning.

Domains of Learning

There are three different paths, or domains, within which people learn: cognitive (knowledge, intellectual skills), psychomotor (physical skills), and affective (behavior, attitude). Learning psychologists inform us that within these three domains, all types of learning can be categorized. This classification provides us with the foundation for understanding how we learn.

Next comes a further classification provided by Professor Bloom. These are the six levels of intellectual behavior used in learning, giving us an easily understood hierarchy of learning within the three domains.[8] The six classifications, taking us from the most rudimentary type of learning to the most complex, are: knowledge, comprehension, application, analysis, synthesis, and evaluation. Examples of each of these six learning levels are:

- Knowledge. You can repeat back facts. The range of knowledge level could be simple, such as the letters of the alphabet, to complex, such as Ohm's Law. You may or may not be able to use the knowledge.

- Comprehension. You have an idea of what the knowledge means. In the above case, you'd have an idea that the letters could be put into words, sentences, and so on; or you'd know how to apply a law to solve a physics problem.

- Application. You can put the knowledge to good use. You actually form a sentence or apply the law to a successful solution.

- Analysis. You can think about it awhile and see different uses for it. For instance, you might see that words could be formed into books or television ads; or that the law may form the basis for solving other physics problems.

- Synthesis. You can apply new uses for the knowledge. This might include being able to develop another language from the letters, or solving other mathematical problems.

- Evaluation. You can determine whether or not the knowledge can be used in abstract ways. This might include using letters or the law as art forms.

What we have just outlined in brief terms is a basic body of educational psychology. It not only helps us understand how we learn, but it fits nicely into the concept of information literacy. For instance, the more advanced the search for information, the farther up the ladder of the six levels of learning we must go. At times, all six levels might be required. This comparison effectively reinforces the soundness as well as practicality of the information literacy process.

Multiple Ways to Learn

Learning is stimulating and fun because it happens in so many different ways. Perhaps we learn because we throw everything we have, body and soul, into the process, devoting countless hours to the cause. But it might also happen purely by accident. We may go to bed at night in a quandary, trying to figure something out, and wake up the next morning with the solution. Sometimes we must work diligently, depending on rote and memorization to help us through to the understanding of a simple truth, yet acquire a complex set of skills with relative ease. Fortunately, the body of knowledge about learning continues to amass, all to our advantage.

One source, for instance, recognizes four learning styles:

- Enthusiastic learners, people who involve their feelings
- Imaginative learners, people who rely on intuition
- Practical learners, people who think, then act
- Logical learners, people who are deliberate learners[9]

Perhaps some of all four types has the greatest payoff over the long haul. After all, learning, like so much else that we do, is situational.

One of the most widely accepted theories of learning styles in recent years is Howard Gardner's multiple intelligences. His original definition of intelligence in *Frames of Mind* was "an ability to solve problems or fashion products valued in one or more cultures."[10] He has since refined it to mean "a biopsychological potential to process information that can be activated in a cultural setting to solve problems or create products that are of value in a culture" in *Intelligence Reframed*.[11] Either way, it means that intelligence can come from multiple sources, and the concept of one intelligence that can only be measured with a standard intelligence quotient (IQ) test is too narrow and limiting. At first Gardner indentified seven basic intelligences but he has added an eighth one:

Linguistic—ability to communicate through language; using language with ease. These are writers, poets, and others who use words to a great extent.

Musical—ability to create and understand meanings made out of sounds; using rhythm, song, and otherwise appreciating music. This includes musicians and composers.

Logical-mathematical—ability to use and appreciate abstract relationships; using conceptual thinking. These are computer scientists, chemists, mathematicians, and others who think in a similar manner.

Spatial—ability to perceive and transform images, then recreate them from memory; using images and pictures. This includes artists and architects.

Bodily-kinesthetic—ability to use all parts of the body in skilled ways; using intuition, gestures. These are dancers, athletes, and others who express things through their bodies.

Intrapersonal—ability to distinguish among own feelings; using creativity to independently develop new ideas. These people are self-motivated, such as philosophers and researchers.

Interpersonal—ability to distinguish among others' feelings; relating and cooperating. These are people who try out their ideas on others for valued opinions and work well with others, such as sales representatives and public speakers.

Naturalist—the ability to distinguish and classify among features of the environment. These are the people, like Darwin and Thoreau, who learn from communing with the environment. This is the newest intelligence added to the list.

The importance of these eight ways of learning, also referred to as the eight smarts, is that they give us great insight into how we learn. By knowing how each of us learns best, we can focus on that method bearing in mind that we likely learn in more than one of the eight ways. For example, we might first hear about something, then actually perform it, thus combining linguistic with kinesetic learning. Numerous examples abound. Various methods, including simple tests used by teachers in classroom settings, exist to help people identify their intelligences. One such tool, *7 Kinds of Smart* by Armstrong, includes information about the first seven of the intelligences, assistance in determining one's strong and weak points, and techniques that develop the so-called smarts.[12] It's but one example of what can be done, and is far more effective than any assistance in raising your IQ.

Multimodality Concept

The concept of multimodality simply means that people learn in many ways. It's closely related to the eight intelligences identified by Gardner and serves to remind us that we need to acquire knowledge and skills in many ways. Doing so ensures that we do, indeed, learn what we need to learn. One way to think of multimodality is in terms of the senses. We see, we hear, and we feel, and all three contribute to learning. A simple illustration of this concept is shown in exhibit 8.1; the more senses are brought into the learning process, the better. In terms of information literacy, it means using as many different vehicles as possible, such as reading, listening, watching, and performing. Each one will reinforce the others, and learning will build.

Generational Issues

How we learn has taken a new twist, and it is possibly the most unique new development in the workplace in general and the training field in particular in some time. It's a mix of employees with not only several decades separating their ages, but representing several distinct generations. The oldest are the World War II folks, the ones Tom Brokaw called "The Greatest Generation."[13] Following behind in large numbers and accumulating a great deal of press along the way are the baby boomers, born shortly after the war. After the boomers, we have Generations X and Y representing the younger folks. You'd think the next generational group would be called Z, but not so. "Generation Next, individuals born between 1977 and 1994, represent a significant challenge to trainers and managers."[14] We hear so much about a mass retirement of baby boomers, yet Next accounts for 26 percent of the population, even though many of them are too young yet to work. Their significance is that they grew up with and are adept at using technology.

With this in mind, picture a number of possible workplace combinations, such as this one: a team leader appointed to the job despite being fresh out of college, but made leader because she's the most proficient person with tech-

Exhibit 8.1
Multimodality Learning and the Senses

Modality	We sense through the	Example
Visual	Eyes	Reading a book or computer screen; observing correct performance of a task
Auditory	Ears	Listening to a tape or lecture; listening to an expert discuss or explain a subject
Tactile	Skin	Touching and using a piece of equipment
Olfactory	Nose	Sensing aromatic features of physical objects
Sixth sense	Extrasensory	Sensing things intuitively, which is enhanced through experience

nology, and technology is paramount to team success; a new hire fresh out of community college who's old enough to be the team leader's grandmother; two men who are nearing retirement age; and a generation Xer who's a conservationist and skateboards to work, and who shows a strong affinity toward entitlement. Right away you can see the challenges—seemingly overwhelming challenges—to workplace success and ongoing learning. Each may perceive information in different ways. To a great extent, the learning habits and styles of these people will be generational. Books to television, to hands on and virtual reality will be among the ways people will want their training delivered.

To make matters more interesting, assume that people with appropriate skills are in short supply, so a part-time worker and two temporary workers are added to the team. Motivation takes on more meaning, and if you had a member or two with disabilities requiring learning accommodations, you get a feel for it the diversity of this group, which needs to be trained as a unit—and we haven't even considered how many of the team members speak English as a second language.

Actually, the situation isn't all that dire, just one requiring a little extra attention. Generation Next members, for example, are "the most educated generation in American history," and "they are sophisticated education consumers."[15] People fifty and over, according to the American Association of Retired Persons (AARP), want "to keep up with what's going on in the world."[16] They, like so many of the people who comprise the workforce, learn by getting their hands on and doing it.

It's tempting to go with the flow and focus on one generation or the other. With technology being what it is, focusing on the youngest who excel at it would be understandable, and in fact, might work just fine. Bankers Trust "was compelled to shift to video game-based training when it realized that traditional training methods were not achieving the desired results."[17] The program's entertainment-oriented, cross-generational appeal, performance measurement, and adaptability are credited with leading to success.

SELF-DIRECTED LEARNING

Learning has a distinctive pattern. From kindergarten through high school, it's highly structured and formal to the point of donning caps and gowns and receiving diplomas, along with encouragement to go out and conquer the world. For those who go on to college, the process continues for several more years. For many people, college and work become blended, stretching the postsecondary portion of education out for several years. For educators, the structured, rigorous, and formal process becomes a way of life—which implies that for most of us, a transition point occurs somewhere along the lifelong learning continuum. We accept responsibility and control over our individual learning. High achievers and those interested in specific subjects start taking control, self-directing their learning, even while in the midst of the formal educational learning process.

This concept is further motivated by the fact that most people, including those employed by organizations, are in charge of their own destinies. This definitely includes implementing continuous learning. An inescapable reality is that you simply have to do it—continuous learning is a twenty-first-century fact of life. What works best of all is when facilitators help the process along. Mentors, coaches, and organizational facilitators can help keep the learning process focused on the most critical skills and knowledge.

Self-directed learning has developed its own nomenclature—SDL. It's a hot topic, as witnessed by these statements: "The emergence of self-directed learning (SDL) is revolutionizing employee training,"[18] and "Companies are increasingly considering self-directed learning (SDL) as an alternative to classroom and computer-based training programs, recognizing that it may be the best way to gain the knowledge required in the highly competitive global market."[19] One claim is that it has achieved savings of 20 to 50 percent, and many organizations are climbing aboard to reap the benefits and savings. Among the advantages are these:

- Relates directly to individual needs
- Flexible time-frame
- Cost of training is reduced
- Available when it's needed[20]

Librarians are great believers in taking charge of their own learning. A study showed that 77 percent of the respondents had undertaken self-directed learning, which equated to three times as much time in this type of training as in formal continuing education.[21]

According to adult learning expert Malcolm Knowles, learners "are responsible for assessing their own learning requirements, developing learning objectives, searching for the resources to satisfy the objectives, implementing a learning plan, and evaluating their success in meeting the objectives."[22] It's a lot of work, but if the need for acquiring the skill is apparent, then people will take the matter into their hands and learn.

There's nothing new here. In the past such terms as *self-paced learning* and *correspondence courses* provided the means for people to learn on their own. The difference with a successful self-directed program, however, is that it must be formalized to the extent that people are provided the resources they need to develop their own plans and objectives, after having assessed what they need. This is where the facilitator comes in. "Facilitators," to be most effective, "help promote change by fostering a learning environment that allows trainees to take their time to learn, tolerates mistakes, offers trainees with feedback regarding their progress, encourage trainees to depart from tradition, and acknowledges the diverse learning styles and abilities."[23] In a sense, this training approach must be formalized to the point of ensuring it works best, but the proof is that people can learn on their own, having taken control of the process that is laid out for them.

Self-directed learning can become reality in a number of ways. One example is using computer games similar to Bankers Trust. Games "allow companies to create customized programs in fulfilling their employees' training needs," and are "fun, engage people on an action and competitive level and foster teamwork."[24] A Long Island report included companies such as Con Edison and Arrow Electronics that use a variety of popular learning games. Owens-Corning Fiberglass Corp. uses the World Wide Web "as a learning medium for its employees," and through a partnership with the American Management Association, the program allows employees "from different parts of the world to link to a special Web site containing the company's clusters of formal competencies."[25] Johnson Controls uses a combination of classroom and computer training, where traditional classroom supplements self-directed learning.[26] Using one of the learning principles stated earlier, variety is, indeed, the spice of life, as well as a good approach to learning.

Self-directed learning looks much like the regular staff development training process. It's just that the staff members become accountable for their own learning, which works well so long as the process is focused on improving organizational performance.

LEARNING HOW TO LEARN

Basic Concepts

Teachers and trainers know how to organize and present new materials to learners in such a way that the material is more easily grasped. Think of the really good teachers you've had and you'll quickly realize this. We can use these same methods for self-learning. The most straightforward way is to outline material into a logical flow, starting with major element "A" and its subordinants, on through to the last major element "n." Next comes the basic step of developing graphics to enhance the outline. Pictures, graphs, diagrams, artistic depictions, and other forms of graphics fulfill the adage that a picture is worth a thousand words. By then mapping the data, combining both outline form and graphics, the best of both worlds are achieved.

These are methods we intuitively use anyway, and by applying them to new subjects and skills, we can continue to learn effectively. Note also that these techniques for learning serve as efficient templates to use during the steps in the information literacy process. Again, learning and being information literate are extensively interrelated.

Smith's *Learning How to Learn*[27] and other sources on the subject identify a number of areas where people can continue to learn—to learn how to learn, starting with taking control of their own learning and spreading out learning over a broad variety of areas. These include the following, showing that a person who has learned how to learn has accomplished part or all of these items:

- Taken control over his or her own learning, not depending on others. Self-directed learning has its place, and perhaps a vital one.
- Has developed a personal learning plan and kept it up-to-date. This, too, is a part of taking personal control over one's destiny.
- Knows his or her own strengths and weaknesses as a learner (e.g., knows which modalities work best, and so on). Perhaps becoming intimately acquainted with the eight multiple intelligences is a great place to start.
- Is familiar with how adults in general and themselves in particular learn best. This is intuitive and not difficult to figure out.
- Doesn't let anything interfere with learning (i.e., obstacles have been removed). Remaining focused, yet flexible, is key to success.
- Sets clear, achievable objectives and goals before starting out on any learning process. This is the road map mentioned earlier.
- Takes advantage of unplanned opportunities to learn. This is simply exercising the right to be innovative and take risks, which can have huge payoffs.
- Learns from everyday life experiences. The school of hard knocks is a good place to learn, provided mistakes aren't repeated.
- Learns from the media. It's also a way to keep updated on the world you live in.
- Participates in potentially fruitful discussions. Others may have just the knowledge you need, and pressing dialog is a good way to seek it out.
- Knows how to ask good questions. It's amazing how this old standby keeps coming up. If there was only way to learn, this just might be the one.
- Has mentors who help him or her learn. That's what they're there for—but remember, it works both ways.
- Knows how to use intuition and possibly even dreams to learn.
- Helps others learn to the best of his or her ability, as in being a mentor.
- Thinks critically. It's the only way to think, unless you want to throw in thinking creatively once in a while.

A review of providers of learning how to learn services and products indicates some of the key ingredients of learning how to learn:

- Interacting with others
- Listening
- Structuring work activities

- Demonstrating interpersonal skills
- Using problem solving skills
- Continually learning new skills
- Thinking critically
- Asking good questions
- Identifying key words
- Outlining and note taking

It is no coincidence that most, if not all, of these are recognizable as keys to being information literate.

Environmental Scanning

Professional planners use the concept of environmental scanning to stay on top of their profession. It simply means taking a look around to see what's happening in their industries, organizations, or other milieus. By anticipating new developments—which could mean anything from new competition to new technology—they can more accurately plan for the future. For example, city governments must stay on top of population growth, scanning the horizon, so to speak, to determine what level of new services they must provide, ranging from water to schools to fire stations. Environmental scanning involves a broad spectrum of searching, including these topics:

- Demographic data
- Futurists predictions
- Political developments
- Consumer trends
- Opportunities and threats
- Strengths and weaknesses
- New developments, particularly technology
- New skills
- New ways that work gets done
- Acquiring new skills when needed

These searches are also done when exercising the information literacy model to seek out, obtain, and use information.

Environmental scanning is like a radar, continually searching to find targets that may have an impact on one's organization. The saying "just coming on the radar scope," applies here. In predigital days it meant that a target, represented by a blip on the radar scope, had just come into radar range. Today it's part of the business jargon meaning something is just being heard about or learned. When information or developments of potential significance are identified, they're evaluated to determine their impact. Doing so will help ensure that there are no surprises when, for instance, a new technology comes along that requires information gathering to stay up to date—by scanning, you would already be up to date.

This metaphor also applies especially well to the information literacy process. People who continually seek information stay in touch with new developments in information seeking in one or more of the following ways:

- Staying on top of industry and professional developments
- Keeping an eye on new books
- News surfing
- Perusing newsletters, newspapers, magazines, and journals
- Networking with others known to be on top of information

If you have a good idea where the information is, you'll get to it much quicker—a great payoff for continuous scanning of what's available.

Education's Role

Schools continue to play a vital part in preparing people to continue to learn after leaving the traditional K–12 and college systems. They're aware that their students will likely be called upon to fill knowledge jobs, which is what the future holds. In fact, these students will be doing much the same thing at work as they did in school—which is to say, being information literate. Knowledge jobs require knowledge workers. Knowledge workers know how to continue their learning. As one institution noted, "Today's new workers will be knowledge workers, who must shift from their manual skills to a set of theoretical and analytical knowledge that can only be acquired through formal schooling."[28] More precisely, this includes knowledge of how to learn—to ask questions, to find answers and critically evaluate them, to adapt as the future demands, and to love learning. No doubt a passion for learning will serve you well.

The College of Marin has a lot to say about learning how to learn. It shows the close parallel between learning in school and lifelong learning; for all practical purposes there is no differentiation.[29] Their recommendations include building good habits: developing the habit of mental self-management, developing the habit of positive thinking, developing the habit of hierarchical thinking, developing the habit of creative and critical thinking, and developing the habit of asking questions.

Exhibit 8.2
Ways Writing Can be Used to Enhance Learning

These are techniques that can both enhance our writing ability and overall learning. The starting point is the beginning of a learning session. Taking the topic and your understanding of it, you would consider these:

- Brainstorming. Write down your ideas for whatever is the problem at hand.

- Definitions. Record your definitions of what is the topic at hand.

- Words. Identify every word that applies to the topic.

- Dialogue. Work with someone else and record your conversations regarding the challenge.

- Directions. Record the directions you intend to take to pursue a particular information search or learning challenge.

- Questions. List as many questions as possible about the task at hand.

- Random thoughts. Record your random thoughts about the process you are going through.[30]

Writing to Learn

Writing is one of the best ways to learn. It forces us to collect our thoughts, organize them, and essentially perform the steps of the information literacy process. Exhibit 8.2 provides some examples of how writing to learn can be a valuable learning tool. Writing has the quality of making ideas more permanent than if we just place them somewhere in the back of our brain. So, too, is writing critical to information literacy as shown in chapter 3. Somewhere along the path to seeking out, acquiring, and applying information, we must place in writing bits and pieces of the process.

Organizational Learning

Organizations, like the individuals who staff them, learn continuously. Organizations that take this concept seriously and positively have the knack for being more successful than their counterparts who don't. This concept, also referred to as the learning organization, was discussed in chapter 1. It has become the subject of popular works, although as previously noted, organizations, particularly successful and long-standing ones, have been learning since organizations began. The significance for continuous learning is that true learning organizations provide excellent foundations for individual development.

Organizational learning can occur in many different ways, and the more ways made available, the better. One author has made a most interesting proposition—that much organizational learning takes place outside of ordinary work spaces. As she notes, "some of our best conversations take place in the hallways."[31] She refers to this as knowledge renewal, a critical part of a successful organization's longevity. Learning organizations thus have the ability to transfer privately held information and knowledge to the collective good of the organization through making it accessible—even in the hallway. This emphasizes the social nature of life, work, and learning. It also underlies some of our problems related to functioning in a digital world.

The next chapter takes up the concept of online help, which includes online tutorials available for a variety of topics and from a variety of sources. You can also go to school on the net, either by visiting a Web page (growing in popularity) or by using a CD-ROM. Since only 16 percent of college students are students in the traditional mode, "the vast majority of today's students are time-crunched adults who must pencil in college diplomas and graduate degrees between hectic jobs and kids' soccer games."[32] Digital learning opens up many resources for learning, as organizations put their training online and training and educational providers go online with their goods and services. It opens up many new learning opportunities, with perhaps the only problem one of determining what's available and what might work best for you.

INTEGRATING THE CONCEPTS

There's no one way to learn. What each of us must do is explore all the ways of learning and identify the ways that work best for us. Most likely, we'll discover that there are several ways, some of which will be dependent on the circumstances. Whatever you do, it will require work, lots of it. People involved in the learning movement note that learning is a task, "something you have to work at," as Jack Gordon has informed us.[33]

A review of this chapter provides the following selection of items to help us continue to learn beyond formal education:

- Be interested in learning. Learning opens doors that lead to more challenges and opportunities for us as we grow and succeed within the organizations within which we work, either as employees or outside providers. Even better, have a passion for it. The payoff is worth every ounce of expended energy.

- Continually seek to learn about new and different things. Variety is, indeed, the spice of life and keeps us young and moving.

- Ask lots of good questions. Socrates taught us such a good lesson, and we should never lose sight of the fact. Who, what, where, what, why, how, and if are eight of the most important words in any language and should be used as often as possible.

- Use all senses and methods of learning, leaving no possibility to chance. We simply learn more by approaching learning in as many ways as possible. Variety keeps life and learning interesting.

- Continually scan the environment for new skills and developments. No doubt the new and different will come along—might as well be ready for it by anticipating it. This follows closely with the concept of continuous learning, by putting us in the driver's seat in determining what we learn.

- Read prolifically. The written word has never been more important than with the development of electronic sources. There are more words generated today, between written media and electronic, than ever before.

- Continue taking courses of all types and through all media. Let others help you discover new areas and new skills, as well as new developments that we might find of great interest.

- Take advantage of every opportunity to teach others, of all ages. The old pros will tell you that teaching is one of the greatest ways to learn. When you consider the diverse knowledge and skills of adults within the continuous learning cycle, it becomes mind boggling how much the teacher can learn from those experienced adults from whom he or she supposedly teaches.

And a last word, there's the crucial consideration that people are now in charge of their own destinies. In fact, consensus is building that places the individual squarely in the driver's seat when it comes to managing careers, regardless of whether it's working for the same company for twenty years or being self-employed. In fact, "There is a growing belief that individuals themselves, not organizations, are responsible for personal well-being and career stability."[34] This a far cry from the way it once was and places full responsibility on the individual for being information literate—ready to tackle all opportunities and turn them to personal as well as organizational advantage.

CHAPTER 9

On-the-Job Help:
A Click Away

What would we do without that friendly question mark at the top of the screen, inviting us to ask any question we might have and quickly find the solution? Better yet, what would we do without the young fellow in the next cubicle, or our teenage daughter who's always there to answer the toughest question about using computers and software? It's easy to purchase a computer, complete with enough software to keep us busy for a few years. With low prices for bare-bones systems and readily available installment payments, or classes at to the local adult learning center or friendly neighborhood library, acquisition of computer power has gotten easier. What hasn't gotten easier is figuring out how to use it. It's one thing to hand over the credit card to the computer store clerk, quite another to call the 800 number to schedule a training class, then actually show up to take it.

Technology pays a bonus to the knowledge worker. It's at our fingertips, literally, primed and ready to perform knowledge work any time, any place. It's part of the computer revolution in which more and more people rely on the personal computer to do more and more of what people do for their livings, including jobs that are still predominantly in the lower skill areas. Online help comes in many forms and can be used in many ways. Combined with the fact that learning and working are increasingly electronic means that the knowledge worker has an exciting future of growing on the job. Technology takes on a dual role: creates the need for training and offers part of the solution.

This chapter delves into one of the most used of all tools for seeking information, on-the-job help. Fortunately, there are plenty of online resources, including the Internet, documentation, books, journals and newspapers, help functions, tutorials, reference resources, company information, and expert systems, that are all discussed in the chapter. Electronic performance support systems (EPSS), a major form of online assistance, is also discussed.

ONLINE RESOURCES

Online resources are prolific. They also cover many broad areas, making it a challenge to determine what's available and what's of value. Common sense would say that the best place to learn about what can be obtained online is to do just that—go online. Indeed, that's how much of the information for this chapter was obtained. However, it's worthy of note that plenty of useful information came from print media, although much of it was also available online. Material that appears in periodicals, newspapers, and books tends to be much more organized, logical, and well-thought out.

There's a wide spectrum of online sources, and they often cross lines, such as when a help site become a tutorial, and so on. However, for discussion purposes, we'll first cover intranets as a primary new source for all online services, then online documentation, electronic books and periodicals, help functions, tutorials, reference resources, company and organization resources, and expert systems.

Intranets

Companies find many uses for intranets, which can be thought of as company-specific Internets available only to their employees (through passwords) and possibly customers. A firewall denies outsiders access, though people can hack into just about any kind of system and sometimes cause excessive damage. One reason for the rise in intranets is that "With companies able to get twice as much accomplished in half the time, intranets are on the verge of becoming as normal as the office computer."[1] DuPont has implemented a common database for its thirty-eight law firms providing legal services. Some fourteen thousand attorneys and their staffs access the "Knowledge Base."[2] Other uses include retail stores tied to corporate offices, paperless payrolls, sales and marketing, personal calendars, and human resources management among many others. As for human resources (HR), the U.S. Postal Service provides a good example of how efficient use of intranets can be. The system is used for processing benefits and compensation, though some companies put their entire HR database online, where all employees have to do to find out how much vacation time they've accrued, find out how much their 401k is earning, or find out about HR policy is to tap into the company's database.[3] Large organizations aren't the only ones employing intranets, as one study has shown. Over half the respondents of companies with two hundred to three thousand employees said they use intranets to provide information to their employees.[4] In addition to security, another downside of intranet use is that they don't always eliminate paper. This is true of any of the online uses discussed in the following sections. As long as printers are available, people will use them for making hard copies of everything from e-mail messages to documents. Nonetheless, intranets provide an exceptionally effective means of providing information online to people who need it. The information can be in the form of any one or all of the following online sources.

Online Documentation

Getting information about online documentation provides an excellent lesson in the trials, tribulations, and challenges of obtaining online information. In some cases, there's too much to go through, in others hardly enough to bother with. Searching the phrase "online documentation" on a variety of sources provides a case in point:

Altavista search engine—59,149 hits

Beaucoup (which searches several search engines)—70 hits

Google—123,000 hits (from an available 1,247,340,000 possible Web pages)

Infoseek—10,654 hits

Lycos—1 hit

Yahoo—12 hits

Hotbot—4,253,800 hits

San Diego Public Library General Business File ASAP Subject search—97 citations

Library of Congress keyword—13 hits

With an array of possibilities like that, where do you begin? For one thing, the articles from the library provide a good starting point. It's logical that if someone took the time to research and write about a subject, and if a trade magazine or journal deemed it fit to print, then the article has a reasonable chance of being worthwhile as an information source. When the information from the articles noted above was synthesized, the picture about online documentation was mixed, meaning it had both its good and bad features. In regard to the good aspects, there's the statement that "Online documentation, which is utilized by companies in informing consumers about their products and reducing cost of such support-related tasks, can also be used as an instructional procedure. Incorporating a reference-based instruction yields fruitful benefits for students."[5] Another: "Through the use of online documentation, exporters can add valuable information to transaction-specific data and retrieve them anytime he wants."[6] And finally, "An embedded system—be it an office copier or a robot—can tap a world of resources if it's connected to the World Wide Web."[7]

And now for the other side of the coin: "An informal survey of computer users reveals that many are upset that software no longer comes with printed manuals and that online documentation can be relatively useless, although some prefer electronic documentation. Books are the best tool for learning about a product, while online help is most useful if the user needs assistance later"[8]; "A user can manage with online documentation, if the user knows the product reasonably well. But for a new product, even a detailed index or full-text search is no substitute for printed documentation"[9]; and "Software vendors take note: Online is not enough when it comes to product documentation."[10] To emphasize the feeling of the last quote, the title of the article is "A document in the hand is better than two online." Yet the practice of putting documentation online grows, and why not? Think how much simpler it is to include a CD-ROM, or, better yet, dedicate a Web page for people to access via the Internet and World Wide Web, than to print documentation that could run to hundreds, perhaps thousands, of pages. An example of this occurred a few years ago when the Galileo airline reservation system was put online, complete with one hundred thousand pages of online documentation.[11]

Most of these examples are for software documentation. However, there have been major breakthroughs in online documentation by government agencies. For instance, the U.S. Internal Revenue Service has made available its collection of documents, the ones that were often difficult to find before the Internet, by simply going to the site (www.irs.gov) and either reading them online or printing a copy. Similarly, the United Kingdom's Social Security office has posted its documents online for easy public access—for those members of the public who have a computer, modem, and Internet Service Provider, or access to them. Universities make documentation of their own material and that of other related organizations available online to students and faculty—and others who can access them. To further illustrate what is available, and perhaps no one will ever have the time to get a complete handle on what is available, here is a sampling from the search engine beaucoup.com:

- Tutorial documentation, a filter for HTTP server that facilitates development of tutorial type questions and presents them to Web browsers

- Siechert & Wood, Inc., who's been providing PC product documentation since 1982

- eMatter from Fatbrain.com, where individuals can publish documents online and be paid a royalty of one-half for online sales

- University of Southhampton, Department of Archaeology, where you can view current research, meet the staff, and preview upcoming events

- JavaServer Group, from Sun JavaServer, including online documentation

- How to survive an unscheduled IRS tax audit, where you learn how to prepare the necessary documentation and following their advice

There were sixty-four more examples from this list one engine alone, but this list gives an idea of what to expect when you go on an online documentation search. Probably the safest thing to say about online documentation is that there's a chance you may find what you're looking for, particularly if it's related to software and computer-related products. With educational institutions, vendors, and interested individuals, among others, offering information, there's lots to find.

Online documentation has other uses besides looking up how to trouble-shoot a faulty circuit board or figuring out how to compute taxes on your home business. "Incorporating a reference-based instruction yields benefits," according to one report.[12] The goal is to develop the skills needed to retrieve information. Online documentation actually teaches the learner how to use the documentation in question. Reported benefits are that it provides hands-on training, skills can be generalized to using other documentation, learning becomes more active, and retention is improved because detailed notes are made available.

Electronic Books

We've heard predictions for decades that paper would disappear and we'd be taking our computers to bed with us for our nighttime reading. Electronic books are finding their niche, even if not replacing printed ones. Many of the ones you'll find these days are of the popular variety, such as those by Stephen King. But if you'll take a look at a list of electronic publishers, you'll find an impressive number of both small and large publishers. Also, library sites feature electronic books, so the list will surely grow. The information seeker's task will be to determine how to best take advantage of them. They can be downloaded and stored for later reading and study.

Electronic books require the reader to have a handheld device to read the e-book (the book is downloaded into the e-book reader). These cost several hundred dollars, though the price will go up and down with competition and the addition of more capabilities. "The publishing industry is gearing up for the great e-book bonanza," announced a *Time Digital* article, "but it's too soon to burn those library cards."[13] The only certainty is that books are now available in a number of formats, which will most likely keep books as popular as they became after Gutenburg invented movable type and brought books to the masses. The article identified many Web sites dedicated to electronic books, indicating that the number of resources is growing. One source noted that about 180 publishers (a number which you can count on to grow), including many of the major publishing houses, have gone online, and libraries more and more are making them available.[14] One site of particular note is that of Project Gutenburg (available at: www.promo.net/pg) which provides public domain texts available for free to the public. Many of these books are of various fiction genres, but reference and other nonfiction works are also available.

As with everything else new and radical, there are problems, not the least of which is copyright. How do you retain a book you've bought electronically? How do you highlight passages you want to quote to a friend or in a report? How does the author get paid? Devices will catch up with many of these possible limitations by making it possible to take notes while you read electronically. Perhaps what we'll have for some time to come is simply an alternative way to read, something that in the long run could further enhance the steady and continuing popularity of books.

Electronic Periodicals

You don't have to go to the online library to find a copy of a magazine, newspaper, or journal article. They have gone online themselves. Some allow you to read for free, others charge to download and copy, and others require subscriptions. Often, subscribers to the actual publication can receive the online version for no additional cost. The *American Journalism Review* online is full of information for journalists (and information seekers performing the same kind of detective work that journalists do) and it also provides links to other online resources. From its Web page (ajr.newslink.org) you can go to an extensive list of online worldwide newspapers, magazines, and radio/tv programs. The list also contains news sites, journalism organizations, and other items of interest to not only journalists, but anyone looking for information retrievable from news sources. Another site, www.newspapers.com, provides newspaper access. Encyclopedias are also online, though you can still purchase CD-ROM versions. In short, there are plenty of direct sources as well as compilations such as libraries. The trick is to locate the ones you need. Chances are there are that a few you can preidentify and call on when you start new information searches.

Online Help

To some of us, the help capability is the old friend we visit any time we hit a snag in the program. This may occur often for novice users. For others, the help function may simply lead to more frustration. Word Perfect, for instance, has been around many years, and the help function has evolved over that period. Even so, if the user isn't reasonably familiar with using it or any other program, the help function may not be as truly helpful as intended. It certainly is no substitute for knowing how to use the program and having deep experience in putting the application to use. Many programs, such as word processors and graphics packages, have so much capability that most ordinary users will tap into but a fraction of the possible functions. The programs are designed for all users, from the newest to the most experienced. Nevertheless, the help function is there for the user, and should be called upon any time there's a question.

Ideally, the purchaser will find out how good the help function is before purchasing a product. Even the most experienced users run up against the wall at times, particularly when attempting to perform complex operations. A clue to how software vendors feel about online help is that often news releases and articles announcing a product will indicate whether or not help is included and possibly offer a pro or con comment about how good it is. A *PC Week* article about a product for Web page development, for instance, noted that it "has the best site management features and a new integrated browser preview, as well as online help for new web developers."[15] An *InfoWorld* article that found fault with several features of one product it reviewed, however, found that among its good features was "good online help."[16]

One way online help can be expanded is to use the Internet, which "is fast becoming a popular medium for untangling user problems, thanks to several advancements in Web-based customer support systems."[17] This takes the user from the program currently in use to the vast expanses of the Internet, where far more information can be made available. New programs to facilitate this help application are appearing as it becomes more proven and useful.

Yet another online help tool is the wizard, "a performance support tool that computer users can resort to to enhance their performance levels more rapidly than through the use of traditional training methods."[18] A wizard can be developed for whatever uses desired, and it actually helps the user perform a task rather than teaches how to do it. We're familiar with wizards that come with word processor packages, as well as presentations and other programs. They provide shortcuts that are time saving and allow users to get by without detailed knowledge they might use only occasionally. The wizard does the work for you, prompting you when there's need for interaction. The key is to learn what wizards are available in the software applications you use, whether you use them often or occasionally. They may save you time later when you're seeking information or trying to solve a problem.

There are other types of online help. Tutorials and documentation are forms of online help, but these would fit a category of items other than tutorials and documents. For example, an insurance company "has created an online Small Business Center that provides a full range of decision-making tools and information."[19] This helps small businesses become informed insurance consumers. High school seniors can get online help to write their college essays, a process that is controversial to some people. The number of organizations providing such services grows, especially as acceptance into top universities becomes more competitive. Cisco's Technical Assistance Center is an example of corporate online help. The service allows customers to work with engineers online.[20] An interesting sidelight to service like this is that electronic white boards, where a person on either end is drawing diagrams or making notes, can appear on the other end of the network. Another corporate online help example is Dell Computer's webPC. Gaining online support on the device has been streamlined to the point where the user presses the "backlit 'E' button on the front of the PC and you'll be taken to the e-Support home page," where you get information, actuate diagnostics, or other types of help.[21] A program used by the metal industry called Scrap Ware 2000 provides a complimentary service of online knowledge base, "where answers and solutions to problems can be found around the clock."[22] Other programs that can be customized by the provider for their products can be incorporated into products, which adds to the growing list of online support already provided by vendors.

An offshoot of online help is the virtual, or live reference, source. Access to these Web sites provides a means for the user to query a real person in order to gain information or get a question answered.[23]

Online Tutorials

The American Heritage Dictionary defines tutor as "a private instructor; one that gives additional, special, or remedial instruction."[24] As the definition explains, it's a special way to learn, and individualized, one-on-one instruction is hard to beat, particularly when the other person is a recognized expert. Move one word down on the dictionary page, however, and the degree of individualization and specialization begins to fade away. Granted, the first definition of the adjective *tutorial* is "of or relation to tutors and a tutor." But the noun version includes books, classes, and software programs that provide instruction. They're individual only because it's you, the learner, and words on a page or screen are guiding you through the step-by-step learning process. Motion, graphics, and all the other modern addenda to online programs can be used, making them somewhat more exciting than words replacing a human being.

People are in luck when it comes to tutorials, with possibly the greatest problem being that of having to wade through the many available and being able to discern which one works best for a specific set of needs. They cover a wide range, from seemingly frivolous to ones that could quickly improve workplace performance by providing access to much needed skills. The *School Library Journal* carried an interesting article about online tutorials. "Looking for good Web tutorials or getting ready to create some for your library? Then check out the following sites, which will amaze, amuse, and inspire you to create some great tutorials of your own."[25]

There are so many tutorial sites that it would be impossible to get a handle on all of them. They cover so many topics, yet you may or may not find the one you need. Professional journals and newsletters often carry articles listing several sites of potential interest to the group. Searching online by topic and tutorial might turn up the one you're looking for. Also, you may find specific ones of interest through networking with colleagues and querying discussion groups you participate in. Also, you will find that some are for sale, while others are free for the taking. There's no authority that certifies any of them, although if you're familiar with the source, such as a manufacturing company or university department, then that will help establish quality and comprehensiveness. Even here, though, you have to make sure it's still current.

As noted, online tutoring is a URL entry away. The Web site of the University of Hawaii's Community College system is a one example. The site, at www.hcc.hawaii.edu/hccinfo/tutorials.html, offers tutorials for the Internet, Pine e-mail, guide to Eudora Mail Package, running a World Wide Web Service, Virtual Library/Cyber Web, official HTML specifications, building Internet servers, and others. The Internet Survival Skills course consists of eleven modules covering such basic topics as electronic mail, File Transfer Protocol, News, Gopher, World Wide Web, and getting connected. Arkansas Tech University, located at library.atu.edu/Onlinehandouts/th.htm, advertises a number of tutorials for library usage, citation, databases, search engine, copyright, Internet and WWW, and Web development. The National Air and Space Administration (NASA), nccsinfo.gsfc,nasa.gov/NCCS/info/tutorial/tutorial.html, offers tutorials in Fortran, C+, UNIX, and other software systems. Some of the Web sites, along with several others to give you an idea of what's available, are found in exhibit 9.1.

Online Reference Resources

Libraries are in greater use than ever. If you don't believe it, drop into your neighborhood library and look around. You'll see people, young and old alike, using often limited Internet access, and they'll be mixed in with children listening to storytellers, people conducting genealogy searches, newspaper readers, students working on research papers, Friends of the Library gatherings, and many others browsing through the stacks looking for all types of books and periodicals. But an amazing thing has happened in recent years—the library has come to you. Encyclopedias can be read by inserting a CD-ROM or by going to the publisher's Web site. One of the world's greatest libraries, the Library of Congress, is available by entering www.loc.gov into your net server's browser.

One of the biggest drawbacks to online libraries and other reference sources is that most information hasn't been digitized and is thus available in print or microform format only. Chances are, it will remain this way, though new materials are automatically available digitally for electronic access, and a lot of older material has been made electronically available. The Library of London, for instance, has undertaken to put its collection online, a major project. The process is time consuming and costly, but regardless, an enormous amount of information is available by clicking your mouse and letting the networks do the work for you.

A logical action for organizations is to put libraries online for employee and customer use. This is in addition to documentation put online. DEC, for instance, "delivers 80 percent of its corporate library content on its global intranet rather than in paper form."[26] Two others among the many corporate

Exhibit 9.1
Sampling of Web Tutorial Sites and What's Available

Note: The following are intended to serve as a sample of available tutorials. This is in no way an endorsement, though in many instances they're ones identified by other sources. Another caveat: there's no guarantee that these sites will be there if you decide to visit any of them. Even reputable institutions like universities change their sites and abandon old sites. These were randomly selected from articles and online search engine results:

Graphics Resources Club—offers as total of thirty-six graphics-related tutorials for subscribers, and users can try for free. www.graphicsresouceclub.com

University of Newcastle—offers tutorials on EndNote, Lynx, Netscape, various Microsoft products, Macintosh, and others. www.library.newcastle.edu.au/training/software.html

Project Cool—features the developer zone, with information for Web site design. www.projectcool.com

Cisco Interactive Mentor—CIM provides instruction on its technology products for a fee. www.cisco.com/go/cim

Learn2—has tutorials for purchase ranging from how to host a baby shower to using Windows 98. www.learn2.com

ehow—15,000 step-by-step how-tos and information on 100,000 helpful products, including tutorial on how to build Web pages and how to start an electronic commerce business.www.ehow.com

learnlots—e-commere and computer related tutorials, with the capability to integrating technical support tutorials into Web sites. www.learnlots.com

Ciberteca—a free online tutorials directory featuring tutorials for programming, Web page design, Internet, telecommunications, science studies, graphics design, commercial software, music, sports, languages, and others. www.ciberteca.net/english

Bob Bowman—list of educational online tutorials, an example of individuals who accumulate potentially useful tutorial information. Advertises such topics as academics, artificial intelligence, desktop publishing, dictionaries, Internet, languages, Macintosh, math, programming, and science. www.user.shentel.net/rbowman/files/online.htm

---

libraries are Chevron Petroleum Technology Corp. and Amgen. The number of items on Chevron's catalog, available via its intranet, runs into the six figures, and represents holdings at several sites. Amgen kicked off its online library by conducting what they called the Roving Librarian program, going to facilities with laptops and demonstrating to scientist users what was available.[27] There are challenges, such as not having the usual and highly desired face-to-face contact with the librarian to help find what's needed and running the risk of not having what's needed in foreign locations.

The Department of the Navy is developing its "Next Generation Library (NGL) that will integrate the virtual library concept with the latest adaptive research retrieval tools." According to Librarian of the Navy Joan Buntzen, it's "a research system that enables users to quickly find distinctly pertinent information, locate and connect to colleagues with similar interests, and share and distribute information with other NGL users."[28]

Data mining. Electronic commerce has brought about a revolution in data gathering. People's buying habits, demographics, and more are obtained when they visit a Web site browsing for purchases. The outgrowth is software called data mining. "Data mining is a form of artificial intelligence that uses automated process to find information" and has "been used successfully for several years in scientific and business communities for tracking behavior of individuals and groups, processing medical information, and a number of other applications."[29] Basically, the program makes choices and calculations for searchers and categorizes the information based on those choices. Another name for this software is Knowledge Discovery in Databases (KDD), which you'll find in more academic treatments of the topic. A model developed and marketed by IBM, for example, can be used to create classification and prediction models, discover associations and sequential patterns in large databases, automate the segmentation of databases into groups of related records, and discover similar patterns of behavior.[30] The program is but one of many on sale by a growing number of software providers. In a sense, it's the quintessence of information seeking, a tool to help digest and present information in a far more useful way. Whereas e-commerce companies can use it to learn more about customer buying habits and thus what to sell them, others can use the same software technology to gather information from what might well be oceans of data that couldn't otherwise be dented. For libraries, the prospect is that they can use data mining to help users find digital materials. The software would perform such tasks as classification and clustering, link analysis, association and sequence analysis, and summarization. Time will tell how widespread the application is for libraries, but it certainly will continue to help make business information-gathering and analysis faster and with potentially more digested and useful results.

New systems will continue to be developed to make libraries even more accessible online. An example is when, a few years ago, the University of California at Santa Cruz started issuing incoming students a wireless modem. It allowed them to do their library searches by sitting under the beautiful redwood trees on campus, rather than spoil it all by having to go inside. Another example is INFOTRAC system used by many libraries, where people can visit the library and obtain full text articles and other research materials from wherever they happen to be—provided, of course, they have the proper equipment and telecommunications setup. CASPR Library Systems "has announced LibraryCom, a complete Internet library Web hosting and directory system," where "school libraries can have their complete library catalog on the

LibraryCom Web site with complete keyword, author, title, and subject searching."[31]

Resources are subscribed to by libraries, corporate and public, and other organizations. They pay, sometimes handsomely, for access to online periodicals, technical journals, newspapers, databases, encyclopedias, and more. Thus the resources aren't available to individuals other than through the library. Exhibit 9.2 briefly describes selected resources used extensively, which illustrates the vast information available through libraries.

At the same time, there will be warnings about online libraries. One critic has likened them to a "virtual popsicle," where "electronic information requires a tremendous amount of energy—with no misstep—to say alive."[32] It revisits the question of how real can digital information be, since it doesn't last nearly as long as that in print.

There's one other online library reference resource available to anyone who wants to use it. It's a human being, actually, and she or he is as close as your telephone or e-mail. Simply contact the person at your public or university library and state your information need. They're on call to make their expertise available.

Exhibit 9.2
Selected Online Library Resources

Following are three sources used extensively by libraries to provide online information to library users. They require fees for their services but are free to the library user (provided he or she has a library card).

ProQuest—A Bell & Howell company providing databases to libraries, including full text documents that come in many categories. A few samples of what they provide include research databases in the sciences, newspapers, newswires, business, overseas business, magazines, medical library, and more. (www.proquest.com)

FirstSearch—Provided by Online Computer Library Center, Inc. (OCLC), a nonprofit, membership, library computer service and research organization. It gives library users over seventy-five databases covering a wide assortment of user needs. WorldCat, for instance, includes not only books in print, but which libraries hold them. (www.oclc.org)

SilverPlatter—A "global leader in providing comprehensive and seamlessly integrated database collections of scholarly reference information in electronic form." Available are over two hundred bibliographic and full text electronic databases. (www.silverplatter.com)

Note: These are but three services, and as well, specific organizations and subject matter areas such as defense, medicine, and others, provided multiple databases for user access. As you can see from the brief description of what is provided, the cost have to be justified by the library selecting the service.

Company and Organization Information

What company, governmental agency, or nonprofit organization doesn't have a Web site? Most do, and they offer an excellent source of online company and organizational information. Financial, investment, prospective client information, and more can be found at your computer terminal. It isn't always as simple as visiting a company's Web site, particularly if you're looking for detailed and potentially confidential information. Other sources are Internet directories, such as Yahoo, and many of the search engines will find possible sites for you. You can search by organization name, industry, trade area, or other key word. If detectives can find all the personal information they need without breaking into off-limit sites, then it's possible for other users can find out organizational information. News groups may have information. There are also people and business finders, such as Four11.com, switchboard.com, and bigfoot.com.[33] One reporter found that by using HotBot.com and InfoSeek, articles on a particular company were quickly found.[34] Combined with library reference resources (see section above), there's an enormous amount of information—provided you push the right buttons.

Library resources also have services that provide company information. They are used by researchers and investors alike and provide a surprising amount of information.

Expert Systems

Thanks to artificial intelligence and expert systems, we can now turn to our computers for help in making many critical decisions. A multidisciplinary consortium of professionals, psychologists, computer scientists, linguists, cognitive scientists, engineers, and others have joined forces to attempt to make computers do everything humans can do. The expertise provided by expert systems are available wherever they're needed, from the doctor's office to the corner store to our homes. Expert systems have a lot to offer in the way of fingertip service. Among the benefits are these: "preservation of expertise, work efficiency and consistency, better decision making, and cost savings."[35] Unbeatable benefits in light of the need to do things faster and cheaper in today's business environment.

As with everything else related to technology, terminology can sometimes get in the way of understanding. The umbrella term is *artificial intelligence*, which in its simplest terms means machines doing the same things done by the human brain. An expert system, which can be at the information seeker's beckoning, is a program that runs on a computer and offers advice. In essence, the way an expert would treat a matter is captured in the program, thus making the human expert's solution available to anyone having access to the program. The basic programming rule of expert systems is "if-then," which is what experts do when they solve problems—they say, "If this is the case, then I would do a particular thing." If it was an expert system for trouble-shooting electronic gear, the logic might be that if an oscilloscope reading was at a certain level, then a certain circuit board is defective. The three main parts of an expert system are:

- Database
- Inference engine (e.g., if-then logic)
- Means of interfacing with the system (e.g., through a mouse and terminal)

The database contains the expert knowledge needed to solve the problem, while the inference engine performs the logic to come to a successful resolution for the given problem.

One other related term you may run across is neural networks. They look at the brain and computer from a different viewpoint, that of the biology of the brain, or its neural networks. Neural networks in a computer would thus attempt to simulate the biological "wiring" of the brain. Depending on your information needs, and especially if they are highly technical, it's possible that there are neural networks available for use. However, our interest here is for the more commonly available expert systems.

Expert System Shells. Shells represent the if-then logic of an expert system. The logic is the same; thus, a shell can be adapted for a number of uses. For example, the basic logic for a program designed for medical diagnosis—the shell—could be used for electronic troubleshooting. A large selection of shells for developing expert systems are available. One source, for example, identifies these:

- Personal Consultant Easy—routes vehicles
- Knowledgepro—for spreadsheet and database files
- First Class Fusion—links to the knowledge base and shows relationships
- Leonardo—for evaluation for how to market products and services
- Financial Advisor—appraises capital investments
- Intelligent Scheduling and Information Systems—schedules complex factory orders[36]

Expert systems have made "a broad impact . . . on organizational America."[37] Here's a random sampling of some of the expert systems:

Schemebuilder Expert—aids hydraulic design by facilitating the creation of fluid power circuit designs[38]

OSHA Advisors—an array of expert systems to help businesses "interpret and apply its standards," including understanding Cadmium standards, identifying hazards in the workplace, and estimating the cost of work-related injuries[39]

ISO 9000—assists first-time users of ISO 9000, as well as identifies the gap between prerequisites and what actually exists, and provides user solutions for an array of quality problems[40]

GCI Alaskan Network—used by GCI to "handle remote electronics in the hostile environment of Alaska"; takes in critical data and makes assessments to avoid costly trips for troubleshooting.[41]

WorldToolKit—a cross-platform program that allows users to create complex three-dimensional visual simulations without having to write extensive code[42]

VARMINT—Vibration Analysis for Rotating Machinery Internals, which helps pulp mill maintenance personnel "quickly diagnose, prevent and eliminate mechanical problems affecting rotating machinery"[43]

ACQUIRE—expert system authoring tool used to build and maintain knowledge bases[44]

Agricultural Expert Systems—expert systems developed in Egypt for use in helping farmers optimize their resources and maximize their food production.[45]

With this randomly selected sampling, you can imagine what else is available for people to use to capture expertise in a shell, then make the respected knowledge about how to solve a vast array of problems.

ELECTRONIC PERFORMANCE SUPPORT SYSTEMS

The electronic performance support system (EPSS) concept is one that has also grown over the past two decades and is projected to continue to do so. It is "forecast to significantly enhance the productivity and efficiency of employees."[46] An EPSS is a system that provides, through a PC workstation, information, online training, tutorials, help, and work-related software that together makes the knowledge worker as independent as possible. Potential components of an EPSS include:

- Online training programs (from a variety of sources)
- Help and tutorials, for the operating systems and all application packages available
- Expert systems and neural networks
- Information, including databases, Internet, intranet, reference systems, and more
- Communications, including electronic, teleconferencing, and more
- Work-related software, including word processing, databases, spreadsheets, graphics, presentations, desktop publishing, and other specialized software to help the knowledge worker do his or her job

- Environmental sensors that will help predict behavior changes
- Hypertext
- Wizards and coaches to help perform the job

One study identified such support structures as searchable references; explanations; context-sensitive help; demonstrations; interactive instructions; tool tips; context-independent help; task guides, wizards, and coaches; application tours, cue cards, and screen tours as being part of installed EPSS.[47]

Three levels of EPSS have been identified: linked support, external (stand-alone) support, and embedded support. Embedded "is tightly integrated into the work flow and interface of an EPSS so that it's transparent to the user"; linked "is loosely integrated into the interface and appears to the user as a separate or secondary surface"; and external "includes classroom training, computer-based training courses, documentation, peer support, help desks, and bulletin boards."[48] To Gloria Gery, the person most responsible for the development of the EPSS concept, "EPSS supports processes and thinking—delivering customer service, for instance—rather than the creation of a product."[49] It's actually more than a training system in that it helps the person learn on the job while providing needed assistance.

In many ways, an EPSS is a mixture of many, possibly all, the online capabilities, plus additional features designed for particular organizations and jobs. In fact, the best way to think of EPSS is that it's a concerted effort to bring everything online that could possibly enhance a worker's performance. It could range from giving the worker a list of places to go via the computer to take a tutorial or gather information, all the way to a specially designed, state-of-the-art capability. Studies show that the growth is not rapid, but those who use EPSS think highly of it. As you can see, the EPSS instantly becomes a key tool in the information literacy process.

Some of the vehicles for learning and getting help on the job include use of the Internet and intranets, electronic performance support systems, using computers in a variety of ways to deliver and keep track of training. These and more systems will be used because organizational America is spending more money than ever on training, as noted elsewhere in the book, and finding more ways to do it. EPSS programs can automate many job-related skills, provide instant instructions for a variety of applications and jobs, and provide assistance to human judgment. Such sophisticated software as artificial intelligence and expert systems, along with simulation, can provide guidance for knowledge workers equivalent to having a personal staff of experts standing by to help.

One of the greatest benefits of EPSS is that training can be delivered at the time it's needed. Think about times when you may have taken a training course, then not had the opportunity to put the new skill or knowledge to use until some time later—after you had begun to lose some of the skills or forget what you'd learned. Or worse yet, you may not have ever used the training. With EPSS, the user stops working and takes the training just before the need to apply it, eliminating costly dead time and any possible chance of wasting the effort. It's literally just-in-time training. *U.S. News and World Report* went so far as to title an article about EPSS "The janitor stole my job: a new software is expanding competition for white-collar jobs."[50] The banking industry points out that bankers should pay attention to EPSS because "these systems are most useful when information needs are divergent and availability of round-the-clock data is considered a priority."[51] Obviously, some people take EPSS most seriously.

A few examples of EPSS at work will help provide further insight into just what they can do and who's using the technology:

AT&T—uses EPSS to coach customer service representatives about which questions to ask the customer, helps make product recommendations based on the responses. The software is proprietary.[52]

Aetna—uses a program to help employees analyze internal management problem-solving and decision-making processes.[53]

FAST—Factory Automation Support Technology enhances human productivity and links factory workers to databases and experts. "The efficiency of workers is supported through the use of electronic performance support systems and by using a wearable, multimedia-capable, voice-activated computer system."[54]

American Express—Financial Advisers Division greatly reduced training time for operators learning how to perform routine banking procedures.[55]

EES—Ethicon Endo Surgery, Inc., a provider of laparoscopic medical instruments, provides marketing staff with information pertinent to selling this technology for performing surgery with small incisions.[56]

It doesn't take much to add a knowledge-based, information-literate touch to an EPSS. It's as simple as adding whatever access would enhance the information and knowledge applications of the user. It well could be as easy as adding access to the library sites most often accessed by the user, perhaps documentation and tutorials likely to be used, and help desks that might be of assistance. Networking with experts, both live and artificially induced, could provide the extra information power the user needs. Online access could be a combination of existing or custom-built systems. Added cost to EPSS development would have to be weighed against how long it takes to effectively become information literate. Information power comes with a cost, which may be well worth it when it comes to getting the information necessary to beat the competition or solve a pressing problem. The prospects are tremendous and will only increase with time as people find newer and more clever ways to click their mouse for virtually instantaneous help in becoming information literate.

Time will tell if EPSS takes on broader acceptance. It is expersive in most cases, and therefore must be considered against alternatives. "The cost of an

EPSS program is justified by the more immediate productivity of employees," with the aim of "erasing the distinction between learning and doing."[57] If it can do that, everyone will be setting them up. In the meantime, they appear to work well for those organizations who have moved forward with them. They do, indeed, give users information power—at their fingertips.

THE INTERNET REVISITED

Much of the previous discussion involves the Internet and World Wide Web. As intranets take firmer hold, it appears that they, too, will incorporate the broad aspects of the Internet. There's no sense limiting any potential information source or potential aids to selection and action taking through acquired information and knowledge. In looking back, we're reminded that there's a lot to know in order to make the most of cyberspace. It's certainly not easy, and no matter how hard many people try, it doesn't meet with complete satisfaction. "People evidently are developing some strange habits on the Internet," we've been told. "Several recent studies have shown that Web visitors spend almost all of their monthly time cycling through the same ten destinations." The report notes that some people never leave America Online and many surfers complain of "wandering through endless links to find one chunk of information," and another study stated that "85 percent of all Web site visitors regularly leave disgusted and unfulfilled."[57] Granted, much of this data refers to people using their systems at home, but there's a fine line between how people use the net at home and at work, and for many people, home is the workplace. The point is that much information-seeking time is wasted, perhaps because of the sheer size and lack of cohesiveness of this enormous system, as well as people's lack of experience. The last could well be because of all the changes that continually occur. It emphasizes the fact that knowing how to use the Internet is an integral part of having information power.

A new development that is appropriately mentioned here is that of Web portals, which was the subject of the article quoted above. They are Web sites that bring information from across the Internet and display it in the browser. Some of these are specialized, such as for financial markets, video, news headlines, and sports. Some of the sites mentioned in the article are as follows:

www.yodlee.com—an assemblage of bank balances, stock reports, and other financial data

www.octopus.com—allows users to drag in other Web pages, special interest publications, and news sites for viewing

www.websplit.com and www.onepage.com—provide a way to monitor constantly updating sites

An adjunct of this type of service are metasearching Web tools, such as Metacrawler.com, that searches multiple engines.

The message is clear for people who want to take full advantage of online assistance in dealing with information and proffering knowledge: get online and get smart about it. One nice thing about learning about being online is that you can learn how online, perhaps by finding a tutorial or e-mailing a friend who can answer questions, or by joining a user group. New developments will continue to be introduced, some that will take some time to become fully accepted, and others that will burst onto the scene.

There Are a Few Problems

Many of the negative aspects of being online are discussed elsewhere, particularly in the following chapter, but will be briefly identified here. The reason is that they impact online use, and future court rulings and protocols may change things dramatically. For instance, copyright law is in turmoil. There's a question in the courts about who owns material that first appeared in print, yet is now available to anyone who wants it. Who owns the music in music libraries, in case your information seeking chores include this genre? And who owns the photos in photo libraries? These questions will likely continue for a long time, and new ones will arise—as is the way with far-reaching technological developments that change lives and work.

Another concern is access. Not everyone can afford a home computer and the trappings necessary to get online, and the waiting list for the neighborhood library's two Internet terminals is usually quite long. Organizations, including Microsoft, are making strides to donate money and equipment for libraries, so the problem is not insurmountable. However, as we become yet more global, how do we communicate with parts of the world that are nowhere near as advanced as we are? These are access concerns related to going online for information that will continue to be of prime interest for some time to come.

A potentially serious problem has to do with power. How long will your laptop battery last when there's a power failure or brownout? We know that fuel crises have been occuring up with shocking regularity, and yet we rely totally on electricity to get into cyberspace. It's something to think about. Could you get your information any other way? Of course, those folks developing new technology are also experimenting with new ways to provide power, so perhaps this isn't such a concern after all. There's also the danger that data files will be lost because of massive power failures. The thought sends shudders simultaneous with the urge to continually back up everything that occurs online. Related is the potential for hackers to get inside a good-sized set of files and obliterate them faster than a power outage might do.

Probably the largest problem related to online resources is credibility. Using the suggested methodology in chapter 3, "Communicating in the Digital Age," and your common sense, the problem can be surmounted. It's an ongoing challenge, and one that must be constantly in the information seeker's sights.

CATEGORICALLY SPEAKING

Stop and think about some of the biggest problems you've had when trying to locate information, particularly online, and you will see a common thread throughout many of those frustrating times. It has to do with categories, or lack thereof. One of the main reasons librarians get master's degrees in library science is to be able to categorize. They do it logically and in ways that make it easier for the rest of us to find. This is not necessarily the case with online resources—except, of course, online libraries. The need for better categorization was illustrated in the first chapter when it was noted that librarians are finding jobs in organizations, including with search engine companies. This will only improve the ability to find what we need, and hopefully the trend to do a better job of categorizing information will continue. Eventually, such problems emphasized by the example of the "online documentation" search described earlier in the chapter will become less common. For the time being, it takes patience to use the online information sources identified in this chapter. And when all else fails, ask a librarian.

CHAPTER 10

Humans Don't Live on Digits Alone: Placing Information Power in Context

INTRODUCTION

Having information power carries a heavy burden: the information itself. Information, made particularly voluminous thanks largely to digitization, threatens to control our lives. It's virtually impossible to get away from information—and the work that goes with it—because of pagers, cellular phones, laptop and handheld computers, digitally enhanced wristwatches, intelligent household devices, wireless communications, and the need to stay tuned in. Or is it necessary to stay tuned in twenty-four hours a day? What would happen if we literally unplugged for a few hours? Would our professional and work worlds come tumbling down around us? What about those who work from home either full time or part time? (Telecommuting is a growing reality for more and more of us these days.) Regarding telecommuting, what about face-to-face, human contact? Don't we need that, too? The answer is yes, we do. Yet for many, unplugging is out of the question. Missing a beat in the flow of information could allow the competition to make a damaging move. Yet how do you solve the problem of human contact when e-mail, satellites, and virtual everything is the order of the day? This is a second challenge regarding information, knowledge, and being information literate. Human contact has taken on a totally new meaning, which in some cases means no human contact at all. As with about everything else technological that's come along over the ages, information has that unique quality of being both the cause and the cure. It's the stuff that weighs us down, literally, and fits the answers we need to be competitive, successful, and, hopefully, happy.

This chapter addresses a broad range of topics related to human aspects of life and work. It includes some of the problems related to information; a description of a whole life concept, which brings in family considerations; and identification and discussion of several whole life tools that have been proven effective.

INFORMATION POWER AND THE WHOLE PERSON

Human contact is necessary, and it must be accomplished even in the most digital, intense work environments. Another phenomenon that has emerged is that there's less and less distinction between the workplace and home. In fact, more and more of us are working at home. This means that blending in all segments of life into a complementary wholeness—a work/life system, if you will—becomes a critical part of being information literate. It may well be the only counter to the high degree of stress that often accompanies work in a competitive, digital world. To complete the picture of information literacy, then, we must address the concept of our work and home lives, including those times when they're one and the same. A theme woven throughout the human element of information literacy is that life and work have become truly fast-track endeavors, mastered by those who can stay competitive by effectively navigating the information superhighway.

Fallout from the Information Age

What we're dealing with here is the potential clash with working in the information age and life. Here's how one reporter stated the problem:

Your business is being webified and dot.commed. Your products have been commoditized. Your margins have been eliminated by Internet exchanges. Your life has become wireless and networked. Your employees chase offers from Internet start-ups. Your e-mail inbox is overflowing. The VCR of your life is on fast forward. And now, in the midst of this wild, wired world of the new millennium, some clown is yammering about the need to get some balance in your life.[1]

To add more realism to the information picture, consider this: "We're working longer and longer hours—208 more hours a year than two decades ago," which means that almost 40 percent of the workforce is working fifty-hour work weeks.[2] So much for technology making things easier and freeing us up by taking over many everyday tasks. Not only are there more hours to do our work, the pace itself seems to have picked up to a whirlwind force. "People's work lives are becoming more frantic as they try to meet their organizations' demands for greater productivity and competitiveness," and people "complain about their fast-paced lives, but actually measure their own importance based on how much work they do."[3] The most likely option to slowing down, however, might not be one a gainfully employed person wants to think about.

The heavy burden mentioned above can be dissected into several specific areas, each with its own unique problems, and, fortunately, solutions. These include stress, concern for health and wellness, family issues, information overload, technophobia, and a sense of community.

Stress. Any idea what is the cost of workplace stress these days? Using the digital form of information gathering, a Web search quickly turned up two sources that provide plenty of reasons why stress is a serious problem. One of the sites, The Institute of Heartmath, provides us with these grim facts: 60 percent of the half-million lost workdays due to absenteeism are attributed to stress; job stress costs an estimated $200 billion in accumulated stress-related reasons; and the majority of visits to health care providers can be attributed to stress.[4] The American Psychological Association offered these startling facts: 43 percent of all adults suffer adverse health effects from stress; stress is linked to the six leading causes of death—heart disease, cancer, lung ailments, accidents, cirrhosis of the liver, and suicide; and the Occupational Safety and Health Administration (OSHA) has declared stress a hazard of the workplace.[5] Even if you're skeptical of these numbers, you might try halving them. They'd still be staggering and costly.

Health and Wellness. When numerous companies purchase Nautilus equipment and rent spaces in gyms for their employees, you know there must be a bottom-line motive behind it. Promoting good health isn't new. What has happened is that organizations are realizing that by investing in it, they achieve a return greater than the original cost because their employees are more productive. It's a straightforward, bottom-line decision, as studies show their value. Firms all over the world are promoting employee wellness. Health insurance in one form or another has contributed to the health and wellness of people covered by it. It's much cheaper to pay for preventive programs fostering wellness than it is to treat unwellness. Whether it be going for a jog after work, taking a noontime walk with workmates, or attending a health foods seminar on company time, there's much going on to improve health and wellness in not only corporations, but all types of organizations. The move is on to make the collective workforce healthier, both mentally and physically, providing it with the wherewithal to deal with work situations that will, if anything, become more stressful.

Family Issues. From the days when corporate family issues may have been confined to an annual family picnic, we've come a long way. Family issues now cover the spectrum of ongoing family life events and activities. Included today are the likes of child care, elder care, maternity and paternity leave, family relations, vacations, two-career couples going in opposite directions, single-parent bread winners, and more—everything you can think of regarding the family. The days where a person went to work and left family matters behind until later that evening, or perhaps until the weekend, are gone, replaced by large numbers of single, working mothers, an increasing number of fathers having custody of their children after a divorce, workers with elderly parents needing assistance, and variations of today's family-work life situations. People take their family problems to work and vice versa. The fact that employers provide counseling through employee assistance programs, on-site child care, and care for elderly parents is a sure sign that families and work matter. They've become a bottom line issue.

Information Overload. One Web site described information overload as "an information Frankenstein."[6] Think about these facts: a million books are published worldwide each year; the English language has reached 540,000 words, five times more than Shakespeare had to choose from; and information doubles every five years, soon to become every four years. Facts such as these abound, particularly since they make such interesting quotations for public speakers. What we end up with is a great deal of anxiety: how do we deal with so much of it? We've all suffered guilt pangs when we threw another magazine or thick report on the "to be read" pile, knowing we'll never get around to it, or perhaps suffered with old things rather than purchasing a newer model—primarily because we know the newer model has been souped up and thus made more complicated.

Technophobia. This is closely related to information overload. Newspapers, magazines, and televisions now incorporate regular features designed to keep us up-to-date on the latest in technological gadgetry, software, and all the other forms technology takes. Computer and technology sections in bookstores and libraries continue to demand more shelf space. For a good example of how rapidly technology changes, and in particular software packages, just browse through a new or used bookstore and note how many computer-related books they feature. Not everyone likes to buy a new computer every year and replace each of several software packages every time there's an upgrade. Nor do they want to replace old appliances, as an example of where new technology is especially active, with newer ones that have more automated features. The language alone is enough to turn most people off, though it isn't uncommon to overhear a white-haired grandmother discussing her computer requirements with a computer store employee, keeping up word for word, bit for byte, with the clerk. Then there's the retired man who plays his daily round of golf on the computer. In fact, it's been reported that people over fifty "are among the most savvy users of the Internet."[7] The point is that technology makes such great leaps and makes them on a time scale that decreases with each new development—and this causes grief and headaches along with the progress.

Sense of Community

Sociologists, psychologists, and our hearts are telling us that we're losing our sense of community. Putnam's study, *Bowling Alone*, chronicled the deterioration of such social elements of volunteering, having dinner with friends, inviting friends over, attending meetings, and the other things we do that require face-to-face encounter, a decline that started at the end of World War II and hasn't stopped since.[8] We depend on electronic means of communicating, a situation that provides easy, quick, and continuous contact, yet deprives us of actually writing personal letters and sitting down for a cup of coffee—with friends or family members. Next time you're virtually parked on the freeway onramp attempting to go from point A to point B, look around and see how many of the cars around you are occupied with just the lone driver. No doubt, we're not as social as we once were, and our electronic communities are far less personal and filled with deep relationships as the actual ones.

Fortunately, there are ways to deal positively with the symptoms of stress, illness, anxiety, and family concerns. The remainder of this chapter will discuss the whole life concept, a concept that provides a state of mind and body prepared to handle information. It also provides a number of tools contributing to mental and physical wellness.

A WHOLE LIFE CONCEPT

Integration is key to successful application of information literacy skills. This includes integrating it with the requisite skills laid out in the preceding chapters, as well as ongoing activities discussed elsewhere in the book. Ongoing activities include: continually scanning the environment for new developments and mastering the ensuing change that goes with it; continuing to learn and incorporating new skills as soon as they are identified; and integrating work life with total life. The result is viewing life in its entirety, everything interrelated—not placing each component in convenient cubby holes where they refuse to stay for long.

People enjoy variety. After all, it's the spice of life as the saying goes. Actually, we have an enigma on our hands. On the one side, we miss our routine when change takes control and forces us to do things differently. Yet on the other side, we need change to keep us on our toes and actively living life to its fullest. This is where the concept of re-creation comes in—we need to continually re-create ourselves by taking time off for fun and games, family, changing jobs, or otherwise integrating all of life's components into one whole life concept. It also means integrating information into the everyday scheme of things.

Holistic Living

For some, holistic living is the motto fulfilled by living life to the fullest, no holds barred, with sayings like "go for the gusto" and "you only go around once." For others, it's such things as "Siberian shamanism, telepathic healing, trance dancing, past-life regression, herbalism, Tantra toning, spirit walking, aura reading, reflexology and aroma therapy."[9] What it actually means, as defined by those who practice and promote it, is to integrate all aspects of life in the promotion of good health and mental well-being. Terms such as *balance, integration, happiness, lifestyle,* and *personal responsibility* enter into the holistic living conversation. An expanded version of the concept includes a variety of items, such as holistic and homeopathic medicine and new physical approaches to health. These elements are depicted in exhibit 10.1.

A number of indications suggest that the concept of holistic living is entering a realm of respectability it has not heretofore experienced. Just the fact that health care providers such as Blue Cross and Blue Shield accept alternative medicinal practices such as acupuncture and homeopathic medicines tells us a lot. If they're willing to pay for these practices formerly shunned by the masses in general and the traditional medical community in particular, then perhaps there is something to it. Why else would a health insurer, in these days of heavily managed and scrutinized health care, pay good money for acupuncture and herbs if they didn't show signs of working?

Exhibit 10.1
Components of a Whole Life Concept

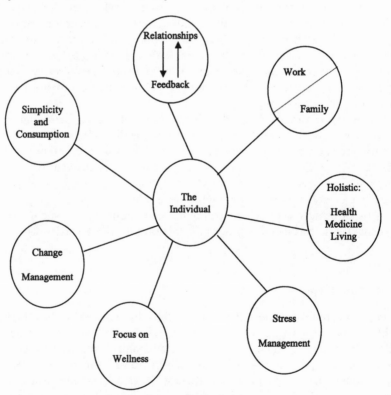

Kenneth Pelletier said that "Holistic approaches lead not only to the pre-vention of stress disorders but to a whole array of new possibilities for the indi-vidual."[10] When these new possibilities improve the quality of life, which could mean anything from feeling less tense to gaining whole new perspectives and enjoyment from being information literate, then holism is a force to be reck-oned with.

What are some of the afflictions brought about by our minds—minds used in the narrowest sense of reacting to the pressure of performance and mo-ment-to-moment living? They include hypertension, arteriosclerosis, mi-graine headaches, cancer, arthritis, and respiratory disease. What this tells us is that we inflict ourselves with many of the most severe health problems known to humans. How can we do these things to ourselves and why do we keep at it? Having to earn a living in the information age has a lot to do with it. Just living in this day and age when much of our culture is defined by what we see on tele-vision, does, too. Fortunately, there are ways to control these. Among those noted by Pelletier are meditation, visualization, autogenic training, biofeed-back, and holistic medicine. Each of these is being proven as successful means of curtailing stress.

Consensus is building for a more holistic approach to life in general. It means integrating all aspects of life into an every-day, twenty-four-hours-a-day way of living. It combines work, play, family, spirituality, rou-tine—everything we do as human beings on a day-to-day basis. Concepts such as holistic living, holistic medicine, and anything else with the term *holism* at-tached to it are praised by some, condemned as worthless exercises by others. However, many of the individual elements comprising these concepts are gain-ing wider acceptance, as previously noted.

Work and Family

There was a time when work and family were as separate as a breadwinner leaving the family and going to work and then returning to the family when the workday was over. These were two quite separate activities, at times dominated by the work element. Nowadays, a mother may well take her child to work with her, and it wouldn't be too far fetched to imagine her spouse dropping off his mother at an elder care center on the way to his work. As it has evolved, today's workplace integrates such concepts as dual-career marriages, child care, elder care, flexible work hours, paternity leave, job sharing, telecommuting and telework, and more. Together, they describe how work and family have been brought together—forced together is more like it, but together just the same. Employers would most likely prefer to ignore family crises, soccer games, pa-ternity and maternity leave, child care, and flex-time, but they can't because these activities ultimately impact the bottom line—such as when a key team player misses a deadline because of a sick child. There are related laws to deal with, as well.

One sign that work and family is a serious concern is that organizations dealing with the situation have been formed. One is the Alliance of Work/Life Professionals, formed in 1996 as a merger of two like organizations.[11] Another is the Families and Work Institute, founded in 1989.[12] Both conduct research in a wide range of work and family topics. The missions of the two organizations provide insight into the much-needed services they provide. The Families and Work Institute is a nonprofit organization addressing the changing nature of work and family life. It is committed to finding research-based strategies fostering mutually supportive connections between work, family, and community. Activities include identifying work-life issues, benchmarking solutions to work-life problems, and evaluating solutions. The Alliance of Work/Life Professionals promotes work/family and personal life balance. It strives to improve professionalism of workers in work/life situations and influence the integration of work and family life. These are but two examples of how work-family are coming together.

Several factors contribute to a successful—meaning situations where work and family mesh cohesively—meeting of the otherwise incompatible aspects of work and family. These include flexibility, understanding from bosses, contingency work, and creative approaches to work when the old model doesn't work.

Balance and Flexibility. Some companies are extended families where employees are referred to as a members of the corporate family. Some bosses, particularly owners of smaller companies, often think about their employees as part of their families. For some organizations, protecting employees can become paternalistic. For some it is merely a sham for trying to make employees become more loyal; for others, the meaning is totally sincere. Then there are the companies that actually are families, with sons and daughters succeeding parents, aunts, and uncles in the business, which becomes extremely interesting if a member isn't pulling his or her share of the load. Either way, people bond at work, for better or worse. Balance is one key, flexibility the other. This at times may well be a tight rope act, such as deciding whether the overtime is worth it when it comes to missing yet another Bobby Sox game or leaving the kids to get dinner on their own.

Here's a sampling of several recent books dealing with work and family, providing an interesting overview of how specific the problems and concerns can become.

From Peters, *When Mothers Work:*[13]

If women are to cultivate their independent identities along with their mothering, they must relinquish some maternal control to partners, grandparents, godparents, and caregivers.

At one time or another 58 percent of American children live solely with their mother. One fourth of American children are born to unmarried mothers, and a quarter of children under three live with a single mother.

As hard as it is for couples to resist their inclinations toward traditional motherhood and fatherhood, those who do are greatly rewarded with marriages that continue to thrive after they have children.

Levine and Pittinsky, in *Working Fathers*,[14] offer the following strategies for working fathers:

- Creating father-friendly workplaces
- Breaking culture collusion
- Managing paternity leave
- Connecting with your family
- Staying connected while traveling
- Connecting through school, day care, and significant others

Balancing the work-family equation for fathers represents one of the greatest challenges—and opportunities—of today.

Supporting men in being good fathers is good for men, good for children, good for women—and good for business.

Hegelsen in *Everyday Revolutionaries*[15] offers this observation:

"The large-scale entry of women into the workplace over the last thirty years, and their subsequent assumption of positions of influence and authority outside the home, is changing how businesses are run," as well as families, communities, and more. He also noted that over 75 percent of women over eighteen are working.

Hochschild's *Time Bind*[16] studied a company noted for being family friendly. The author found that,

"The more attached we are to the world of work, the more its deadlines, its cycles, its powers and interruptions shape our lives and the more family time is forced to accommodate to the pressures of work." Moreover, he learned, that the company has family friendly options, but working women do not take full advantage of them, choosing instead to work additional time.

Hersch, in *A Tribe Apart*,[17] chronicled changes in teenage life. This study followed eight teenagers for an extended period, noting that society has created for them a separate life cutoff from their families:

"The most stunning change for adolescents today is their aloneness."

Self-Employment and Self-Empowerment

The days of twenty years of satisfactory performance rewarded by a nice pension and gold watch presented at a banquet are long gone, replaced by the new age of self-empowerment. What this really means is that it's every man and woman for him or herself. The old career model of going to work for someone else and, by working hard and striving for advancement, being promoted for your efforts, and all the while fully expecting the company will take care of you through thick and thin, simply doesn't exist anymore. There are, of course, exceptions, but that's just what they are—exceptions. Look at how many organizations are pulling back on pensions and related health benefits and the picture becomes clearer. Global competition, where companies from overseas (or next door) have stepped in and taken over a significant portion of the business, primarily because of cheaper labor, has had a major role in this change. Balances of power, such as in manufacturing, are shifting around the globe. Just look at how many products and parts once made in the U.S.A. are now made in Guadalajara or Kuala Lumpur.

More and more people these days are self-employed, even if they work for someone else. Organizations of all types have discovered the advantages of contingent work forces and have come to rely on them to an ever greater extent. Such forms as part-time, both temporary and permanent; temporary help, both temporary and permanent; contract labor; leased labor forces; and outsourcing of more and more work, have redefined the workplace. Even chief executives may be brought in for one particular phase of a company's existence, moving on when the task is completed.

Telework is another factor in the move to self-employment. People can now do more work from home, plugging into the company's computer and working away while tending to the laundry and kids. Done properly, which means establishing rules and discipline, working from remote stations can be most rewarding for both employer and employee. Setting work goals and then accomplishing them is the first step toward success. It also saves the company a lot of money. One of the keys is to have readily available the resources (e.g., fax, PC, telephone line) needed for information searches.

Relationships and Feedback

Behavioral scientists tell us that we owe much of our humanness to the fact that we interact with other humans. How else would language develop, for instance, if it wasn't from the infant having a parent speaking to it? Our existence as a human species started out as bands of hunter-gatherers, people who fully depended upon one another for survival. In Western civilization, we have a reputation for being individuals and tending to be more self-centered. Even so, we still seek out and acquire relationships of a variety of types with others. Just ask a parent, for example, how many groups does he or she belong to. You might hear about the Parent Teachers' Association, soccer league, church, Sunday school, professional business association, social club, adult softball league, civic organization, charity organization, and possibly several work-related groups. The study by Bella and others titled *Habits of the Heart,* which delved into the relationships of love and marriage, psychotherapy, public life, and political activism, noted that Americans are still concerned with finding meaning in life primarily through "intense relations with others." They stated further that "we are . . . not a collection of private individuals," and that "it does make a difference who we are and how we treat one another."[18] It's been noted that not only do people need other people, they need to have a sense of touch as noted by the growing popularity of such programs.[19]

A common question that arises regarding telecommuting to work is "but what about face to face, human contact? Don't we need that, too?" We already know that the answer is yes. But how do you solve the problem of human contact when e-mail, satellites, and virtual everything is the order of the day? The significance of basic human behavior is that we need interactions and that oftentimes, because of electronic elements, we stay literally a workstation away from others with whom we work closely with. Organizations that initially promoted telecommuting, where their employees accomplished essentially all their work from remote sites, have changed their minds and started requiring that employees actually come into the office periodically.

Religion at Work

Church and state may be separated, but not so church and the workplace. We've long had religious holidays, where people got Christmas Day off whether they were Christian or not. As the Academy of Management reported, "technology, global competition, downsizing, and reengineering have created a workforce of employees seeking value, support, and meaning in their lives that finds expression not only at home but also on the job." They further noted that "This search for religious and spiritual meaning in the workplace is a departure from the more traditional business mentality."[20]

One study differentiated between spirituality and religion in the workplace, the latter considered to be inappropriate at work. Spirituality deals with realization of full potential, working in a good and ethical organization, working with good colleagues, and serving the community.[21] Spirituality has also been defined as "The basic desire to find ultimate meaning and purpose in one's life and to live an integrated life."[22] If was felt that management must deal with spirituality in order to develop the workforce's greatest potential. Businesses have been known to have chapels on the premises, and many employers are generous in recognizing the religious beliefs of employees who are of other faiths. In today's diverse workplace, it's not uncommon for Jews, Muslims, Protestants, Catholics, Buddhists, and others to be working side by side. The term *Protestant work ethic* may still be bandied about, but the ethic is made up of many flavors these days. The key is for the workplace to be adaptive to whatever are peoples' spiritual needs as long as they don't interfere with work. The long run may prove that people need to have their spiritual selves supported in order to put their religious beliefs—whatever they may be—into the whole life perspective. Religion and spirituality provide an excellent reason why you can't separate the workplace mind and spirit from those that go home at night or to worship at another time. It's also important to bear in mind that people may have a strong sense of spirituality without ever setting foot inside a church. Along with diversity must come religious tolerance.

WHOLE LIFE TOOLS

Humans create problems for themselves but also have a great knack for providing solutions to them, though oftentimes not until much later. Following are some of the solutions that have been used successfully.

Wellness and Health

Wellness and health programs have two major objectives: (1) to keep healthy and therefore more productive, and (2) to help people deal with existing health problems. Successful programs include education, awareness, checkups, and participation in a broad variety of activities. They may be done on personal time, company time, or both. All aspects of health are addressed. Such holistic health items as acupuncture and homeopathic medicine, as noted previously, are included as well.

Wellness programs generally consist of components such as these:

- Healthy heart—cholesterol; blood pressure; heart rate
- Diabetes
- Diet
- Exercise and fitness
- Posture and back injury prevention
- Self-care
- Skin care
- Cancer
- Substance abuse
- Smoking cessation
- Stress management

YMCAs and YWCAs commonly provide excellent health and wellness programs. As one example, a YWCA in Charleston, West Virginia, provides these programs:

- Aerobics, fitness, and aquatic programs
- Weight room, pool, sauna, and Jacuzzi

- Child care and youth activities
- Swimming and water exercise programs
- Gymnastics, martial arts, and dance classes
- Basketball and volleyball[23]

Eli Lilly, winner of a C. Everett Koop National Health Award for success in significantly reducing employee health care costs by improving health through wellness programs and education, provides another example of what can be done.[24] The programs are judged on health risk appraisals and screening, support for stress reduction and smoking cessation, fitness activities and preventive care. An interesting sidelight is that one study showed that men were less apt than women to adopt healthy attitudes. Reflecting the increased concern for wellness is the growing number of online health and medical sites. As reported by *The Wall Street Journal*, 22 million adults representing almost 40 percent of those online "used the Internet to seek health related information."[25]

Here's a sampling of other wellness programs, providing evidence that organizations are taking the situation seriously:

- Coors Brewing Co. has had a wellness center since 1981. Originally founded solely for employee wellness, it was later discovered that health care costs were reduced.[26]
- Sara Lee Knit Products Inc., Northwestern Mutual Life Insurance Co., and Chattanooga State Technical Community College, "effectively transformed their employees into well-conditioned, active and healthy individuals."[27]
- Indiana companies that provide $120 discount on health insurance if employees agree to use stairs instead of the elevator; get a $50 gift certificate by agreeing to wear a seat belt to work every day; quit smoking and save the company $1,100 a year; start an exercise program and save the company $260 a year; and for every $1 spent on wellness programs, receive $2.51 back.[28]

The programs work, employees are healthier and happier, and money is saved. What better way to help blend work and life.

Stress Management

Stress comes in many forms and from many directions, and comes as easily from things we enjoy doing as well as from those we don't like. It has always come with work, but with job and family and other parts of life all intertwined, the potential for stress has increased exponentially. An important consideration is that stress can be reduced, perhaps controlled, but not totally eliminated. One of the outfalls is anxiety, which is a good example of why we can never eliminate stress—change simply keeps coming along too rapidly.

Information and Technology Anxiety. "Too much work and too little time" is how one author states the condition that leads to information anxiety.[29] Succinct and true. We simply haven't been prepared for this deluge of information pushed along by constant change sometimes bordering on orders of magnitude and usually having to do with technology. It's a quantum leap to move from learning how to deal with the flight or fight syndrome—i.e., dealing with a saber-toothed tiger standing in the path ahead of us—to coping with information and technology. Words like *anxiety, threat, speed, obsolescence, complexity,* and *coping* are used often to describe what we feel and are. Technology too often has taken the role of the modern-day saber-toothed tiger.

Stress Management Techniques. A number of techniques have been applied successfully to reduce and even to control stress. These include deep relaxation, self-hypnosis, and meditation. Sometimes simply taking several deep breaths will do the trick by slowing down our breathing and heart rate to speeds more in keeping with calmness. One favorite exercise is to start with muscle groups at the top of the head and concentrate on first tensing them, then letting them go. By working from head to neck to shoulders, to back and chest, and so on, the entire body can become relaxed by the time you work your way to your toes. These can usually be learned by following printed or audio instructions for a time or two.

Bearing in mind that going online can be a major contributor to stress, mental as well as physical, there's a most interesting twist. Employers are offering tips on wellness programs, ranging from "skin cancer to how to cook chicken,"[30] and they're making them available online. Coupled with the growing number of Web sites mentioned above, we now have the potential of health information overload, not to mention reliability and all the others concerns.

Self-hypnosis and meditation require more formal training, but aren't difficult to do. After all, our minds are capable of trailing off into other states when we least expect them to do so. Our subconscious minds are always at work (e.g., being creative), and both types of programs utilize this fact by placing positive thoughts that reduce stress into the subconscious. You can learn either of these by reading about them, listening or watching videos, and by attending training sessions conducted by qualified instructors. Find one that works, and it will make you far more information literate simply because it will free your mind of extraneous worries and headaches.

A sampler of what can be done to hold down stress includes these:

- Sleep longer. A study at the University of Westminster in London showed that the earlier people wake up, the higher are their cortisol levels, which is the body's main stress hormone.[31]

- Put on party hats and funny noses, as Community America Credit Union does to let off steam and keep everyone happy, which may take but ten or fifteen minutes.[32]

- Women.com offers five quick fixes: breathe, massage your feet, use scents (rubbed into the temples), juice up (as in orange juice), and stretch.[33]

- Cincinnati and Northern Kentucky firms have taken advantage of "Meditation and Desktop Yoga," to reduce stress, which take as little as ten minutes.[34]

- Cigna Energy uses relaxation therapy in the form of massage, reporting that absenteeism went down 9 percent and resignations fell off by 7 percent a year after implementing the program.[35]

Simplicity and Consumption

Stories have been told and songs sung around the theme of the simple life—as in why can't life be made simpler, why must it not only be complex, but get more complex over time. There are true sagas of women who have walked away from promotions to the executive suite in order to be closer to their families. And of men cashing in their worldly belongings, perhaps folding up a professional practice, and setting out to circumnavigate the globe on their sailboats. One of the most acute examples of the longing for simplicity occurs when the novice PC user attempts to load a software upgrade, or walks into the library to discover that the wooden cabinets filled with card stock yellowed by the constant touch of human hands have been replaced by a computer; and where the five-thousand volumes in the neighborhood library have grown to hundreds of thousands and more online.

Leading a simpler life is a personal choice, but not one easily made. Sacrifices must be made, but with care and discretion. Simplicity does have its place when attempting to counter the rigors and stress of the information age. Such problems as materialism, conspicuous consumption, narcissism and self-serving behavior, no-holds-barred competition, popular culture worship, and dependence on lawyers and other experts are among the causes of stress often cited. Eliminating or reducing any one or many of these would remove the clutter from our lives. The question is, how dependent are we on these things? Simplicity is actually a state of mind, where such things as concern for ecology and the environment, redefining quality, and being aware of all that goes on around us will go a long way toward simplifying life.

The point to be made is that one way to ease the way for the hurly-burly, instantaneous, electronic, and drastically changing world of work we live in is to simplify as much as possible. Here's a synthesis taken from a variety of sources espousing the philosophy of living a more simple, less cluttered life:

- Most millionaires live below their means.
- Live frugally—in all aspects of life.

- Be sensitive to ecology and conservation issues.

- Be concerned about others.

- View the earth as a system, with everything having a place and role.

- Avoid the trappings of affluence.

- Avoid stress—stay relaxed.

- Choose an occupation you feel good about.

- Think historically.

- Realize that many of the poorest people today have far more worldly goods than some of their most well-off ancestors.

- Also realize there are problems and circumstances in the world which are beyond your ability to do anything about.

Gaining Control

Getting back to the problem of information anxiety, there are solutions. From among both the people who have taken on the task of confronting exploded information and technology and those who seem to go with the flow, we can find words of wisdom to help us along. As one person said, "Fortunately, human beings are intelligent, innovative, and resilient."[36] A synthesis of proven recommendations gives us a starter set of rules to follow to reduce anxiety, if not eliminate it to a great extent. These are short, but powerful mindsets for information literacy practitioners.

Get Organized. This includes removing clutter, using computer tools to keep schedules and help plan, and more. Considering that "a recent study shows that the average white collar worker spends six weeks a year looking for things in the office," getting organized takes on a whole new meaning.[37]

Filter. This includes information of all kinds. It's relatively easy to take a quick glance at a piece of information (e.g., newspaper article, book, e-mail) and determine its immediate and long-term value to you. Throw it away unless there is a reasonably good chance it will be of some value in the near future, or unless you want to read it for the sheer pleasure or out of genuine curiosity. If you're organized as noted above, you'll have a way to put the information away so that it can easily be found when you do need it.

Stay on Top. This means to keep abreast of new technological developments and your own skills—information literacy skills they turn out to be. See chapter 8, "Learning How to Learn." The concept of environmental scanning will help considerably.

Get Help. Networks are one of the most reliable and fastest ways to get help in dealing with information and technology. When you have a technician you can trust, for example, ask that person about a new hardware development you're worried is going to pass you by. And don't forget the friendly neighborhood librarian, perhaps the most information literate person around, and most willing to help.

Plan for Change. This will give you a far better chance to deal with it when it comes, and undoubtedly, some of it will slip through and catch you unawares, no matter how hard you try to be prepared. (See Managing Change below.) Of course, you've already figured out that the best defense against anxiety is to be fully and truly information literate.

Time Management

People usually do a lousy job of managing their time. The fact that bookshelves abound with time management books and that seminars and workshops on the topic are relatively easy to find provide insight into how critical it is that people manage their time efficiently. The title of the first chapter of Covey and Merrill's *First Things First* says it all: "How many people on their deathbed wish they'd spent more time at the office?"[38] The message of this book, is that our lives become the consequences of how we deal with our seemingly limited time. By tying time to values—e.g., what do you value most at any given time, prioritizing, and setting goals—we can do a much better job of it.

Arthur Andersen implemented a program to save time on such activities as proposal and report writing, presentations, research, and making work plans. The program "translated into annual savings of $1.3 million in sales and marketing and $12 million in engagement performance activities."[39] Not bad for a time savings program, and it certainly proves the old saying that time is money.

Many programs call for keeping a log of how we spend our time. Perhaps a quicker way is to do an information search for studies that have been conducted, then accepting this as our starting point. However, by establishing what's important to us and setting goals and schedules about how much time will be devoted to these things, we'll have taken a major step toward using our time more efficiently, as well as more enjoyably.

One typical program includes these objectives: analyze daily routine, understand the effect of attitude on productivity, develop time management strategies, communication skills, assertiveness skills, problem solving strategies, and stress management techniques.[40] You can easily see that being information literate will take care of many of the things we need to do to be more time efficient. This particular course, by the way, included time management techniques of prioritizing, delegating, setting personal prime time, and getting organized. It's uncanny how closely these, too, resemble being information literate and having the requisite skills.

Some people liken managing their lives to juggling acts. Situations where both significant others work, particularly in high-visibility jobs, can mean seeing one another on occasion at best. Juggling schedules helps, and ironically, online calendars can be of assistance. One woman executive had to take her children to a public housing development to show her children what their lives might be like if she didn't work and stayed at home with them, and this is but one example of many things that working mothers have to do to balance earning a living and managing a family.[41] A consensus of the articles, studies, and other things developed about time management seems to include the common theme of cutting out unnecessary interruptions, which isn't easy to do; otherwise it wouldn't be a problem. *Forbes* magazine recommends this: "Don't read time-management books or attend seminars on the topic," which may or may not be tongue-in-cheek.[42]

Managing Change

The fact that constant, sometimes radical change is one of the major challenges faced by today's organizations is a given. Information and knowledge workers who staff these organizations must be capable of dealing with it in one manner or the other. In fact, organizations that do so are apt to be the ones that not only remain viable over the long haul, but often are the ones at the top. There's a direct and positive relationship between the ability to meet change head-on and organizational success. Getting back to Collins and Porras, their study *Built to Last* proved this quite convincingly.[43] The eighteen companies in their study have survived extreme change and turned it into their strategic advantage over a long number of years, and they continue to do so today as they face many of the global, technological, information and knowledge challenges mentioned throughout this book.

The body of knowledge for organizational change is called organization development (OD). A simple definition of OD is that it is planned, managed change. In other words, rather than just reacting to change, it is anticipated and controlled to the organization's advantage. For example, rather than waiting for the next wave of new telecommunications technology to come along, then having to hurriedly decide how to respond, a change-oriented company might be alert to what technological changes are coming along and have a decision in place long before others who are floundering as they try to determine what to do.

Thanks to radical and continuous change, "An overnight demand has arisen for exotic new skills that were once on the fringe of the labor pool."[44] These exotic skills do the trick, provided you've learned what they are and how to use them. There's good reason to be concerned with change. Technology alone makes it mandatory to keep up with new developments, not to mention competition and the globally driven economy. The idea that continuous change is the only event you can predict with certainty isn't so far fetched.

When it comes to change, there are numerous ways to deal with it, ranging from ducking from its path to turning it into a plan of action for you and your organization. The most tempting way to face change is to ignore it. Unfortunately, it has a way of coming back to haunt us when left to its own devices. Change is going to occur, whether we're ready for it or not. In reality, it tends to move along and leave us behind when we put on our blinders. As the author of the quotation above notes, we usually micromanage, look at the short term, fix rather than reorder, or misunderstand the culture. An interesting observation: there is a direct relationship between having the right information and being able to manage change.

Lying at the other extreme of the change reaction spectrum is the best way to react. It's called planned, managed change. This is easy to say, much more difficult to do. Other alternatives, such as to react, lie in between. (See exhibit 10.2 which identifies possible change reactions.)

Personal Change Model

By adapting the organizational change model, we can derive an approach to help information gatherers in handling change. The components include these:

- Be information literate.
- Stay updated on new technology.
- Continually scan the horizon to see what others in your business or expertise are doing.
- Network with other professionals.
- Use an accepted model to deal with change.

For the latter, the traditional model of problem solving works well. By determining what is the situation you want to exist, then determining the one that actually exists, you have started the process. The next step is to determine what

Exhibit 10.2
A Spectrum of Change Reactions

Ignore	Fight	Minimum adaptation	Plan & Manage
Take high risk	May be a losing battle	Less risk—might work/ might not	Results are what you want them to be.

Example: Compliance with new workplace law that would require you to make extensive information search and accomplish change in policies and procedures to be fully compliant.

Ignore	Fight	Minimum adaptation	Plan & Manage
Employees file complaints	Possibly go to court	Employees will know, even if you get away with this	No complaints or court appearances; employees react more positively.

is the best strategy to get from where you are to where you want to be. Then simply implement the change, taking pains to prepare yourself and others affected by it to operate in the new mode. Exhibit 10.3 illustrates this simple change model.

Integral to the ability to plan for and manage change is systems thinking—thinking of the whole even while examining its parts. The system in question is often the entire organization, such as a manufacturing company, military unit, insurance agency, or service club. It could also be a work group within the organization, but even then it's critical to view the entire organization while focusing on the subpart. Also, when viewing the organization as a whole, it's equally critical to view it within the framework of the environment within which it operates. A commonly stated way to describe systems thinking is seeing the forest and not just the individual trees within it. Knowing how the parts of a system operate as a whole helps us to manage change.

Only by seeing the whole can change be most effectively implemented. Systems thinking is also part of the ABCs of business literacy. (See chapter 7, "Subject Matter Expert.") Understanding the bottom line is one of the outcomes of systems thinking. You can also see the close relationship between systems thinking and information literacy. Information and the knowledge it leads to don't exist within a vacuum.

Change is one of the main reasons people at work have to pursue information and knowledge within organizations, either to deal with it or to cause it to

Exhibit 10.3
A Simple Change Model

STEP 1—Where do you want to be?

• Fully describe where you want to be—what new situation do you want to become a reality? This could cover a wide range of possibilities, form major change (e.g., enter a new profession) to minor (e.g., take a spreadsheet course).

STEP 2—Where are you now?

• Identify your present position with respect to where you want to be. If you know nothing about the new profession, you'll have to conduct research before you can make any moves. Take a course, all you need to do is see how much you can afford to pay to take it.

STEP 3—What will it take to get there?

• Plan—determining what resources it will take, how long, and so on.

• Implement—make the change.

• Monitor—to make sure it works out the way you wanted, making any necessary adjustments.

Note how similar and compatible this is with the information literacy process.

happen. This alone is a pressing reason to know as much as possible about change, particularly the proactive kind.

A LAST THOUGHT ON WHOLE LIFE THINKING

What has happened in the workplace is that we've mixed the wonder of technology with the wonderful experiences of being human. The mix isn't always good, although some would say that technology can solve everything. The solution sounds simple enough—be careful how you mix them; but organizations and what they do for a living have a life of their own. And technology certainly has a life of its own, one that seems to run amok at times and never slows down. One advisor listed three things you can do to "regain control over your technological tools and save your sanity: don't let technology replace the human touch; don't let civility and respect escape your life; and schedule a block of time to communicate."[45] This excellent advice blends both of the wonders noted above.

People are concerned with the "elusive art of getting a life."[46] Fortunately, organizations are paying more attention to this fact. The main message from this chapter is that life is different these days. It requires that we bring into consideration everything we do as humans—work, play, family, volunteering, politics, religion, personal interests—whatever it is that makes us "us." By addressing all aspects of our being, we can better prepared to deal with life as professional information gatherers and users. Given the fact that employers are recognizing the need to include the whole person at work—through elder care, child care, flexible work hours, working at home, and more—there's no reason why we all can't more seamlessly blend the two concepts—work and family—into a lifestyle that supports the best parts of both.

CHAPTER 11

The Future: Maintaining Information Power

INTRODUCTION

The radar analogy mentioned in chapter 8 serves us well when it comes to the future. Keeping our eyes on the scope, that is, looking for new ideas, developments, and trends, is a powerful tool to keep us in touch with what might happen in the future. It's what futurists do for a living. Their radars are constantly scanning the horizon and beyond. Taking a risk here and there will further the cause of being ready for the future. It's the people who have taken the most risks, when they were well prepared to do so, who have enjoyed continual success at work and at beating the competition. It's not easy to predict the future. We can, however, assess where we are now and project where this may lead us, which will undoubtedly be toward an exciting, and markedly changed, workplace, one demanding high skill levels and the ability to acquire new ones at a moment's notice. Where do we go from here? Have we identified the set of skills that will carry us through the new age and beyond? The answer is that we have established the framework. Being information literate, staying current, and continuing to learn will provide staying power leading to continued information power. It requires constant alertness to what's going on around the workplace and marketplace, all senses focused on both the present and looking well down the road to what may be in store.

This final chapter takes a look at the future as it relates to information power and literacy. The picture is as what you would expect—more technology, more information, more demand, more of everything. A number of predicted developments in technology, jobs, skills, and knowledge are reviewed, followed by a discussion of related problems which must be dealt with. Tips on how to prepare for the future and information literacy are identified, and the chapter ends with a brief summary of the total skills set required to be fully information literate.

Information literacy isn't a new concept. It's just that it means so much more these days as hand tools and machinery have given way to information and knowledge as the primary wage earning means. Even today's tools and machinery are often computer driven. As Peter Drucker said, "We are rebuilding organizations around information";[1] "Our biggest challenge will continue to be obtaining this outside information so that we can make good decisions"; and "Times change, and we must change with them." No doubt information literacy is the skill of choice for those who want information power and the path to success.

WHAT ARE THE PREDICTIONS?

A 1995 prediction for work in the year 2020 was that "There are no more workers, no more managers, no more jobs—only teams of people who bring their skills to constantly changing projects. Many of these work teams never meet physically" but through technology, and "They don't all have the same employer—some even work for four or five companies."[2] It goes on to say that few people will work in a traditional corporate setting. Some of this has happened, and some hasn't. We work through technology and we work in corporate settings. The only thing for certain is that change will continue to be dramatic.

Technology

Technology continues to take the lead in knowledge, change, and information literacy in that it virtually upgrades itself. Every day we seem to make new breakthroughs in size, capacity, speed, and more. Yet there's an interesting result. "It's rather ironic," we're told, "that as the information age finally closes in around us, organizations are becoming more dependent on *people* than ever before."[3] Technology is a two-edged sword. It as often as not creates new problems as fast as it solves old ones—a treasure trove and Pandora's Box all in one. One researcher has asked two critical and pertinent questions about information and its relation to technology: What information must we have to be effective? And How can technology make it available to us when we need it—and not a moment before?[4] Technology can become the pull effect, the research continues, rather than the push. It can be used to pull up just the information we need, rather than continually push more information than we can confront at any given time.

Numbers can be impressive. They can also be undigestible, but by limiting them here, we can get a quick glance at what technology is predicted to do in the future. Improvements in optical transmission of digital signals are on the road to being able to transmit the contents of the Library of Congress in five minutes.[5] Whether we understand terabits or not, that's fast. Microprocessor chips will contain, we are told, one hundred times more transistors in the future than they now can. For some of us, they already hold too many.

The U.S. Department of Commerce in its report "Understanding the Digital Economy" notes that the digital revolution is just beginning, stating that there will be extensive growth in Internet use (as many as one billion people served by 2005); $300 billion worth of electronic commerce; increased digital delivery of goods and services; and increased ordering of goods. A drastic change in skill requirements is also predicted, with "workers with information technology skills are needed across the economy."[6] They predict a growth from 7 million instructional technology workers now to 9 million. We already see this exemplified by the dichotomy between skilled worker shortages alongside large layoffs.

Jobs

The concept of work teams not only grows, but grows more interesting. Perhaps the greatest common theme regarding the future of jobs is that of the virtual team. One term given this is the *collaborative virtual workspace*, which is defined as "an office automation environment that enables people to converse, collaborate, and interact regardless of their geographic location."[7] Thus, teams will not only thrive, but will be made up of people at a variety of locations, people who may never see one another on a face-to-face basis, other than via television monitors. Not only that, but the composition of them can change on a regular basis as long as the new members are online.

Chief of information technology, possibly changed to a more glamorous and modern-sounding title, will continue to grow in importance as a job in future organizations. Certainly, each person will be chief of his or her own information domain, with responsibilities as great as their corporate counterparts. People who have grown up digital and have read online magazines (e-zines) just as their parents read comic books as youngsters will be ready to fill them. Jobs in the future will be more digital in nature. But as noted throughout the research efforts for this book, people and basic people skills are still what it will take to competently fill jobs on an ongoing basis. The reason is simple—jobs of the future will require more highly trained, skilled, and adaptable people than ever before. "As the business world globalizes and the Internet grows," Nicholas Negroponte tells us, "we will start to see a seamless digital workplace."[8] Information seeking, as opposed to passively receiving information, is one answer to the future. It has been noted that "increasing responsibility" has been put on individuals "to become active seekers, rather than passive recipients of information, especially for decision support and problem solving."[9] This author goes on to state that technical workers and managers who are adept at identifying sources of information and developing approaches to getting it are the ones who will succeed. Of course, a few problems must be worked out, such as how to deal with so many choices.

Knowledge

The knowledge worker, though not new, is certainly a person who stands in the limelight these days. How important is this person? It has been noted that "America's future prosperity rests upon the education of all our citizens." Another hint: "When people share knowledge, the group's effectiveness and productivity increase."[10] A major challenge is that because of the tremendous growth in knowledge jobs—and predictions for it to grow more—is an acute one: where do you find them?

As noted in the Department of Commerce's economic report cited above, an additional 2 million information technology workers (i.e., highly skilled and information literate) will be needed by 2007.[11] One thing that might help ease the shortage of knowledge workers is that students will hopefully graduate from high school with the skills needed to fill these gaps. They should be expected to be computer literate as well as information literate, at least as far as the library applications are concerned. If so, this will be a boon to the workplace, helping to offset the shortage of people who have the requisite skills for the future.

Statistics abound about how much information and knowledge we are confronted with compared to people just a few generations ago. The trick is to filter through what there is to glean that will be of the greatest use and act upon it. Knowledge will not diminish, nor will the need for it. The key will continue to be to manage it—to use it to advantage.

Skills

In looking to what skills will be needed for the future, the American Psychological Association (APA) offers a few surprises. They note that employers will be looking for people who can be motivated under extreme circumstances and stay with the job, yet are able to go with the flow of change. Constant training will be the norm. They speak of concentrating "in the next century on better understanding and nurturing the human side of business."[12]

Companies will continue to need better educated people, meaning information literate people. Finding and solving problems, it's predicted, will be a fundamental part of this required education. Another view of what skills are needed comes from the United Kingdom. The topics available for this program include planning, culture, relationships, information, technology, communications, managing change, creativity, and personal development. You can see the similarities in all the skills discussed to this point. Employers want, and are testing for, "responsibility, openness to learning, initiative, and emotional stability."[13] These requirements sound familiar because they're the skills needed to be information literate.

Diversity

Diversity impacts information seeking in two distinct and dramatic ways. First, a widely diverse workforce changes the baseline for dealing with information and knowledge because of the diversity itself—some people speak other languages and come from cultures that treat them differently; the spread of information literacy skills may be quite broad; and the resulting influence on information is that it will be more challenging to share it. Second, because of the global nature of gathering information, the technology may or may not be in place to get information about, for example, a foreign market that is critical to your plans to expand. Not every country and organization in the world has had the opportunity to digitize information to the extent the Western world has, and even if the technology exists, there could be language barriers to obtaining and analyzing it.

Much of the work done today is accomplished on a team basis, and diversity is one of the greatest—and fortunately one that works in teamwork's favor—challenges to work. Simply learning how to work together must be done before information can be exchanged. One government labor official stated the situation clearly when he said that "Diversity is and will be the major driving force in the 21st century" and that the "downside to low-level unemployment is that it's hard to find the skilled, trained workers you need."[14] As more international workers enter the U.S. workforce, and particularly those taking on high technology jobs, the impact of information literacy will grow.

A Few Predictions

Here are some future predictions that will impact information power as reported by *The Futurist:*

- Information may go from doubling to quadrupling within one lifetime.
- Monumental investments will be made in developing the information superhighway (beyond what's already been spent).
- Computers will become even more widespread.
- Telecommuting will continue to grow as more people work from home.
- Continued breakthroughs will take place in all aspects of electronics.
- Education costs will rise.
- People will have more leisure time (provided you can deal with four times as much information).[15]

Another prediction from *The Futurist* noted the following items. It should be noted at this time, however, that the future has already arrived:

- Virtual organizations, which rely at times solely on information and the combined knowledge of those who work together digitally. A profound statement about computer technology was that it "has eliminated financial float, and it has also eliminated decision float."[16] All the more reason why having information power has become the way of life of successful organizations.

- Just-in-time work force, a sign of the contingency workforce times.

- Ascendancy of knowledge workers, which we've discussed at length earlier in the book.

- Computerized coaching and electronic monitoring, which has also been discussed, particularly in chapters 8, "Learning How to Learn," and 9, "Online Help."

- Growth of worker diversity, which becomes obvious when we take a look around us at work.

- Aging work force, but we know that senior citizens can become as information literate as anyone else, provided they're given the opportunity.

- Birth of the dynamic work force

Another prediction is that the young people entering the workforce will come equipped with the computer skills they need, and will have climbed a long way up the ladder of being information literate. As one author said, "The children of today possess an aptitude for computers that is expected to change the future workplace. Their generation will bring into the workplace a high level of computer literacy the likes of which have never been seen before."[17] A disclaimer must be added to this prediction: not all young people have access to the technology needed to make them so computer literate. This problem will be discussed later in this chapter.

Other predictions include one from Michael Dertouzos that the World Wide Web "has an integral role in the future workplace" and that the Web "will be used to deliver human work."[18]

To put predictions into proper perspective, here's what Herman Kahn noted that we could expect down the road:

- Emphasis on technology
- Greater dependence on consensual techniques for getting work done
- Rise of the learning society
- Other manifestations of a coming postindustrial society
- Automatic data processing being used to generate national income and wealth

- Computerized countrywide and worldwide commerce that is instantaneous
- New worldwide feedback mechanisms
- New varieties of worldwide organizations[19]

What makes this truly interesting is that he published these predictions in 1974, showing that people do have insight into what to expect. It's also important to note that Kahn predicted that there would be mistakes associated with the dependence on technology and that information would be misused. It certainly has.

WHAT ARE THE PROBLEMS?

As with anything that contributes to progress, there's the other side of the coin. As change steamrolls its way through our lives, and technology continues to drive us to becoming ever more reliant upon it—all in the name of information literacy—accompanying problems, too, demonstrate a snowballing effect. In other words, attendant problems are exacerbated, adding to the challenge to stay on top of knowledge by being information literate. Some of the problems are perplexing—trying to cope with, let alone stay on top, of change. Others are more insidious and threaten to widen the already huge gap between those who are well off and those who are not. The following discussion will introduce new problems and summarize the ones mentioned previously in the book.

Widening Gap between the Haves and Have-Nots

Studies, including ones made by the United Nations, show that there is a rift between nations of haves and nations of have nots as far as wealth and worldly goods, including the most basic ones, are concerned.[20] They show the disturbing fact that this gap is widening. Living standards become more disparate between rich and poor, even within the same geographic regions and countries. Technology and access to information—and the knowledge it brings—is a significant cause for this widening gap. There's a bit of irony here, as the cost of a PC with all the trimmings for the knowledge worker is falling. Internet access is available through Internet service providers (ISP) for reasonable monthly fees, and the existing telephone line can be used for Internet connection. As an alternative, cable companies and others provide telephone-free connections as part of the monthly fee. In short, to have the minimum system, communications, and software, along with the expertise to use it all, is within reasonable reach of many Americans. But how about those for whom it is not? What is accessible and affordable to us simply is not to many people living not all that far away from us. If a family in a developing country has an income the equivalent of ten dollars a month, even a hundred, where will it be spent—with the food provider or the Internet service provider? Mergers of the key players may well aggravate the problem.

As MIT's Dertouzos stated, "The poor nations and poor people, by contrast," when it comes to widespread technology growth, "can't even get started."[21] Underuse and lack of funds to pay for the technology is stated as the culprit, and these people will "gain no such leverage. They will stand still, which in relative terms means falling exponentially further behind the rich."[22] By contrast, Negroponte is optimistic that with 20 percent of the world consuming 80 percent of its resources, the gap will be healed at least partly because "Digital technology can be a natural force drawing people into greater world harmony."[23] Indeed, it would be most rewarding if technology could become an equalizer rather than a chasm builder. To make matters worse, though, the technology-propelled economy has further widened the gap.

Stress

Each individual must determine his or her level of stress and stay on top of how to manage it so that it doesn't take a toll. Being information literate and using technology as a means to an end will go a long way. So, too, will knowing a good relaxation or meditation technique and how to take time off when the going gets too rough. (See chapter 10, "Humans Don't Live by Digits Alone.") Unfortunately, there are no easy solutions. The power of information and knowledge, particularly as it continues to grow in depth and importance, will tend to at least keep the chasm there, if not push it wider apart. Perhaps the answer lies in how accessible the information becomes to the have nots. Certainly, school systems are taking steps to provide online access to all their students. As long as libraries, and especially those in neighborhoods, are supported, this will keep the lines of communication between all people and the information highway open.

Sense of Community

This has been discussed in previous chapters and is definitely a subject bearing attention. There are two schools of thought, one that technology is everything, and one that we must use technology to our advantage, but not to the detriment of human beings. Work is done through people, and it isn't likely we will make such an extreme adaptation in a generation or two that will change people to the point where they don't need others around. Dertouzos, for example, states that "working from home is both undesirable and unproductive," and he isn't the only one who feels that way.[24] Through collaboration, compromise, and common sense, technology can be applied where it does the most good and brings the least harm to human relations.

INFORMATION LITERACY AND THE WORKPLACE

Successful organizations have always been able to provide their employees with information power. It may have been called information technology, computer literacy, or something else—or nothing at all other than good business. However, taking on information literacy within the definition given in chapter 2 and surrounding it with the skill set discussed in the subsequent chapters is a new concept. Organizations have traditionally dealt with computer literacy, information technology, and related topics. Yet a few are beginning to address the issue head on. Two are the U.S. Navy and Dow Chemical. Here's an overview of their programs, and they're programs that will be repeated in the future in a variety of forms, all for the purpose of giving people information power.

U.S. Navy

Through the Office of the Librarian of the Navy, the U.S. Navy recognizes the need to do everything possible to enhance servicewide information literacy. It's quite a challenge, considering how widespread are the needs. Goals of the program include promoting and facilitating information and online literacy for all Navy and Marine Corps personnel; servicewide information resources; servicewide information resource sharing and communication; support for force readiness; and life-long learning and a knowledge-centric culture.[25]

Dow Chemical

Dow Chemical Company has launched an information literacy program that will serve globally as part of its ongoing business improvement objectives. When employees spend as much as twenty hours a week looking for information, the program shows great promise with its purpose of establishing competencies and learning resources to help employees become effective users of information.[26] Starting with current research, a baseline of information literacy is being determined. These findings will be used to judge which aspects of information literacy are needed (e.g., which skills are most in demand, what enablers of information are in place and which ones are needed, and what are best practices). For a company that is already in the knowledge management business and does it well, this will be a step to providing greater information power for anyone at Dow who deals with information and knowledge.

A critical observation about information literacy and information power: both these programs emphasize the importance of sharing information, which is an additional trait of the truly professional information literate person.

SUMMARY

The Required Skills: A Review

Where will our skills come from in the future? Information literacy skills are shown in exhibit 11.1. There are people who claim that the Internet is a "killer" application for learning. In fact, "Tele-learning is making connections among persons and resources through communication technologies for learning-related purposes."[27] Admittedly, it's easily accessible and offers a great deal of power for delivering skills training. Combined with all the other methods in existence—and new ones that will surely come about—opportunities for keeping up with information literacy skills abound.

Integration is key to successful application of information literacy skills. This includes integrating with the requisite skills laid out in the preceding chapters, as well as ongoing activities throughout the book. Think of this demanding array of skills as a continuum. Each individual is somewhere along it,

Exhibit 11.1
Information Literacy Skills, A Summary

Information Literacy is the ability to

- recognize that accurate and complete information is the basis for intelligent decision making,
- recognize the need for information,
- formulate questions based on information needs,
- identify potential search strategies,
- develop successful search strategies,
- access sources of information including computer-based and other technologies,
- evaluate information,
- organize information for practical application,
- integrate new information into an existing body of knowledge,
- use information in critical thinking and problem solving.

Other Skills:

Communication, basic, electronic, diversity aspects
Thinking skills, strategy, critical, problem solving, decision making
Advanced thinking, creativity, innovation, risk taking
Computer literacy, basic system, operating system software, applications software, Internet, communication, administrative
Continuous learning
Whole person, whole life concept
Dealing with the future, business literacy, managing change

with a personal program to steadily move further along the scale towards competency, mastery if at all possible. It works best to concentrate on those aspects most needed at the time rather than be overwhelmed with trying to master all of them at once. The corollary to this is the tremendous personal satisfaction of knowing you're information literate and will continue to acquire the skills and knowledge you'll need for all life's purposes now and in the future. There's nothing like confidence and success to beget more of the same.

Part of the "wow" factor of work today is that when you put this set of skills together, they make a formidable, perhaps daunting, impression. Yet these are the skills "Employers in most industries—across every job category—are seeking."[28] It wasn't all that long ago that help wanted ads seeking these skills would be for engineers and computer scientists. But not anymore. The higher up the scale you are, the more gainful will be your employment.

Educational systems are doing their part to infuse kindergarten through adult education with information literacy skills. Instruction, technology, and opportunity to put the skills into action are becoming integral parts of school curricula. Yet there's more to it than this: "we must realize that even after we graduate, our education is never complete."[29] It's incumbent on each of us to accept full responsibility for continually refreshing our information literacy skills.

The Future of Information

Being information literate and maintaining information power will be a continuing requirement—because information will take on a larger role in the knowledge-driven market and workplaces and because technology and continued organizational and marketplace change will change the tools and the rules. The impact will continue to be on the processes of information, and the skills related to computer use, thinking, decision making, and creativity. We will become more digitized, yet there will remain an enormous amount of information that will not be available online and will be critical at times. There will be more information, and more technology to deal with it. It's up to the user to make sure that tools don't get in the way, but are instead put to good use. There will be, as previously noted, more diversity of information. Unfortunately, there will be continuing problems, and new ones to join them. Perhaps the greatest of these will be the chasm between the information-technology haves and have nots. Maintaining a balance in life and work will be more pronounced as the line between work, Web, and home becomes more fuzzy, completely disappearing for more and more of us. Information literacy will remain a challenge—and it will also be our ticket to success.

Yes, there is one skill for workplace success, and it's a big one, but worth every bit of the effort to master. Information power, through information literacy, will serve you well.

Notes

A note on references: The majority of periodical references were obtained online via the San Diego Public Library's General Business File ASAP.

PREFACE

1. Z. Ercegovac, and E. Yamasaki, "Information Literacy: Search Strategies, Tools and Resources," *ERIC Digest*, ED 4221178, May 1998.

2. T. Stewart, *Intellectual Capital* (New York: Doubleday, 1997), p. ix.

3. P. Drucker, "The New Society of Organizations," *Harvard Business Review*, September–October 1992, pp. 95–104.

CHAPTER 1

1. T. Stewart, "Knowledge, the Appreciating Commodity," *Fortune*, October 12, 1998, p. 199.

2. M. Moynihan, *The Coming American Renaissance* (New York: Simon and Schuster, 1996), p. 275.

3. M. Park, *InfoThink* (Lanham, MD: Scarecrow Press, 1998).

4. T. Stewart, *Intellectual Capital* (New York: Doubleday, 1997), p. x. See also his works in *Fortune* magazine on this and related topics.

5. L. Edvisson, *Intellectual Capital* (New York: HarperBusiness, 1997), p. 11.

6. "Measuring Intellectual Capital," David Skyme Associates, April 20, 2000, available at www.skyme.com/insights/24kmeas.htm, October 15, 2000.

7. D. Leonard-Barton, *Wellsprings of Knowledge* (Boston: Harvard Business School Press, 1995) p. xiii.

8. M. J. Earl and I. A. Scott, "What Is a Chief Knowledge Officer?" *Sloan Management Review* (winter 1999) p. 29.

9. J. C. Linder, "Today a Librarian, Tomorrow a Corporate Intelligence Professional," *Special Libraries* (summer 1992): pp. 142–44.

10. S. DiMattia and N. Oder, "Knowledge Management: Hope, Hype, or Harbinger?" *Library Journal*, September 15, 1997, pp. 33–35.

11. K. L. Spitzer, *Information Literacy* (Syracuse, NY: ERIC Clearinghouse on Information and Technology, 1998).

12. J. Stuller, "Chief of Corporate Smarts," *Training* (April 1998): p. 28.

13. M. Corcoran and R. Jones, "Chief Knowledge Officers? Perceptions, Pitfalls, and Potentials," *Information Outlook* (June 1997): p. 30.

14. M. Pedler, J. Burgoyne, and T. Boydell, *The Learning Company* (New York: McGraw-Hill, 1991), p. 1.

15. P. Senge, *The Fifth Discipline.* (New York: Doubleday, 1990).

16. J. C. Collins and J. I. Porras *Built to Last* (New York: HarperBusiness, 1994).

17. P. Drucker, *Post-Capitalist Society* (New York: HarperBusiness, 1993), p. 183.

18. "Marconi plc Chooses the Forum Corp. to Develop Global Learning Organization," *PR Newswire*, August 29, 2000, p. 9,229.

19. "Knowledge Workers in Demand through Year 2000," *Managing Office Technology* (January 1997), p. 22.

20. G. James, *Business Wisdom of the Electronic Elite* (New York: Random House, 1996).

21. J. Wilson, "Another San Jose Finds Its Way to Software Fame," *Financial Times* (January 26, 2000): p. 8.

22. M. R. Nelson, "We Have the Information You Want, But Getting It Will Cost You," *Crossroads*, ACM Electronic Publication at info.acm.org/crossroads/xrds 1–1/nmelson.html, January 23, 1999.

23. R. Tetzeli, "Surviving Information Overload," *Fortune*, July 11, 1994, pp. 60–65. See also "Glued to the Screen," Reuters Studies, December 1997, available at about.reuters.com/rbb/research/addict.htm, and P. Lymay and H. R. Varian, "How Much Information is Enough?" available at www.sims.berkeley.edu/how-much-info, 2000.

24. D. Clark, "Managing the Mountain," *The Wall Street Journal*, June 21, 1999, p. R4.

25. P. Pascarella, "Harnessing Knowledge," *Management Review* (October 1997): p. 37.

26. C. Handy, *The Age of Unreason* (Boston: Harvard Business School Press, 1989), p. 51.

27. S. Zuboff,. *In the Age of the Smart Machine* (New York: Basic Books, 1994).

28. R. N. Bellah, et al., *Habits of the Heart* (New York: Harper and Row, 1985).

29. R. Crawford, *In the Era of Human Capital.* (New York: Harper Business, 1991). p. 10.

30. S. Davis, and B. Davidson, *2020 Vision* (New York: Simon & Schuster, 1991), p. 12.

31. D. Leonard-Barton, *Wellsprings of Knowledge* (Boston: Harvard Business School Press, 1995).

32. U.S. Department of Commerce, *A Framework for Global Electronic Commerce.* (Washington, D.C.: U.S. Department of Commerce, May 28, 1999), chapter 7, p. 3. Source: www.ecommerce.gov/executiv.htm

33. D. R. Tobin, *Re-Educating the Corporation* (Essex Junction, VT: Omneo, 1993), p. 21.

34. E. J. Kazlauskas, "Use of Electronic Information Systems—Another Perspective," ERIC Document, ED 363 340, 1993, p. 3.

35. E. Hayes and J. Johnson, "Knowledge Workers Command Premium Pay," *Los Angeles Business Journal* (September 7, 1998): p. 1.

36. "Facts on Illiteracy in America," January 10, 1997, available at http://indian-river.fl.us/living/services/als/facts.html.

37. *Training* magazine, October 2000.

38. "Workweek Column: Skills Sought," *The Wall Street Journal*, May 11, 1999, p. A1.

39. C. Carr, *Smart Training* (New York: McGraw-Hill, 1992).

40. "Information Power," American Library Association, available at www.ala.org/aasi/ip-nine.html, November 16, 1998.

41. C. S. Doyle, *Information Literacy in an Information Society* (Syracuse, NY: ERIC Clearinghouse, 1994), p. 2.

42. "Information Power," *American Library Association*, available at www.ala.org/aasl/ip–nine.html, November 16, 1988.

CHAPTER 2

1. R. J. Todd et al., "The Power of Information Literacy," ERIC Document, ED 354 916, July 1992, abstract.

2. E. Plotnick "Information Literacy," *ERIC Digest*, ED427777, February 1999.

3. P. S. Breivik, *Student Learning in the Information Age* (Phoenix: Oryx Press, 1998), p. 3.

4. C. S. Doyle, *Information Literacy in an Information Society* (Syracuse: Clearinghouse on Information and Technology, June 1994), p. 3.

5. P. S. Breivik, "Education in the Information Age," *Information Literacy: Developing Students as Independent Learners* (summer 1992): p. 6.

6. M. Eisenberb and B. Berkowitz, "The Big6 (tm) Skills Information Problem Solving Approach," www.big6.com, February 25, 2000.

7. P. Iannuzzi, C. T. Mangrum, and S. S. Strichart, *Teaching Information Literacy Skills* (Boston: Allyn and Bacon, 1997), p. 147.

8. "Information Seeking and Retrieval," University of Buffalo, available at www.sils.buffalo.edu/faculty/tu/Lis566b/566b1/sld001.htm, no date.

9. E. M. Beck, ed., *Familiar Quotations* (Boston: Little, Brown & Co., 1980), p. 83 (as quoted in *Apology*).

10. L. Brenner "Establishing a Sales Relationship," www.svobodamag.com/features/1110estab.html, October 15, 2000.

11. L. Roth, "Educating the Cut and Paste Generation," *The Library Journal*, November 1, 1999, p. 42.

CHAPTER 3

1. P. Sandwith, "Building Quality into Communications," *Training and Development* (January 1994): p. 55.

2. T. W. Goad, Personal experience while attending a reading tutor workshop.

3. R. Jana, "Doing a Double Take—IT Professionals Who Work Abroad Often Need to Re-examine Their Communication Skills, Business Practices—and Retool," *InfoWorld*, February 14, 2000, p. 100.

4. J. Diamond, *Guns, Germs, and Steel* (New York: W. W. Norton, 1997), p. 27.

5. T. W. Goad, Personal experience from conversation with a U.S. professor who was teaching overseas.

6. "Write On!" *HRFocus* (August 1993): p. 94.

7. "An Added Joy of E-mail: Fewer Face-to-Face Meetings," *Wall Street Journal*, July 14, 1998, p. A1.

8. B. Cole-Gomolski, "Chat Rooms Move into Boardrooms," *Computer World* (November 1997): p. 1. See also *Forbes*, December 15, 1997, pp. 46–47 for other examples.

9. D. Tapscott, *Growing up Digital* (New York: McGraw-Hill, 1998).

10. K. Zetter and H. McCracken, "How to Stop Searching and Start Finding," *PC World* (September 2000): p. 129.

11. D. Keating, "Tips and Tricks for Finding Information on the Internet," *Knight-Ridder/Tribune News Service*, January 21, 1998, news release.

12. J. December, *The World Wide Web 1997* (Indianapolis, IN: Sams.net, 1997).

13. C. M. Brown, "Refining Your Internet Searches," *Black Enterprise* (February 2000): p. 73.

CHAPTER 4

1. B. Pascarella, "The Secret of Turning Thinking into Action," *Management Review* (May 1997): p. 38.

2. J. M. Iedtka, "Everything I Need to Know about Strategy I Learned at the National Zoo," *Journal of Business Strategy* (January–February, 1997): pp. 8–11.

3. J. A. Byrne, "Strategic Planning," *Business Week*, August 26, 1996, p. 46.

4. C. Loehle, *Thinking Strategically* (Cambridge: Cambridge Press, 1996), p. 1.

5. O. Harari, "Catapult Your Strategy over Conventional Wisdom," *Management Review* (October 1997): p. 23.

6. Byrne, "Strategic Planning," p. 46.

7. F. F. Pritchard, "Negotiating and Using Frames to Develop Specific Critical Thinking and Writing Skills." (paper presented at the annual meeting of the Center for Critical Thinking at Sonoma State University California, August 1993).

8. Q. Spitzer and R. Evans. *Heads You Win* (New York: Simon and Schuster, 1997), p. 11.

9. "The Definition of Critical Thinking" at http://www.sonoma.edu/cthink/k12library/definect.nclk, 1996.

10. W. W. Reeves, *Cognition and Complexity* (Lanham, MD: Scarecrow Press, 1996), pp. 57–58.

11. I. I. Mitroff, and H. A. Linstone, *The Unbounded Mind* (New York: Oxford University Press, 1993).

12. R. Kaufman, *Identifying and Solving Problems*, 3rd ed. (San Diego: University Associates, 1982), p. iii.

13. A. Rjan, et al., "Take It from the Top," *People Management*, October 23, 1997.

14. C. Tauhert, "Crossing Chasms: Can CIOs Become CEOs?" *Insurance and Technology* (July 1997).

15. A. C. Martinez, "Transforming the Legacy of Sears," *Strategy and Leadership* (July–August 1997).

16. P. Proctor, "New Strategy Focus Drives Boeing Transformation," *Aviation Week and Space Technology*, April 28, 1997.

17. C. A. Hale, *The Leading Edge* (New York: Irwin, 1996).

18. T. Pollock, "To Solve a Problem, Ask the Right Questions," *Supervision* (May 1999): pp. 18–20.

19. L. R. Miller. "Better Ways to Think and Communicate," *Association Management* (December 1997): pp. 71–73.

20. V.S.L. Tan, "Develop Strategic Thinking Skills," *New Straits Times*, April 25, 2000.

21. D. Wilson, "Critical Thinking," *Plant Engineering* (February 1998): p. 31.

22. Ibid., p. 32.

23. S. D. Brookfield, *Developing Critical Thinkers* (San Francisco: Jossey-Bass, 1987), pp. 116–17.

24. A. Quesada, and S. L. Summers, "Literacy in the Cyberage," *Technology and Learning* (January 1998): p. 30.

25. Kaufman, "Identfying," p. 96.

26. W. B. Rouse, "Technology for Strategic Thinking" at http://ess-advisors.com/column9. htm, no date.

27. L. J. Thompson, *Habits of the Mind* (Lanham, MD: University Press of America, 1995), pp. 130–31.

CHAPTER 5

1. W. Bennis, "Cultivating Creative Genius," *Industry Week*, August 18, 1997, p. 84.

2. P. Thorne, *Organizating Genius* (Oxford: Blackwell Publishing, 1992), p. 9.

3. M. Csikszentmihalyi, *Creativity* (New York: HarperCollins, 1996), p. 1

4. J. M. Higgins, Innovate or Evaporate," *The Futurist*, (September–October 1995): pp. 42–48.

5. D. J. Boorstin, *The Discoverers*. (New York: Random House, 1983), p. xv.

6. "Employers Learn the Benefits of Lateral Thinking," *Personnel Journal* (August 1994): p. 44.

7. J. C. Collins, and J. I. Porras, *Built to Last*. (New York: Harper Business, 1994).

8. "Beyond Creative Thinking," *Working Age* (January–February 1995).

9. See Collins and Porras for more on Hewlett-Packard.

10. Bennis, "Cultivating Creative Genius," p. 84.

11. E. deBono, *Lateral Thinking* (New York: Harper and Row, 1970), p. 11.

12. Ibid., p. 10.

13. N. Hermann, "Brain Dominance Theory," in R. L. Craig, ed., *Training and Development Handbook, 3rd Ed.* (New York: McGraw-Hill, 1987), pp. 349–59.

14. G. M. McEvoy, "Organizational Change and Outdoor Management Education." *Human Resource Management* (Summer 1997), pp. 235–250.

15. A. Classe, "The Great Outdoors," *Computing*, November 5, 1992, pp. 32–33.

16. L. Jacquette, "Red Lion Builds Teamwork with Outdoor Training," *Hotel and Motel Management* (April 8, 1991): pp. 2–3.

17. "Company Profile," at http://www.cot.com.au/profile.htm., Computer Outdoor Training Corporation, no date.

18. J. Sample, and R. Hylton, "Falling off a Log—and Landing in Court," *Training* (May 1996): pp. 66–70.

19. A. Hills, "African Adventure for Executives," *The Financial Times*, September 3, 1995, p. 11.

20. "Intelligent Risk Taking," at http://www.barnesconti/programs/RT.html, 1995.

21. "Risk Taking," at http://pentium.intel.com/intel/oppty/why/values/risk.htm, 1998.

22. E. Ramstad, "How Trilogy Software Trains Its Raw Recruits to Be Risk Takers," *The Wall Street Journal.* September 21, 1998, p. A1.

23. N. A. Fontenot, "Effects of Training in Creativity and Creative Problem Finding upon Business People," *The Journal of Social Psychology* (February 1993), pp. 11–22.

24. "Industry Report 2000," *Training* (October 2000).

25. H. Schultz, and D. J. Young, *Pour Your Heart into It* (New York: Hyperion, 1997), p. 1.

26. J. P. Kotter, *Matushita Leadership* (New York: The Free Press, 1997).

27. C. M. Solomon, "Creativity Training," *Personnel Journal* (May 1995): pp. 65–71.

28. J. King, "Supr CIOs," *ComputerWorld*, August 4, 1997, pp. 1, 24.

29. A. G. Robinson, and S. Stern, *Corporate Creativity* (San Francisco: Barrett-Koehler, 1997).

30. J. W. Holt, J. Stannell, and M. Field, *Celebrate Your Mistakes* (Chicago: Irwin, 1996).

31. A. K. Gupta, and A. Singhal, "Managing Human Resources for Innovation and Creativity," *Research Technology Management* (May–June 1993): pp. 41–48.

32. Solomon "Creativity Traninting," p. 66.

33. J. J Kao, The Art and Discipline of Business Creativity," *Strategy and Leadership* (July–August 1997): pp. 6–11.

34. J. N. Shields, "Six Tips for Generating Group Creativity," *Association Management* (February 1997): p. 24.

35. R. von Oech, *A Whack on the Side of the Head* (New York: Warner Books, 1983), p. 55.

36. Csikszentmihalyi, *Creativity*.

37. H. Lancaster, "Managing Your Career," *The Wall Street Journal*, September 16, 1997, p. B1.

38. E. de Bono, *de Bono's Thinking Course, rev. ed.* (New York: Facts on File, 1994), p. 23.

39. M. Michalko, *Thinkertoys* (Berkeley, CA: Ten Speed Press, 1991).

40. S. Parnes, *The Magic of Your Mind*. (Buffalo, NY: The Creative Education Foundation, 1981). p. 97.

41. K. Albrecht, *Brain Power* (Englewood Cliffs, NJ: Prentice-Hall, 1980), p. 231.

42. "Self-improvement Online's Creativity Training," available at www.selfgrowth.com/creativity.html, no date.

43. S. G. Bulruille, ed,. "Discovering and Developing Creativity," The American Society for Training and Development *Info-Line*, 1989, p. 5.

CHAPTER 6

1. *The Wall Street Journal*, April 27, 1999, p. A1.

2. G. Koretz, "The Payoff from Computer Skills," *Business Week*. November 3, 1997, p. 30.

3. L. J. Bassi, and M. E. Van Buren, "The 1998 ASTD State of the Industry Report," *Training and Development* (January 1998): pp. 21–43.

4. K. Mazzoni, "California's Schools Need More Tech Training," *Sacramento Business Journal*, September 1, 2000, p. 47.

5. S. Davis, and J. Botkin, *The Monster under the Bed* (New York: Simon and Schuster, 1994).

6. C. C. Ashley, "Training for Software Success," *Bests Review—Life Health Insurance Edition*. October 1997, p. 87.

7. M. M. Kennedy, "Computer Incompetents, Beware," *Across the Board* (October 1998): p. 51.

8. S. Evans, "Everything's Up-to-Date at Kelly," *Modern Office Technology* (November 1998), p. 56–57.

9. P. Gilster, *Digital Literacy* (New York: John Wiley and Sons, 1997).

10. H. E. Allerton, "Hard Drive," *Training and Development* (August 2000), p. 18.

11. P. Davis, "What Computer Skills Do Employees Expect from Recent College Graduages," *T.H.E. Journal* (September 1997): pp. 74–78.

12. J. D. Thomerson, "Applied Educational Computing: Putting Skills to Practice," Eric Publication, ED 415 219, 1998.

13. B. Ziegler, "On Their Own," *The Wall Street Journal*, June 27, 1994, p. R14.

14. I. H. Bernstein, and P. Havig., *Computer Literacy* (Thousand Oaks, CA: Sage Publications, 1999).

15. J. Pemberton, and A. Robson, "The Spreadsheet—Just Another Filing Cabinet?" *Management Decision*. (December 1995): pp. 30–35.

16. S. C. Galbreath, J. A. Bocker, and B. C. Adams, "Sharpen Spreadsheet Skills," *Journal of Accountancy* (October 1998), pp. 39–46.

17. *The Learning Space Foundation*, available at: www.learningspace.org:88/instruct/literacy/definition.htm., January 14, 2000.

18. M. A. Hepburn, "Media Literacy," *The Clearing House*, (July–August 1999): pp. 352–57.

19. A. Quesada, and S. L. Summers, "Literacy in the Cyberage," *Technology and Learning* (January 1998): pp 30–36.

20. C. Seiter, "Lotus Notes Release 5," *Macworld* (May 2000): p. 42.

21. R. D. Putnam, *Bowling Alone* (New York: Simon and Schuster, 2000).

22. D. Tapscott, *Growing up Digital* (New York: McGraw-Hill, 1998).

23. S. Birkerts. *The Gutenberg Elegies* (New York: Fawcett Columbine, 1994).

24. B. Henderson, ed., *Minutes of the Lead Pencil Club* (New York: Pushcart Press, 1996), p. 233.

25. P.G.W. Keen, *Shaping the Future* (Boston: Harvard University Press, 1991).

26. A. Ehrenshaft, "The User Group Turns East Tennessee Gal into a PC Guru," *InfoWorld*, July 27, 1992, p. 49.

27. M. Walsh, "For Executives, a New Chain of Commands," *Crain's New York Business*, August 4, 1997, p. 15.

CHAPTER 7

1. S. Hays, "Labor-Management Partnerships Boost Training," *Workforce* (April 1999): p. 80.

2. S. L. Stokes, "Blueprint for Business Literacy," *Information Systems Management* (spring 1993): p. 73.

3. L. Wenzel, "Workplace Literacy at High Liner Foods," avaliable at www.nald.ca/naldnews/99summer/highline.htm, no date.

4. "Ohio State University Developing Unique Program That Links Businesses, Spanish Majors," available at www.state.oh.us/obes/ossuspanish.htm, no date; "The Ohio Workforce Excellence Awards," available at www.obes.org/award.htm, no date.

5. "Sacramento Area Literacy Coalition," available at www.interaptiv.com/salc/directory/index.cfm, no date.

6. "Workplace Literacy Survey," available at www.state.de.us/dedo/publicaitons/literacy/tsld007, no date.

7. "Palm Beach County Literacy Coalition," available at www.gopbi.com/community/groups/literacy, no date.

8. "Workplace Literacy," Michigan State University, available at www.msu.edu/lvcalc/workplace.html, no date.

9. S. Hays, "Basic Skills Training 101," *Workforce* (April 1999): p. 76.

10. K. Tyler, "Tips for Structuring Workplace Literacy Programs," *HRMagazine* (October 1996): pp. 112–17.

11. S. P. Robbins, *Management*, 4th ed., (Englewood Cliffs, NJ: Prentice-Hall, 1994). p. G-3.

12. Ibid., p. G8.

13. S. Bing, "Yes, You Can Survive Career Death," *Fortune*, October 28, 1996, p. 65.

14. "Why Layoffs Are Getting Lighter," *Fortune*, March 2, 1998, p. 224.

15. C. Harris, "Learning in Action," *The Academy of Management Executive* (August 2000): p. 145.

16. D. James, "Regional Managers and the Push toward Cultural Literacy," *Business Review Weekly*, February 2, 1998, p. 74.

17. R. H. Rosen, "In Growing Global Economy, Boost Cultural Literacy," *ComputerWorld*, April 24, 2000, p. 35.

18. D. Stamps, "English as a Second Priority," *Training* (February 1998): p. 53–58.

19. Ibid.

20. "Diversity and Workplace Literacy," Clackamas College, available at webster. clakamas.cc.or.us/instruct/ctds/diversit.htm, no date.

21. K. Fay, "Workplace Literacy," College of DuPage, available at www.cod.edu/BPIWork-Lit.htm, no date.

22. "Workplace Testing and Monitoring," *Management Review.* (October 1998), p. 31.

23. B. Costello, "Teach for Tomorrow Aims at Math and Literacy", *Providence Business News,* October 11, 1999, p. 4.

24. H. H. Wehmeier, "The Business of Science Literacy," *Industry Week,* October 7, 1996, p. 56.

25. J. Baggot, "Too Much Phun Can Be Bad for You," *New Scientist,* March 25, 1995, p. 47.

26. A. Michaels, "Stepping up the Corporate Ladder," *Manage* (July 1994): p. 16–17.

27. Business Literacy 2000. Available at www.readersindex.com/b2000/home.html, no date.

28. R. McGarvey, "EQ and You," *Kiwanis* (February 1999): p. 35.

29. M. N. Martinez, "The Smarts That Count," *HRMagazine* (November 1997): p. 72.

30. K. Tauber, "Corporate Awareness of EQ Will Transform Workplace," *Houston Business Journal,* June 16, 2000, p. 48.

31. J. E. Smigla, and G. Pastaria, "Emotional Intelligence," *The CPA Journal* (June 2000): p. 60.

32. D. Ryback, *Putting Emotional Intelligence to Work* (Boston: Butterworth-Heinemann, 1998).

33. H. Weisinger, *Emotional Intelligence at Work.* (San Francisco: Jossey-Bass, 1998), p. xvii.

34. D. Goleman, *Working with Emotional Intelligence* (New York: Bantam, 1998), p. 3.

35. R. K. Cooper and A. Sawaf, *Executive EQ* (New York: Grosset/Putnam, 1996): p. xxvii.

36. Martinez, "Smarts," p. 75.

37. E. Mendes, "Developing Emotional Intelligence in Organizations" (flyer appearing in June 1999 issue of *Training Trends*).

38. L. Murray, "High Performance Teaming Basis of EQ vs. IQ Training," *Business First-Columbus,* March 10, 2000, p. 39.

39. J. Case, *Open-Book Management.* (New York: Harper Business, 1995).

CHAPTER 8

1. J. W. Verity, "The Next Step: Reengineer the Classroom," *Business Week,* February 28, 1994, p. 88.

2. J. P. Kotter, *The New Rules* (New York: The Free Press, 1995), p. 5.

3. J. Moad, "Front-Office Payoff," *PC Week,* December 8, 1997, p. 85.

4. S. Davis, and J. Botkin, *The Monster under the Bed* (New York: Simon and Schuster, 1994): p. 16.

5. *Training,* October 2000 (issue dedicated to results of nineteenth annual industry training survey).

6. A. H. Maslow, *Motivation and Personality*, 2nd ed. (New York: Harper and Row, 1970).

7. T. W. Goad, *The First-Time Trainer* (New York: AMACOM, 1997), p. 46.

8. Bloom's Taxonomy, available at numerous online sites, including weber.u.washington.edu/~drumme/guides/bloom.html, no date.

9. "Learning Styles," available at http://rick.dgbt.doc.ca/~jean/english/4types.htm, October 1966.

10. H. Gardner, *Frames of Mind* (New York: Basic Books, 1983): p. x.

11. H. Gardner, *Intelligence Reframed* (New York: Basic Books, 1999): p. 33.

12. T. Armstrong, *7 Kinds of Smart* (New York: Plume, 1993)

13. T. Brokaw, *The Greatest Generation* (New York: Random House, 1998).

14. A. Wellner, "Get Ready for Generation Next," *Training* (February 1999): p. 42.

15. Ibid., p. 43.

16. M. Dolliver, "Unlike the Young, the Old Don't Yet Know Everything," *ADWeek Eastern Edition*, August 7, 2000, p. 52.

17. M. Prensky, "Bankers Trust," *HR Focus* (September 1998): p. 11.

18. P. J. Guglielmino, and R. G. Murdick, "Self-Directed Learning." *SAM Advanced Management Journal* (summer 1997): p. 10.

19. R. Zemke, "In Search of Self-Directed Learners," *Training* (May 1998), p. 60.

20. Guglielmino and Murdick, "Self-Directed Learning," p. 11

21. J. Varlejs, "On Their Own," *Library Quarterly* (April 1999): p. 173.

22. T. G. Hatcher, "An Interview with Malcolm Knowles," *Training and Development* (February 1997): p. 37.

23. T. G. Hatcher, The Ins and Outs of Self-Directed Learning," *Training and Development* (February 1997): p. 34.

24. J. Martorana, "More Companies Using Interactive Games to Train Staff," *LI Business News*. July 20, 1998, p. 11.

25. J. Gordon, "Outsourcing on the Web," *Training* (June 1998): p. 98.

26. C. Miles, "Training for Tomorrow's Technologies," *Plant Engineering* (March 1997): p. 112.

27. R. M. Smith, *Learning How to Learn* (Chicago: Follett, 1982).

28. L. Graff, "A New Transformation in the World of Work," *On the Horizon*, available at http://sunsite.unc.edu/horizon/pastissues/voll3no2/social.html, December–January 1995–1996.

29. D. Martin, "How to Be a Successful Student," College of Marin, available at www.mrin.cc.ca.us/don/~Study/3learning.html, no date.

30. J. S. Hile, "Getting the Lead Out," *Training and Development* (April 1992): p. 55–58.

31. N. M. Dixon, "The Hallways of Learning," *Organizational Dynamics* (spring 1997): pp. 23–34.

32. C. Frazier, "Log on to Learn," *Time Digital* (December 2000), pp. 54–57.

33. J. Gordon, "Learning How to Learn," *Training* (May 1990): p. 54.

34. K. D. Ryan and D. K. Oestrech, *Driving Fear out of the Workplace*, 2nd ed. (San Francisco: Jossey-Bass, 1998), p. xx.

CHAPTER 9

1. J. Greer, "Increasingly More Companies Embrace Private Networks," *Memphis Business Journal*, April 21, 2000, p. 52.

2. J. Bell, "Worldwide Sharing," *Business First Columbus*, July 28, 2000, p. 15.

3. J. Hutchens, "The U. S. Postal Service Delivers an Innovative HR Strategy," *Workforce* (October 2000): p. 116.

4. P. Troiano, "Intranet Booms for Midsize Companies," *Management Review* (February 1999): p. 8.

5. M. A. Hughes, "Online Documentation in Reference-Based Instruction," *Technical Communication* (February 1997): p. 58.

6. F. Reynolds, "Computer Documentation Can Be a Blessing, Albeit It Mixed at Times," *Journal of Commerce and Commercial*, October 29, 1997, p. 2C.

7. D. Shean, "Putting an Embedded System on the Internet," *EDN*, September 17, 1997, p. 37.

8. E. Foster, "Which Suits Your Technical Manual Fancy: Print or Online Documentation," *InfoWorld*, September 1, 1997, p. 68.

9. E. Foster, "When Buying Technical Wares, Some Want Vendors to Throw the Book at Them," *InfoWorld*, June 16, 1997, p. 106.

10. G. Wilburn, "A Document in Hand Is Worth Two Online," *Computing Canada*, April 6, 1998, p. 9.

11. T. Mayor, "Galileo Makes Manuals Minus the Paper," *PC Week*, March 17, 1997, p. 37.

12. Hughes, "Online Documentation," p. 58.

13. R. S. Boynton, "You Say You Want an e-book Revolution?" *Time Digital* (December 2000): p. 39.

14. C. K. Oka, "NetLibrary.Com," *Library Journal*, May 1, 2000, p. 161.

15. J. Rapoza, "HTML Authoring Improves on Three Fronts," *PC Week*, January 24, 2000, p. 27.

16. M. Avery, "Gasp Will Not Leave You Breathless," *InfoWorld*, June 14, 1999, p. 37.

17. L. Pender, "Primus Online Help with SolutionSeries WebPack," *PC Week*, March 22, 1999, p. 123.

18. S. Carliner, "Designing Wizards," *Training and Development* (July 1998): p. 62.

19. "Small Firms Get Online Help," *National Underwriter Property and Casualty-Risk and Benefits Management*, May 24, 1999, p. 36.

20. J. Madden, "Cisco Speeds Support with Better Online Help," *PC Week*, January 17, 2000, p. 3.

21. C. Venezia, "A Simpler Way to the Web," *PC Magazine*, January 18, 2000, p. 47.

22. "ScrapWare Offering Online Help," *American Metal Market*, February 25, 2000, p. 10.

23. See, for example, www.lssi.com/virtual and www.sanford.edu/staff/infocenter.liveref.html.

24. *American Heritage Dictionary*, 3rd ed. (New York: Houghton Mifflin, 1992).

25. G. Junion-Metz, "Teacher Knows Best," *School Library Journal* (May 2000): p. 37.

26. E. Callaway, "Online Corporate Libraries Stack Up," *PC Week*, January 26, 1998, p. 80.

27. K. Commings, "Library Access via Corporate Intranets," *Computers in Libraries* (March 1997): p. 26.

28. J. L. Buntzen, "Next Generation Library," *Chips* (fall 2000): pp. 32–34.

29. K. Banerjee, "Is Data Mining Right for Your Library?" *Computers in Libraries* (November 1998): p. 28.

30. "IBM DB2 Intelligent Miner for Data," IBM software, available at www-4.ibm.com/software/data/iminer/fordata.html, no date.

31. "CASPR's LibraryCom Brings Libraries Online," *Computers in Libraries* (April 1999): p. 12.

32. M. Schuyler, "The Virtual Popsicle," *Computers in Libraries* (February 1998): p. 28.

33. D. Keating, "Tips and Tricks for Finding Information on the Internet," *Knight-Ridder/Tribune News Service*, January 21, 1998, news release.

34. D. Gladstone, "Searching for Data," *Home Office Computing* (August 1997): p. 47.

35. M. L. Trencher, "Expert Systems Come of Age to Help Drive Insurers' Business," *National Underwriter Property and Casualty-Risk and Benefits Management*. August 24, 1998, p. 3.

36. A. A. Qureshi, J. K. Shim, and J. G. Seigel, "Artificial Intelligence in Accounting and Business," *The National Public Accountant* (September 1998): p. 13.

37. T. W. Goad, *The Handbook of HRD Technology* (Amherst, MA: HRD Press, 1993).

38. "Expert-System Module Assists Hydraulic Designs," *Hydraulics and Pneumatics* (March 1998): p. 22.

39. M. J. Blotzer, "Expert Advice from OSHA Advisors," *Occupational Hazzards* (December 1998): p. 53.

40. M. K. Khan, "Development of an Expert System for Implementation of ISO 9000 Quality Systems," *Total Quality Management* (January 1999): p. 47.

41. A. Stewart, "Expert System Tames Alaska Network," *Communication News* (January 1999): p. 37.

42. B. Talley, "World Tool Kit," *InfoWorld*, October 28, 1996, p. 97.

43. I. Liddle, and S. Reilly, "Expert Systems Offer Precise Analysis, Diagnosis of Mill Rotating Machinery," *Pulp and Paper* (February 1993): p. 53.

44. "ACQUIRE," Acquired Intelligence, available at www.aiinc.ca, no date.

45. "The Central Laboratory for Agricultural Export Systems," available at potato.claes.sci.org, January 4, 1999.

46. S. E. Malcolm, "Where EPSS Will Go from Here," *Training* (March 1998): p. 64.

47. G. Benson, "A New Look at EPSS," *Training and Development*. (January 1997): p. 48.

48. S. Cohen, "EPSS to Go," *Training and Development*. (March 1998): p. 54.

49. R. Ganzel, "Getting a Grip on the Digital Future," *Training*. (February 1998): p. 62.

50. P. J. Longman, "The Janitor Stole My Job," *U.S. News and World Report*, December 1, 1997, p. 50.

51. A. Zolper, "New Technologies for Credit Training and Information Management," *Commercial Lending Review* (winter 1996): p. 6.

52. S. Caudron, "Your Learning Technology Primer," *Personnel Journal* (June 1996): p. 120.

53. J. J. Ockerman, L. J. Najjar, and J. C. Thompson. "FAST." *Computers in Industry*. (January 1999): p. 53.

54. E. Foster, "Training When You Need It," *InfoWorld*, February 24, 1997, p. 51.

55. K. Cole, O. Fischer, and P. Saltzman, "Just-in-Time Knowledge Delivery," *Communications of the ACM* (July 1997): p. 49.

56. T. Mayor, "Doing Equals Learning," *CIO*, January 15, 1996, p. 52.

57. D. Bedell, "Doorways to the Net," *San Diego Union-Tribune*, November 7, 2000, p. 6.

CHAPTER 10

1. L. Secretan, "Integration, Not Balance," *Industry Week*, June 12, 2000, p. 29.

2. L. Zuckerman, "Whistling While We Work," *U.S. News and World Report*, January 24, 2000, p. 29.

3. B. Moses, "The Busyness Trap," *Training* (November 1998): p. 38.

4. "HeartMath Technology in Business," *Research Overview*, January 19, 1999, available at http://www.heartmath.org/ro/hro/hbiz1.html.

5. "Stress in the Workplace," *Psychology at Work*. available at http/helping.apa.org.work/stress5.html, 1997.

6. "An Information Frankenstein," available at http://inst.augie.edu/~asmith/frankenstein.html, no date.

7. K. Ballint, "An Age of Change," CumputerLink, supplement to *The San Diego Union-Tribune* June 1, 1999, p. 6.

8. R. D. Putnam, *Bowling Alone* (New York: Simon abd Schuster, 2000).

9. S. C. Gwynne, "Is My Aura Showing" *Time*, October 20, 1997, p. 4.

10. K. R. Pelletier, *Mind as Healer, Mind as Slayer* (New York: Dell, 1977) p. 301.

11. "Mission and Goals," *About AWLP*, available at http://www.awlp.org/about/index.htm, 1998.

12. "Welcome to F.W.I," *Families and Work Institute*, available at http://www.familiesandwork.org/index.html, no date.

13. J. K. Peters, *Why Mothers Work* (Reading, MA: Addison-Wesley, 1997), p. xiii.

14. A. Levine, and T. L. Pittinsky, *Working Fathers* (Reading, MA: Addison-Wesley, 1997) pp. 227, 234.

15. S. Hegelsen, *Everyday Revolutionaries* (New York: Doubleday, 1998) pp. 5, 15.

16. A. R. Hochschild, *Time Bind* (New York: Metropolitan, 1997), p. 45.

17. P. Hersch, *A Tribe Apart.* (New York: Fawcett, 1998), p. 19.

18. R. N. Bella, et al., *Habits of the Heart* (New York: Harper and Row, 1985), pp. 291, 282.

19. J. Burne, "Harnessing the Power of Touch," *Financial Times*, January 15, 2000, p. 11.

20. K. C. Cash and G. R. Gray, "A Framework for Accommodating Religion and Spirituality in the Workplace," *The Academy of Management Journal* (August 2000): p. 124.

21. I. I. Mitroff, and E. A. Denton, "A Study of Spirituality in the Workplace," *Sloan Management Review* (summer 1999): p. 83.

22. J. J. Salapek, "For God and Company," *Training and Development* (March 2000): p. 77.

23. "Health Promotion," *YWCA Charleston, W.V.*, available at http://www.ywcachaswv.org/health.htm, no date.

24. "C. Everett Koop National Health Award Winners Announced," *Lilly Company News*, available at http://www.lily.com/company/news/981016.html, 1999.

25. "Workers Go Online in Search of Health and Fitness Tips," *The Wall Street Journal*, March 23, 1999, p. A1.

26. F. W. Clifford and R. J. Diaz, "Wellness on Tap at Coors," *Financial Executive* (March–April 1995): p. 83.

27. G. Flynn, "Companies Make Wellness Work," *Personnel Journal* (February 1995): p. 63.

28. "Fiscal Fitness," *Indiana Business Magazine* (July 1998): p. 17.

29. J. Fox, "Conquer Information Anxiety," *Amtrak Express* (March–April 1995): p. 10.

30. "Workers Go Online in Search of Fitness Tips," p. A1

31. H. E. Allerton, "Whack!" *Training and Development* (October 2000): p. 88.

32. "Every Day's a Party," *Credit Union Journal*, October 2, 2000, p. 18.

33. C. A. Sturken, "Fast Relief for Job Stress," *Meetings and Conventions* (September 2000): p. 21.

34. J. Williams, "Meditating on the Job," *Business Courier Serving Cincinnati-Northern Kentucky*, June 9, 2000, p. 33.

35. R. Dreyfack, "Treasure Chest," *Supervision* (June 2000): p. 20.

36. Fox, "Conquer Information Anxiety," p. 36.

37. Ibid., p. 12.

38. S. R. Covey, A. R. Merrill, and R. R. Merrill, *First Things First* (New York: Fireside, 1994).

39. "Knowledge Is Money," *Journal of Business Strategy* (November 1999): p. 4.

40. A. Pollak, "Time Management," ERIC Document, ED 368 976, 1994.

41. "Executive Moms," *Forbes*, July 6, 1998, p. 20.

42. K. Baron, "Tips on How to Not Waste Time," *Forbes*, October 16, 2000, p. 158.

43. J. C. Collins, and J. I. Porras, *Built to Last* (New York: Harper Business, 1994).

44. J. H. Want, *Managing Radical Change* (New York: John Wiley, 1995), p. xi.

45. J. While, "Regain Control over Technological Tools and Save Your Sanity," *The Business Journal*, September 1, 2000, p. 43.

46. A. Maitland, "The Elusive Art of Getting a Life," *Financial Times*, January 13, 2000, p. 24.

CHAPTER 11

1. P. F. Drucker, "Infoliteracy," *Forbes*, August 29, 1994, p. S104.

2. M. A. Verespej, "A Workforce Revolution?" *Industry Week*, August 21, 1995, p. 21.

3. J. Hope, and T. Hope, *Competing in the Third Wave*. (Boston: Harvard University Press, 1997), p. 65.

4. K. D. Ryan, and D. K. Oestreich, *Driving Fear out of the Workplace*, 2nd ed. (San Francisco: Jossey-Bass, 1998).

5. G.T.T. Molitor, "Trends and Forecasts for the New Millennium," *The Futurist* (August–September 1998): p. 55.

6. U.S. Department of Commerce, *A Framework for Global Electronic Commerce* (Washington, D.C.: U.S. Department of Commerce, May 28, 1999). Chapter 7, p. 1. www.ecommerce.gov/executiv.htm

7. "Collaborative Virtual Workspace," avaliable at http://cvw.mitre.org/anews.html, April 13, 1999.

8. N. Negroponte, *Being Digital* (New York: Vintage Books, 1995), p. 228.

9. P. Pascarella, "Harnessing Knowledge," *Management Review* (October 1997): p. 38.

10. "Knowledge Workers in Demand through Year 2000," *Managing Office Technology* (January 1997): p. 22.

11. U. S. Department of Commerce, A Framework," p. 1.

12. P. A. McGuire, "Wanted: Workers with Flexibility for 21st Century Jobs," *APA Monitor*, available at http://www.apa.org/monitor/jul98/factor.html, July 1999.

13. L. Parch, "Testing . . . 1, 2, 3." *Working Woman*, October 1997, p. 74.

14. S. M. Poole, "Georgia Labor Official Says Diversity Will Drive Future Workplace." *Knight-Ridder Tribune Business News*, May 28, 2000, news release.

15. R. Barner, "The New Millennium Workplace," *The Futurist* (March–April 1996): p. 14.

16. Ibid., Barner, p. 15.

17. T. L. Beard, "The Kids Are Right," *Modern Machine Shop*, February 1998, p. 6.

18. J. Levine, "The Web and the Workplace," *Forbes*. June 2, 1997, p. 178.

19. H. Kahn, ed., *The Future of the Corporation* (New York: Mason and Lipscomb, 1974).

20. "Issue 3: The gap in living standards between. . . ." available at http://www.geocities.com/~acunu/millennium/Issue 3–2.html, no date.

21. M. L. Dertouzos, *What Will Be* (New York: HarperCollins, 1997), p. 241.

22. A. Murray, "In the New Economy, You've Got Scale," *The Wall Street Journal*, January 11, 2000, p. A1.

23. Negroponte, *Being Digital* p. 230.

24. As reported by Levine, "The Web," p. 178.

25. Joan Buntzen, librarian of the Navy, interview by author, San Diego California, September 1, 2000.

26. Julie Oman, Dow Chemical Company Business Intelligence Center, telephone interview by author, February 6, 2001.

27. B. Collis, *Tele-Learning in a Digital World* (London: International Thomson Computer Press, 1996), p. 9.

28. L. G. Fitch, "High-Tech Skills: Not Just for Engineers Anymore," *The San Diego Union-Tribune.* May 16, 1999, p. Employment-1.

29. K. L. Spitzer, M. B. Eisenbert, and C. A. Lowe, *Information Literacy* (Syracuse, NY: ERIC Clearinghouse on Information and Technology, 1999), p. 227.

Index

About the Author

TOM W. GOAD is an organizational consultant, trainer, and author. A past president of the San Diego Chapter of the American Society for Training and Development, he lists among his consulting clients a variety of educational institutions, businesses, and an archaeology project. He holds a doctorate in organization development and has taught on the graduate school level.